MICHAEL R. MYLER   2 —

The Politics of Oil in Venezuela

FRANKLIN TUGWELL

The Politics of Oil in Venezuela

STANFORD UNIVERSITY PRESS

1975 Stanford, California

Stanford University Press
Stanford, California
© 1975 by the Board of Trustees of the
Leland Stanford Junior University
Printed in the United States of America
ISBN 0-8047-0881-9
LC 74-25930

For my parents

Preface

AS THIS BOOK goes to press the Venezuelan government is busy preparing to nationalize the petroleum industry operating within the country. When the necessary legislation has been approved and implemented—almost surely before the end of 1975—the era of privately managed oil development in Venezuela, which has lasted more than half a century, will come to an end. Since this is a book about that era (especially its final decade-and-a-half) and about the forces that have brought it to an end, it seems especially appropriate that it should appear at this time.

The book itself is the product of research that has spanned many years. It is based upon materials I gathered during three visits to Venezuela between 1966 and 1974 (involving a total of more than a year's residence there)—first as a doctoral candidate in political science at Columbia University, and later as a visiting researcher at the Instituto de Estudios Superiores de Administración.

Research of the kind reported here depends to an unusual degree on the cooperation and assistance of other people, and I am pleased to have the opportunity to express my gratitude to those who answered questions, opened their files, and facilitated my work and travel in many other ways. First mention in any acknowledgment, of course, must go to my wife, Sandra, and to my parents, Grace and Rexford Tugwell. Without their continuing support, encouragement, and wise counsel, neither this study nor the research venture on which it is based would have been possible at all. Many who helped me understand the complicated story of petroleum policymaking in Venezuela are named in the endnotes;

others, at their own request, must remain anonymous. I received financial support from Columbia University, the Foreign Area Fellowship Program, and Pomona College. The Instituto de Estudios Superiores de Administración provided an office in Caracas and, more important, a challenging academic environment in which to carry on my work.

Among those who read the manuscript with a critical eye, I am indebted especially to Gene Bigler and Juan Pablo Pérez Alfonzo for their detailed and exacting commentaries. For assistance of many different kinds I thank Enrique Tejera Paris, Alirio Parra, Kim Fuad, David Blank, Norman Gall, David Myers, William Luers, and, last but far from least, George Hall, friend and adviser to generations of students and researchers in Venezuela. Ruth Rice and Mary Gammons earned my gratitude and respect for their good will and attention to detail in typing and proofreading.

Finally, I should add, the usual disclaimers apply: none of the institutions or individuals mentioned here is in any sense a sponsor of this work or responsible for its interpretations or conclusions.

F. T.

Contents

Tables and Figures

Appendix Tables

Figures

Abbreviations

AD	Acción Democrática
Bs	bolívares (see Appendix Tables E and F)
COPEI	Comité de Organización Política Electoral Independiente (Christian Democrats)
Cordiplan	Oficina Central de Coordinación y Planificación
CVP	Corporación Venezolana del Petróleo (Venezuelan state company)
FDP	Fuerza Democrática Popular
Fedecámaras	Federación Venezolana de Cámaras y Asociaciones de Comercio y Producción
FND	Frente Nacional Democrático
GDP	gross domestic product (market value of output produced within Venezuela)
GNP	gross national product (market value of output accruing to residents of the nation)
IPAA	Independent Producers Association of America
LNG	liquefied natural gas
MBD	million barrels per day
MEP	Movimiento Electoral del Pueblo
OAS	Organization of American States
OLADE	Organización Latinoamericana de Energía
OPEC	Organization of Petroleum Exporting Countries
TRV	tax reference value (a standard figure per barrel of a given petroleum product, on which tax is figured irrespective of realized price)
URD	Unión Republicana Democrática

The Politics of Oil in Venezuela

Introduction

THIS BOOK is a study in the determination and implementation of public policy toward a massive, foreign-controlled export industry. More precisely, as the title indicates, it is an attempt to come to grips with the politics of Venezuelan oil—with the pattern of conflict and bargaining among the major contenders in the oil policy system, and with the ways this pattern has been shaped by (and in turn has shaped) the rapidly changing political process, especially during the years of democratic government since 1958. Thus it focuses on the strategies adopted by Venezuelan leaders in pursuit of petroleum policy objectives, on the efforts of the international oil corporations to defend their profits and retain access to Venezuelan resources, and on the consequences of these activities for the overall pattern of development in the country.

In recent years, scholars concerned with the problems of Latin American development have become increasingly interested in the influence of transnational actors, and foreign corporations in particular, upon political and economic events in the countries of the area. "Dependence" has become a prominent theme in the work of social analysts, and studies of multinational corporations and their intervention in domestic decisionmaking have become fashionable. Belatedly, the social-science community has begun to acknowledge the theoretical significance of dominant-subordinate relationships and patterned inequalities, economic as well as political, private as well as public, and to recognize the artificiality of analytical models that neglect or underestimate these phenomena.[1]

Among the practitioners of development statecraft themselves the formal management of ties to the international system has likewise begun to assume top priority; indeed for many countries it has taken on an importance equivalent to that accorded military security on the policy agendas of developed superpowers. This is especially true for countries that depend heavily on the sale of one or a very few products—the "export economies," as Jonathan Levin has called them.[2] It is becoming increasingly clear, however, that the policy problems posed by such dependence are complicated and formidable, requiring extraordinary skills in bargaining and favorable political conditions both at home and abroad. Unfortunately, they are also problems that have received little attention until quite recently.

Although many countries in Latin America depend on primary-product exports, Venezuela and her oil in many ways symbolize the extremes of this condition. The figures are well known: petroleum has in recent years accounted for more than 90 percent of the country's export earnings by value, for 20 percent of the gross national product (GNP), and for more than 65 percent of the government's income. In 1975, as a result of recent price increases, oil is likely to account for as much as 40 percent of GNP and 85 percent of government income. Moreover, the production and export of oil in Venezuela has been controlled almost entirely by branches of the world's most powerful and affluent multinational corporations, among them Exxon, Royal Dutch Shell, Gulf Oil, and Texaco. These ship nearly 3 million barrels of crude oil and petroleum products from the country every day, most of it going to the more developed nations of the world, especially the United States. The wealth made available by this trade has transformed Venezuela in a few decades from a quiescent agrarian society to one of the most developed nations in Latin America. The sheer pace of change has been dizzying: between 1936 and 1958, per capita GNP grew at an average annual rate of 7 percent; and the current level, just over $1,500, is the highest in Latin America and nearly triple the regional average.[3] This extremely rapid growth has also been unbalanced and crisis-ridden, closely following the fortunes of the international oil market.

Although the impact of Venezuela's oil is most visible in the spectacular changes in her economy, her social and political life has also been affected. Petroleum income has stimulated headlong social mobilization, uncontrolled urbanization, and a rapid rise in political participation; it has facilitated an unprecedented expansion in the size and power of the state; and, to a degree unusual in a tradition-bound continent, it has freed the government from the grip of established elites. More recently, wealth derived from petroleum has helped to sustain a rough-and-tumble democracy. And on a broader level it has helped shape a pervasive style of politics—a "politics of fiscal saturation"—at the heart of which is an institutionalized addiction to rapidly expanding public resources.

Venezuela's experience is especially instructive because her policymakers have experimented with a number of different strategies designed to influence the behavior of the companies controlling the oil industry. These companies, in turn, have explored new ways of adapting to changing domestic political conditions and to escalating government demands. In the last half-century the relationship between government and companies has followed a course from extreme submissiveness on the part of the state to the recently declared decision to nationalize the industry completely. In sum, Venezuela has had a rich and varied experience in the design and implementation of policy toward a massive, foreign-controlled export industry.

After the energy crisis of the early 1970's no one needs reminding that oil is a commodity of enormous global significance—by value, it is the most important product moving in international trade. Among oil-exporting countries, Venezuela has led in the design of new means of appropriating surplus profits and placing limitations on corporate freedom of action. The now-famous Organization of Petroleum Exporting Countries (OPEC), which occupies a central place in world energy affairs, owes its existence in large measure to the efforts of a Venezuelan Oil Minister. For decades Venezuela has been a principal source of imported oil for the United States. In recent years Venezuelan supplies have accounted for more than 10 percent of all petroleum products consumed in that country. The conduct of oil policy in Venezuela, then, has had and will continue to have widespread impact beyond her borders.

My goal in this book is to analyze and evaluate the performance of Venezuelan authorities in handling their country's most important development problem and to relate their actions to the operation of the political process. Where possible, I have sought to identify the conditions of success and failure that obtain in development policymaking generally, as well as the more limited conditions affecting the management of export dependency. I have also sought to clarify the context of choice in which the future of the Venezuelan petroleum industry will be decided. These concerns are reflected in the principal themes of the book: the pattern of bargaining and conflict between government and oil companies, and its impact on policy; the role of ideology in the selection of alternative courses of action; the ability of public policymakers to adjust their behavior as a result of lessons "learned" in practice; the interdependence of the domestic political process, petroleum policy, and rapid, oil-tied social change; and the extent and efficacy of multinational corporate intervention in Venezuelan domestic affairs. I have emphasized the post-1958 period because it is intrinsically more interesting in terms of these themes and because much of the available information on oil policy in earlier years—and this is very little in the case of the Pérez Jiménez era—has been assembled in other works. Chapter 2 provides a summary of this historical background in order to set the stage for the subsequent analysis.

In coming to grips with the politics of oil in Venezuela, I have made a deliberate effort, in the style pioneered by Albert O. Hirschman and Charles Anderson, to search out the more subtle implications of behavior, to use more flexible yardsticks in measuring policy outcomes.[4] Thus, for example, I have tried to remain alert to the constructive aspects of conflict and dissension, and to distinguish between short-run and long-run costs and benefits. From this broader perspective, Venezuela has been more successful in the conduct of petroleum policy than most observers have been willing to admit; but her success has been due to a remarkable mixture of acumen, skill, and outright luck. Until recently few analysts have tried to place themselves in the position of a developing country's public authorities as they confront the organizational and financial monoliths of the petroleum world. It takes only a brief exercise in this more empathetic approach to convey a sense of the enormous difficulties involved in the conduct of oil policy. Indeed, from this perspective the more common "extreme" solutions —xenophobic expropriation or passive collaboration—appear seductive because they avoid the profound technical and political problems posed by more constructive and responsible alternatives.

A final caveat is in order. Largely owing to recent international developments, Venezuela in 1975 stands at the most important threshold in her modern history. The old pattern of ties to the world oil market has run its course, and policymakers must now construct a completely new set of relationships. And they do so in the full knowledge that the future of their country will be profoundly affected by their decisions. Oil, democracy, and a coherent, equitable development of the country remain closely interlocked and will continue to be so. Indeed, in her decisions on petroleum policy, Venezuela is taking charge of her fate in a way few nations have. This makes it all the more imperative that her statesmen accurately interpret the lessons available from past experience.

1. The Policy Setting

IN THE ANALYSIS of any public-policy system it is important to begin with an understanding of the distinctive characteristics of the issue area involved, as well as the strategic context for decisionmaking, that is, the actors, political relationships, and doctrines involved in shaping outcomes. This is especially true in the case of petroleum policy, where alternatives are often highly technical in nature and where the policy system itself is inordinately complex and includes contenders with widely differing objectives and means of influence.

First, let us consider the issue area. There is widespread disagreement about the actual contribution that primary commodity exports make to a nation's development, especially when they are generated by direct foreign investment. This disagreement is perhaps most intense in the case of mineral-extractive operations, since these are often carried on in isolation from the rest of the economy and have fewer backward or forward linkages to stimulate activity in other sectors. When "enclave" industries of this kind are controlled by large-scale multinational corporations, as is often the case, the issue becomes still more difficult. Most analysts would agree that this method of exploiting resources is at best a mixed blessing in a developmental sense, and that it is preferable for entirely domestic concerns to undertake the job if at all possible. More important, most would concur that once foreign-controlled extraction has been initiated—and in most cases this method has been chosen because alternative means are thought to be impracticable at the outset—its effect for good or ill on the development of the host country will depend on the ability of that country to shape the resulting relationship.[1] Except in a few extreme cases, autarky (i.e., pure independence) will never be an available alternative. International economic exchanges will continue, and so will vulnerability to decisions made by powerful external actors, private and public. Dependence, unless it is defined away by theoretical gymnastics, is usually a function of rather enduring geopolitical circumstances. As Peter Evans has put it: "For most poor countries, greater autonomy must mean increased control over external economic relations, not their absence."[2]

In abstract terms, the successful management of a dependency of this kind involves several key tasks: first, capturing income, technology, and skills from the profit-making activity; second, controlling the conditions of resource development to assure a steady income and to insulate the country from the vagaries of the international market; third, in the case of nonrenewable resources, using captured earnings to establish alternative sources of income and growth, gradually decreasing the relative role of primary exports in the economy. An additional task, more controversial but implicit in the successful accomplishment of the first three, is domesticating the industry, that is, eventually supplanting majority foreign ownership entirely. All of these, of course, are essentially political tasks. To understand how Venezuela has approached them we must examine the strategic context of her oil policy.

For present purposes, the strategic context may be divided into three distinct but closely interrelated components. The first is the relationship between the Venezuelan government and the foreign oil companies, a relationship marked by continuous conflict and interdependent bargaining. The second is the Venezuelan political system as it has evolved since the outset of the age of petroleum, and especially since 1958. Here also, the watchword is conflict. Historically, Venezuela's politics have been filled with strife; but in recent years conflict has become more intense as the country's leaders have attempted to establish a working democracy under conditions of rapid social mobilization. As the political system has changed, petroleum policy has become increasingly enmeshed in the day-to-day haggling of party and governmental disputes. The final component is what might be termed "ideology" or "development doctrine" (or perhaps "philosophy," since it contains strong normative elements and propositions). This comprises the rather distinctive ideas and beliefs about oil and the international petroleum system, and about Venezuelan economic and political development, that have informed the decisions of policymakers. In practice, these three components have worked together to determine the options available in oil, and they provide a rough conceptual framework helpful in understanding the formulation and implementation of policy.

The Companies and the Government: Interdependent Bargaining

In modern history, relationships between host governments and foreign investors in developing countries have been notoriously hostile and disruptive. The examples that most often come to mind are cases of sudden and complete expropriation, such as those prominent in the diplomatic chronicles of the Russian, Mexican, and Cuban revolutions. But alongside these spectacular actions, which in a sense put an end to the relationships involved, there have been numerous examples of continuing struggle and disharmony, the foreign investors complaining about unfair treatment and broken contractual agreements, and the host governments complaining about excess profits and corporate intervention in domestic affairs. As a number of analysts have noted recently, a close look at these relationships reveals that the conflict is usually something more than the random outcome of irresponsible nationalism or xenophobia; in fact, it is often a patterned relationship, a process of interdependent bargaining with a rather clearcut internal logic.[3] This is true especially in the case of large-scale mineral extraction that weighs heavily in the overall economy of the host country.

The bargaining involved in the company-government relationship is similar in many ways to the "mixed motive" games that have been described by Thomas Schelling; it also shares many of the characteristics normally identified with bargaining between sovereign powers.[4] To this foreign-investment "game" the foreign corporation brings capital, managerial skills, and sophisticated technology. The government brings the advantages that sovereignty always endows: the legal right of access and the power to set the terms under which foreign capital must operate.[5] In Venezuela's case this power has been extensive, since, according to the inherited Hispanic legal tradition, the state is the inalienable owner of all subsoil resources. Thus when foreign companies invested in Venezuela in the 1920's and 1930's, they did so as concessionnaires rather than as owners of resources, and their agreements with the state simply gave them the privilege of exploiting public resources in return for royalty payments.*

The contenders in this "game" are typically mutually dependent, in that each relies on the other for the continuation of productive activity and its resulting benefits. The companies receive profits and continued access to resources; the government gains essential fiscal receipts and developmental impetus for the economy. Beyond this interdependence, the most important characteristic of the relationship is its inherent instability. Put another way, it contains the seed of its own destruction—an internal dynamic leading ultimately to replacement by some new arrangement. To be understood, therefore, episodes of conflict and bargaining, as well as government and company strategies, must be analyzed within the context of continuing metamorphosis. Fixed equilibrium points, represented by agreements on new tax codes or altered concessions arrangements, must be regarded as temporary and evaluated in terms of past and future changes. The timing and form of the relationship's evolution, however, is likely to vary, and is itself susceptible to a considerable degree of policy guidance.

In order to grasp the reasoning behind these statements, it is necessary to look at the actors involved and their motivations. Consider first the petroleum industry.[6] Although nearly 30 com-

---

* In Venezuela's case the royalty payment involved a percentage of the product itself, made in kind or, at the discretion of the state, in money equivalent.

TABLE 1

*Companies Holding Concessions or Producing Oil in Venezuela,
December 31, 1973*

Company	Parent organization	Concessions held (acres)	1973 production	
			Barrels per day[a]	Percent of total production
U.S. Subsidiaries				
Amoco	Standard, Ind.	13,591	32,194	0.96
Charter Venez.	Charter Venezuela	17,297	10,976	0.33
Chevron Venez.	Standard, Calif.	192,399	46,023	1.34
Continental Venez.	Conoco	1,969	3,235	0.10
Coro	Texaco	138,042	–	–
Creole	Exxon	1,433,827	1,495,342	44.43
International Venez.	Exxon	15,155	101,325	3.01
Mene Grande	Gulf	1,467,151	202,652	6.02
Mobil de Venez.	Mobil	355,958	106,336	3.16
Phillips	Phillips	97,476	30,227	0.90
Sinclair Venez.	Atlantic Richfield	96,571	–	–
Talon	Kirby	148,673	3,298	0.10
Texas	Texaco	271,579	70,260	2.09
Texaco Maracaibo	Texaco	7,776	54,806	1.63
Venez. Atlantic	Atlantic Richfield	47,782	79,977	2.38
Venez. Sun	Sun	49,420	79,543	2.36
Other U.S. interests	various	–	65,915	1.96
SUBTOTAL		4,354,666	2,382,109	70.77
Other Interests				
Caracas	Ultramar (Br.)	68,476	9,388	0.28
Corporación Venez. del Petróleo	Venezuelan Govt.	2,914,144[b]	73,993	2.20
Mito Juan	Mito Juan (Ven.)	83,458	3,176	0.09
Petrolera Mercedes	Texaco-Ultramar (U.S.-Br.)	220,436	–	–
Shell de Venez.	Royal Dutch Shell (Br.-Neth.)	730,625	897,345	26.66
SUBTOTAL		4,017,139	983,902	29.23
TOTAL		8,371,805	3,366,011	100.00

SOURCE: Creole Corp. Rept., 1974, p. 8.

[a] Standard, 42-gallon barrels of crude oil.

[b] This land was assigned directly by the government to the state corporation for petroleum development, not allotted by concessions agreement, as was the case with other acreage listed.

panies operate in Venezuela, oil production up to the early 1970's has been controlled almost entirely by several highly integrated subsidiaries of multinational corporations (see Table 1). In 1973 two companies, Creole (controlled by Exxon) and Shell of Venezuela, a subsidiary of Royal Dutch Shell, dominated the industry, producing more than 70 percent of the oil. The next largest company, Mene Grande (controlled by Gulf, with minority holdings by Shell and Exxon), produced only 6 percent. Other branches and subsidiaries of international "majors," such as Mobil and Texaco, accounted for another 11 percent of production, and smaller independents controlled the remainder.

The parent companies of these enterprises operated in every phase of the industry, from drilling to marketing finished products, and they worked closely together, cartel-like, in a basically oligopolistic market setting. As a group they represented one of the greatest concentrations of economic and organizational power in the world, by almost any measure. In 1970 the parent companies of the five largest enterprises producing oil in Venezuela had combined worldwide sales of more than $45 billion, larger than the GNP of all but 10 countries and greater than the government revenues of all but three. Standard of New Jersey (after Nov. 1, 1972, Exxon) and Royal Dutch Shell together accounted for just over $27 billion, or nearly three times the entire GNP of Venezuela in that year.[7]

Much of the strength, independence, and efficiency of these multinational organizations stems from their ability to coordinate the entire range of their operations in order to maximize profits. From the point of view of a highly dependent country like Venezuela this has serious implications. First of all, Venezuelan policymakers cannot assume that the profit calculations of the oil subsidiaries in their country, which are the entities subject to Venezuelan taxes, have been made in such a way as to maximize the taxable earnings to which they have legal access. The prices paid, the amount of petroleum produced, and even the form of production and processing undertaken within the country are all affected by extra-national considerations. Each of the corporations operating in Venezuela controls an immense network of operations, pays a host of taxes (many of which can be discounted against each other), and sells thousands of products in dozens of different countries. Profit maximization demands that these activities be coordinated to earn the largest total sum of money for the overall operation, taking due account of such things as security of resources, corporate growth, and managerial satisfaction. Each of the major oil corporations is capable of supplying a portion of its crude-oil needs from other locations if oil from any one area becomes unavailable or less profitable. Indeed, in order to maximize profits companies have always had to play producing countries off against each other when practicable. There is a compelling efficiency in using such opportunities to bring costs down: as Michael Tanzer has pointed out, it would be a breach of the stockholders' trust for managers to do otherwise.[8]

Clearly, for a country overwhelmingly dependent on the earnings of a few branches of such organizations, there can be little assurance that the outcome of their activity will be consistently beneficial unless they are held under tight control. This, in fact, is precisely the concern of the social scientists who have watched this form of economic enterprise spread with such astonishing speed in recent years.[9] Whatever a host country's interest in the particular economic activity, a multinational corporation, if it is efficient and responsible, does not and should not act to enhance that interest—although it may do so purely by chance.

A further problem arising from the nature of petroleum companies is the nearly unbelievable complexity of their activities (and their profit calculations). The increasing use of computer-based data processing has contributed to this complexity, at least from the perspective of the outside observer. Add a deliberate secrecy about every phase of operations, and it is easy to see why so few people outside the corporate offices feel they really know how the industry works. It is also easy to understand the sense of despair that so often grips the policymaker of a small, dependent country as he faces off against the industry.

Consider, for example, the problem of deciding whether a corporation has charged an adequate price for oil in a recent contract (a problem that has been of central importance in Venezuela). One must take account of such things as the kind of crude, the state of reserves and expected future production at the source, the point of destination, refining schedules, and national quota systems for distribution—all this in comparison with other kinds of crude moving at various tanker rates over different distances to different refineries. Moreover, the corporation will evaluate these factors in terms of the tax advantages involved in taking more or less profit at the point of production, the refinery, or the outlet. Since a large proportion of petroleum sales are sales by one branch of a company to another branch of the same company, this kind of cost and price juggling is easy. To be sure, shortcuts for working out and analyzing pricing policy can be, and are, devised. But coming to know the going rate is far different from figuring out whether the rate of a particular contract is the best available to the host country as a return for its resources—and the problem may involve millions of dollars.

From the point of view of Venezuelan policymakers, these characteristics of multinationals create a high level of continuing uncertainty about the country's prime source of livelihood. They must assume that in many circumstances their country's welfare will be sacrificed by externally based decisionmakers; and worse, that it will usually be impossible, in practical terms, for them to know whether or not this is being done at any given time. This alone would seem to provide sufficient reason to avoid a continuing dependence on the subsidiaries of multinational corporations, as is the case in Venezuela. But here, as in many underdeveloped countries, the dependency was established and consolidated under public authorities who knew little about the difficulties they would encounter. By the time these difficulties became evident the relationship between government and companies had become one of deep mutual dependence, and both contenders had established great stakes in the continuity of the production and profit-making process. In 1971, for example, even before the "energy crisis" price hikes, the government of Venezuela received directly from the companies nearly $2 billion in taxes and royalties. This amounted to about $160 for each Venezuelan—no small sum when one realizes it is equal to half or more of the per capita GNP in nine other Latin American countries and greater than the per capita GNP of some 45 countries around the world in that year, among them India, China, Indonesia, and Nigeria. The oil companies, for their part, held assets in 1971 worth more than $2.6 billion and were producing 3.5 million barrels every day.[10]

This condition of mutual dependence did not keep the relationship between the government and the companies from changing; on the contrary, it is clear in retrospect that it contained a sort of inner dynamic pushing it toward increased state control and increased Venezuelan participation in the division of profits. This evolutionary process acquired much of its distinctiveness from the nature of the bargaining game itself, a game whose rules and logic formed boundaries within which government policymakers had to operate.

Foreign investors in extractive industries such as petroleum must receive favorable initial terms if they are to take the risks involved in exploration and bringing new sources into production. These terms usually include the guarantee of a high rate of return, a promise normally contained in the concession agreement itself. But, as a number of economists have observed, once the raw material has been discovered, extractive facilities built, and production begun, there comes a time—usually within a few years—when the high returns conceded in the original concessionary agreement begin to appear unjustifiably generous.[11] In many cases these returns are double or even triple the earnings available on other forms of investment; this has been especially true in petroleum, where the profitability has traditionally been enormous.[12] In time, the producing companies become vulnerable to demands for change in the distribution of earnings between themselves and the state. To an extent they have become captives of the agreement; their risks have been taken, and they have sunk capital in the enterprise. Gradually, the bargaining terms tend to shift in the government's favor, and it becomes increasingly likely that the government will ask for—and the companies will have to hand over—a larger share of the earnings. Thus over time the relationship of the host government to extractive corporations tends to be a dialectical one: clashes in which old agreements are challenged and new ones worked out alternate with relatively quiescent periods, though in the long run there is a steady redistribution in favor of the state.

In practice the actual relationship is usually much more complicated than this image of two-party bargaining over profits would indicate. And it is the complicating conditions that prevent an eventual stabilization, or equilibrium, in the relationship, instead impelling it toward its own transformation. There is, above all, the problem of uncertainty, which pervades the relationship and is a prime concern of both contenders. The government remains uncertain about nearly everything to do with the companies: what they earn and how, what their short- and long-term plans are, how they make their choices, and how they will respond to government policies. The companies are also affected. As the bargaining process gets under way, corporate sense of security, especially about future earnings, begins to erode rapidly. Contracts acquire a special character in situations of this kind, since it is nearly inevitable that they will be questioned in one way or another before their term is up. Any given agreement actually represents only a single moment's accommodation, the most recent readjustment in a continuing process. Other government tactics, such as making retroactive tax claims, add to the difficulty of predicting return on operations in any reliable way.

Closely tied to uncertainty as a complicating factor is government intervention in industry operations, including pricing, choice of production methods and quantities, and allocation of product. Governments seek to control corporate policies because they want more income and cannot abide the neglect of domestic interests that is built into corporate decisionmaking. Companies hate such controls because they impede profit maximization, reduce flexibility, and force upon them unwanted priorities; moreover, they create even more uncertainty.

Still another complication is new investments. Continuous large-scale extraction of resources requires periodic new investments, sometimes very large, to explore and prove new fields, to introduce new production methods, and to expand or redesign refining processes. This need creates short-term subprocesses within the overall pattern of company-government interaction. Often the companies raise the price of new capital; and the government, after the initial agreement has been signed, has additional incentive to attach the high, "excess," profits that result. This cycle will usually feed back into the smoother, long-term trend of shifting government-company bargaining in various ways: it will shift the strategies of the contenders toward certain techniques, such as tax incentives for investment, that compensate for its effect; and it will reduce the time span between episodes of open conflict (i.e. adjustment of disequilibrium) in the relationship, since companies will change their calculations of time and risk because of it.

The most important long-term effect of the need for periodic reinvestment, however, is its creation of a kind of degenerative tendency in the industry itself. Reinvestment, along with multinational production-source options, is the big bargaining card in the hands of the industry, and as such it will be used in trying to block the erosion of a company's position within a given country. As the tendencies in this relationship work themselves out over time—as uncertainty feeds upon itself, as the margins for adjustment begin to narrow, as short-term calculations come to predominate, and as reinvestment becomes more costly—the physical health of the industry itself becomes the final stake. The industry can easily be trapped in a dangerous "write-off" spiral.

At this point the question of changing the basic agreement for resource exploitation begins to take on critical importance for both parties. The new arrangement proposed may take an extreme form, such as total control by state agencies or joint company-government enterprise; or an intermediary solution, such as government-regulated service contracting, may be adopted. Whatever solution seems attractive, it is likely that decisionmaking authority will shift still further toward the domestic arena, most probably to the state iself. Only such a transformation, it would seem, can resolve the conflicts and tensions that have built up over time in the old relationship.

In broad outline, Venezuela's experience in modern times

conforms to this rough model. Since the early 1920's, when the government's share of profits was roughly 15 percent, Venezuelan governments have repeatedly revised their policies to increase their income and their influence on company decisions. Major changes often leading to bitter disputes with the companies, occurred in 1942–43, 1949, 1958, 1966–67, 1970–71, 1972, 1973, and 1974; and interspersed among these were numerous minor readjustments. At present, the government's overall share of company profits is at or near 85 percent, and its influence over company decisionmaking has increased correspondingly. Company investment policies have tended to change in response to these adjustments (see Appendix Table A, pp. 179–81).

But the model developed so far, though a useful explanatory framework, specifies no more than the general reasons for the overall trend in company-government relations. It does not delineate either the timing or the form of change; it does not touch on matters such as income division or the nature and extent of government control; and, most important, it cannot detail the end result of the process of transformation itself. All these things vary according to public policy decisions, which are in turn responsive to the domestic political process.

The Political Process

The Venezuelan political system is difficult to analyze in any condensed fashion. Events in Caracas succeed each other with bewildering speed, leaving the observer with an impression of turbulence but with little sense of an overall pattern. At the risk of oversimplifying, however, it is possible to identify four broad trends that have been important in shaping petroleum policy. The first of these—a kind of general conditioning factor—is the extremely rapid social and political mobilization the country has experienced over the last four decades, as first the middle class and then the urban and rural lower classes have become important forces in national politics. The second is the appearance and rise to power of a reformist party, Acción Democrática (AD), which first became the organizational vehicle for a number of newly mobilized groups and then fragmented, contributing to the transformation of the party system itself into a multiparty pattern. The third trend is the rapid growth of the Venezuelan state as an independent power center in the country, mostly owing to its fiscal receipts from petroleum. Finally, there is the emergence of a complex system of private-sector groups and associations, topped by an influential and cohesive peak association, reflecting the strong desire of economic elites to acquire greater influence in economic policymaking.

Large-scale oil development began in Venezuela shortly after World War I (many oilmen set the date at the opening of the famous Los Barrosos gusher in 1922). At this time Venezuela was a highly traditional society. More than two-thirds of the population lived by agriculture, illiteracy was high, and the economy depended mostly on the export of a few cash crops. Political affairs, such as they were, were under the firm control of Juan Vicente Gómez, one of the most primitive and despotic dictators in Latin American history. The war, however, dislocated trade patterns and stimulated economic and political change throughout Latin America. Venezuela's wealth of petroleum attracted oilmen from Europe and the United States in growing numbers as the world's appetite for energy increased, and along with them came capital for the purchase of lands, for bribery, and for the payments needed to obtain mineral concessions from the government. Opportunities for education and employment, both private and public, gradually expanded, and so did the turmoil and dislocation so often associated with the expansion of political participation in a developing nation.[13]

When Gómez died in 1935 the government passed into the hands of his Minister of War, General Eleazar López Contreras, who ruled on behalf of Venezuela's small traditional oligarchy. In the decade that followed, a generation of new, middle-class leaders (many of them associated with a series of 1928 student protests against Gómez), began to take advantage of the more open political climate, forming poltical parties and pressing the government of López Contreras and his successor, Isaías Medina Angarita, for wide-ranging political and economic reforms.[14] Between 1935 and 1945 the pace of change accelerated. The ruling elite sought to accommodate growing demands for change by enacting a series of gradual reforms, including a partial expansion of suffrage and important modifications in economic policy. The most prominent of the latter was a complete redefinition of petroleum policy, completed in 1943. Venezuelans are divided among themselves regarding the responsiveness of governments of this era to the demands of new groups. The government did allow the formation of political parties and seemed inclined to move ahead with reforms, but not quickly enough for many.

By 1944–45 a number of young leaders belonging to AD (including Rómulo Betancourt, Raúl Leoni, Juan Pablo Pérez Alfonzo, and many others who would have prominent roles in the post-1958 period) had become deeply frustrated with the slow pace of change and with their own lack of access to the charmed circle of elite politics. And when a group of young military officers decided to move ahead with a reformist coup, these civilian politicians allied with them. For most of them, this was the most important decision of their lives; certainly it was an important one for the future of Venezuela.[15]

During the next three years, a civil-military junta, and subsequently an elected government headed by Rómulo Gallegos, attempted a far-reaching program of structural reforms in Venezuelan society and economy. A series of decrees provided for agrarian reform and for extensive programs in public health, housing, and education. The government also pursued a much more assertive petroleum policy (which I will examine in Chapter 2). Simultaneously, the leaders of AD mobilized both workers and peasants, and linked them to the party through national confederations.[16] The support of these two lower-class groups was largely responsible for AD's overwhelming victory in the free elections of 1947. This alliance of organized workers, peasants, and middle-class leaders was to remain the dominant coalition in Venezuela's democratic politics until the late 1960's. While it lasted, it offered leadership opportunities that few Latin American countries have experienced; and, most important from our standpoint, it provided a solid basis for an aggressive and consistent petroleum policy after 1958.

Between 1920 and 1943 the size of the Venezuelan government, as measured by its income, doubled roughly every ten years. Beginning in 1943, however, the public sector expanded even more rapidly: indeed, real fiscal income (in constant *bolívares*) increased fourfold between 1943 and 1947 (see Appendix Table B, p. 182). Unlike many reformist regimes, the first AD government had plenty of funds to support its activities. And nearly all of this increase in wealth came directly from the oil industry. During the same four years Venezuela experienced the largest increase in oil exports in her history, mainly owing to the growth in demand stimulated by World War II. In subsequent years, government income continued to grow at a somewhat slower rate, again reflecting the fortunes of the petroleum industry. Except for a brief recession in 1960, oil income has never accounted for less than 90 percent of Venezuela's total export revenues at any time during the past 30 years. The very fact of such striking fiscal expansion, as well as the manner in which it has occurred, has had profound consequences for the course of Venezuelan political development and for petroleum policy, as later chapters will illustrate. Because of it, the state has been simultaneously assured of a large measure of independence from social and economic elites and an enormous role in the country's overall economy.

Despite its multiclass support and its enviable financial condition, the AD-military experiment did not survive long. Its leaders were inexperienced, overzealous, and intolerant of criticism, besides incurring the inevitable hostility of the traditional elites, the older military officers, and the foreign petroleum corporations. A climate of bitter conflict and public criticism took hold, and in 1948 the military stepped in again. After two years of rule by military junta, the government fell to the control of Lt. Col. Marcos Pérez Jiménez, who did his best to refashion a centralized autocracy like that of his predecessor Gómez. Corruption and peculation flourished, along with increasing police repression as the government sought to eliminate "politics" from public affairs. One by one, beginning with AD, the dictatorship outlawed parties and exiled their leaders or forced them underground.

From a still-expanding treasury, the dictatorship poured funds into flamboyant urban construction projects—and into the pockets of administrative officials and sycophants—meanwhile neglecting the rural areas of the country. As one writer has put it, the regime "went about as far in misappropriating abundance as was possible under the circumstances."[17] But financial mismanagement, brutal repression, and a series of disastrous political blunders (including a farcical attempt to demonstrate popular support by means of a rigged plebiscite) gradually alienated virtually every sector of Venezuelan society; and in 1958 Pérez Jiménez succumbed to a combined military and popular insurrection and flew off to exile, his luggage full of pilfered funds.[18] Still another junta then took power, pledging to hold elections within a year.

While still in exile, the leaders of the country's major political parties—among them Rómulo Betancourt of AD, Jóvito Villalba of the Unión Republicana Democrática (URD), and Rafael Caldera of the Christian Democratic Party (Comité de Organización Política Electoral Independiente, COPEI)—agreed to cooperate after the fall of the dictatorship in order to prevent a repetition of the destructive competition that had had such disastrous consequences for their country. And after returning to Venezuela they began to search for a political formula to accomplish this goal. A series of right-wing coup attempts against the interim junta reinforced their commitment; and after trying in vain to agree on a single "unity" candidate for the elections scheduled for late 1958, they agreed in a special pact that whoever won would form a coalition government and adopt a program generally acceptable to all parties.

As had been expected, Betancourt of AD won the presidency, gaining 49 percent of the vote (14 percent more than his closest competitor). In addition, AD won 73 of the 133 seats in the Chamber of Deputies, and 32 of 51 in the Senate. This victory, however, was far short of the more than two-thirds majority AD had received in 1947. Significantly, 67 percent of the vote in Venezuela's six large urban centers (those of over 100,000 population) went to

the junta president, Wolfgang Larrazábal, and only 26 percent
went to AD; it was the rural areas, which gave Betancourt 59 percent of the vote and Larrazábal 25 percent, that supplied the margin of victory. (Larrazábal, a vice admiral under Pérez Jiménez,
had acquired widespread popularity in Caracas owing to the generous public assistance funds his interim government had made
available to the poor and the unemployed.) The outcome of this
election was the first sign of an urban distaste for the more institutionalized parties that has plagued Venezuelan governments
ever since.[19]

Immediately after the elections Betancourt set about forming
the coalition government required by the interparty pact, and
managed to distribute cabinet seats, administrative positions, and
state government posts to obtain a reasonable balance of power.
The new president's announced program reiterated his commitment to the reformist goals that had guided AD during the 1945–48
period; but this time he used more moderate language, reflecting
a decision among the top AD leaders to avoid directly threatening
the established powerholders in the country and instead to work
around them, using the state's oil income as the source of developmental impulses. For the most part, Betancourt made clear, existing privileges and prerogatives, most notably those of the private
economic elites, would remain untouched while the government
sought to build a modern, egalitarian, and democratic Venezuela.

The administration immediately launched an ambitious program of planned development to accomplish its aims. This included: first, a continued but more diversified industrialization,
guided by the state but with a substantial role for private enterprise, with the objective of reducing the country's dependence on
petroleum exports; second, an extensive agrarian reform program
with provisions for easy credit, technical aid, and marketing assistance; and third, widespread improvements in education and social welfare. The government also resumed its search, suspended
during the dictatorship, for a new relationship between the state
and the foreign oil companies—in essence, for one that would provide Venezuela with greater control over her oil industry than was

possible under the existing concessions system. To plan and coordinate these ambitious programs, the government established a central-planning agency with direct ties to the executive: the Oficina Central de Coordinación y Planificación (Cordiplan).

Almost as soon as the inaugural ceremonies were over, however, the new administration encountered serious and unexpected problems. To begin with, the economy went into a severe slump. This was caused in part by the sharp drop in prices for Venezuelan oil that occurred just after the Suez Crisis (see Appendix Table C, p. 183), in part by the unbalanced growth and fiscal irresponsibility of the dictatorship and the interim government, and in part by the panic of many private investors who foresaw disaster in the government's new programs. A rapid flight of capital drained off needed resources, and unemployment mounted, especially in the urban areas. Though unsure how to respond, the administration took strong measures—at first deflationary, including exchange controls and substantial budget and salary cuts, and then expansionist, including public works. Within three years the economy was well on the way to recovery, but the period of scarcity and budgetary contraction had left its marks on the political system.

As the government struggled with economic problems, the coalition began to break up. The first serious defection came in the spring of 1960, when a group of younger AD members, upset by the moderation of the "old guard" leaders, left the party and formed the extremist Movimiento de Izquierda Revolucionaria (MIR), committed to violent revolution. Shortly thereafter URD, the second largest party, also left the coalition. Its leaders felt themselves slighted in the distribution of government posts, and they opposed the government's policy of stern opposition to the course of the Cuban Revolution. Their differences with AD came to a head over the decision to break relations with Cuba in the fall of 1960, and they left the government.

URD's departure confirmed the rapid polarization of Venezuelan society, which proved to be the most vexing problem facing the administration. Dissidents, first on the Right and later on the Left, mounted repeated violent attacks on the state, keeping it constantly off balance as it sought to handle complex problems of economic policy. The right-wing conspiracies, which began to proliferate as soon as Pérez Jiménez fled, culminated in an abortive attempt to assassinate Betancourt in June 1960. In the same year leftist insurgents began a campaign of rural and urban terrorism that increased steadily in intensity for three years.

Still another defection from the coalition occurred in early 1962, when a second faction within AD, having failed in an attempt to take control of the party's apparatus, left the government. This loss was a serious blow to the coalition (now composed only of the AD old guard and the COPEI) because it now lost its majority in the Chamber of Deputies, and further meaningful legislation became impossible until the election of 1963. By this time, however, most of the major reform bills had already been passed. In the end, in spite of economic crisis, defection, conspiracies, and terrorism, the coalition managed to survive, carry out many of its programs, and hold free elections on schedule in 1963. Under the circumstances, this was a remarkable feat, marred only by the fact that the government had been forced on several occasions to suspend constitutional guarantees.

At the polls, AD again suffered a substantial drop in popularity, from 49 to 33 percent of the vote; but its candidate, Raúl Leoni, won without difficulty. COPEI increased its vote to 20 percent (from 15 percent in 1958). The main opposition parties (URD, Fuerza Democrática Popular, and Independientes Pro Frente Nacional) repeated their landslide victories in the urban areas, registering 44 percent of the overall vote. Most important, the election revealed that the urban-rural coalition forged by the AD leaders in the 1940's could no longer sustain the party's majority: of 177 congressmen and 45 senators, AD elected 65 and 21 respectively; and for the first time it obtained less than a majority of the rural vote, some 40 percent, while its support in the large urban areas dropped to 18 percent.[20]

Thus the 1963 election was an important threshold in Venezuelan politics, confirming the demise of the dominant-party system and initiating a decade of multiparty politics—more typical of

Latin America—in which the president could not command a legislative majority and was thus dependent on the support of other parties to pass his programs. This breakup can be traced in part to rapid urbanization, which in the few years after 1958 had transformed Venezuela from a rural nation into one of the most urban in the world, with more than two-thirds of its people living in cities.[21] The new residents who crowded the urban shantytowns had left behind their peasant ties to AD and its peasant associations, and party leaders found it difficult to reassimilate them. Though important participants in the polity, the urban poor tended to remain "up for grabs" by orators who could capture their vote at election time with rhetoric and the promise of "bread and circuses."

The 1963 election itself, however, was followed by a period of moderate, relatively stable government. The leftist revolutionaries, having failed to prevent a strong popular commitment to legitimate government, almost immediately abandoned their campaign of violence, and after a brief episode of urban terror in the late 1960's gradually disappeared as a significant force in Venezuelan politics. AD, seriously weakened, again turned to the other parties for support and, following drawn-out negotiations, formed a new coalition. This included the URD, which eliminated many of its more radical members after 1963, and a new party, the Frente Nacional Democrático (FND), headed by Arturo Uslar Pietri, a conservative intellectual whose participation was symbolic of the more moderate cast of the regime. AD's old ally, COPEI, decided not to remain with the government and formed what it called a "loyal" opposition, expecting thereby to improve its chances in the election of 1968—and calculating correctly, as it turned out. The new coalition suffered its first defection when Uslar Pietri, angered by his failure to influence petroleum and fiscal policies, joined the opposition in the spring of 1966. In addition, just before the election of 1968, AD itself again split over the issue of too-moderate government policy. This final schism was the principal reason for the victory of COPEI leader Rafael Caldera in the next presidential race.

TABLE 2
Election Results, 1968

Party and presidential candidate	Percent of Presidential vote	Congressional		
		Percent of vote	Senators elected	Deputies elected
Acción Democrática (Gonzalo Barrios)	28%	26%	19	63
COPEI (Rafael Caldera)	29	24	16	59
Movimiento Electoral del Pueblo (Prieto Figueroa)	19	13	5	25
Cruzada Cívica Nacionalista (Pérez Jiménez)[a]	–	11	4	21
Unión Republicana Democrática[b] (Burrelli Rivas)	22	9	3	20
Fuerza Democrática Popular[b]	–	5	2	10
Frente Nacional Democrático[b]	–	3	1	4
Others	1	9	2	11

SOURCE: Consejo Supremo Electoral.
    [a] Backed Pérez Jiménez for legislature; no presidential candidate.
    [b] Coalition supporting Burrelli Rivas in presidential race; separate congressional candidates.

As can be seen from Table 2, in the 1968 presidential race Caldera won with less than one-third of the vote, actually just over 30,000 votes more than his AD rival. In the legislative race the results were even more fragmentated. AD won more seats in the Chamber of Deputies and the Senate than COPEI, but still not enough to control either house. And a surprisingly large proportion of the vote went to smaller, personalist parties—again reflecting the temper of urban residents.[22] Especially embarrassing was the fact that former dictator Pérez Jiménez won a Caracas senate seat. (He was promptly declared ineligible owing to a technicality in the voting law, and has since been barred from any elective office by a constitutional amendment excluding those convicted of crimes while in public office.)

True to its democratic commitments, AD turned over affairs of state to Caldera and the Christian Democrats. The changeover was quite a landmark: for the first time in Venezuelan history an opposition presidential candidate won an election and was permitted to take office. But AD, which considered itself the originator of democratic politics and social reform in Venezuela, found the defeat a bitter pill to swallow, and its tactics as the dominant opposition party revealed this clearly. From the outset, AD leaders operated with the 1973 elections foremost among their concerns.

Caldera, for his part, intensified interparty hostility by choosing to break precedent and dispense with the coalition mechanism by which AD had coopted its potential opponents and shared with them some of the prerogatives of victory. This decision left him in a difficult position, since he had received the smallest electoral mandate and the slimmest margin of victory in the country's history. In place of a coalition, he relied on working arrangements and informal alliances in the legislature; but he kept a tight grip on cabinet and administrative positions, and shortly after the elections his followers began cleaning out the bureaucracy to make room for COPEI party loyalists. The stage was thus set for an extraordinarily complex interplay of political forces, much of it in the legislative arena, which touched nearly every aspect of public policy.

Because of the intense political conflict and the partial immobilization of the government after 1969, the election of 1973 was regarded as a critical threshold for Venezuelan democracy. AD was determined to regain its former power; and its candidate, Carlos Andrés Pérez, Minister of the Interior during the violence-torn years of the early 1960's, poured all his energy into rebuilding the badly fragmented party. Betancourt, too, returned to the country and went to work mending fences and persuading departed leaders to come back to the fold. COPEI, of course, was just as determined to stay in power and to build a legislative base strong enough to end the opposition's parliamentary stranglehold. Political leaders maneuvered endlessly; a surprising number even traveled openly or surreptitiously to Madrid to solicit the endorsement of the exiled Pérez Jiménez. AD and COPEI mounted extravagant and highly professional media campaigns, using TV spots, radio jingles, posters, and sound trucks. For all the intensity of the campaign, however, there was little bitterness; and indeed, there was an air of good feeling about the whole affair.

TABLE 3
Election Results, 1973

	Presidential		Congressional		
Party	Candidate	Percent of vote	Percent of vote	Senators elected	Deputies elected
AD	Andrés Pérez	48.6%	44.3%	28	102
COPEI	Fernández	36.8	30.3	13	64
MAS	Rangel	4.2	5.2	2	9
MEP	Paz	5.1	5.0	2	8
URD	Villalba	3.1	3.2	1	5
Others	–	2.1	12.0	3	12

SOURCE: Consejo Supremo Electoral.

On election eve most experts, relying on rather extensive polls, forecast a continuation of the existing distribution of electoral strength, with COPEI and AD together retaining roughly the same percentage of the overall vote or perhaps even slipping some. Most speculation focused on the possibility of a breakthrough (perhaps up to 15 percent of the vote) by the Movimiento al Socialismo (MAS), a coalition of the left somewhat comparable to the Chilean Unidad Popular, or upon the possibility that Pérez Jiménez would influence the chances of one of the half-dozen populist leaders vying for his favor.

The results stunned everyone. Carlos Andrés Pérez took the presidency with a resounding 48.6 percent of the vote, and AD won an absolute majority in both legislative houses (see Table 3). Equally important, the election reversed the long-term trend toward political fragmentation in Venezuela, introducing a polarized, two-party arrangement. AD and COPEI together took more than 85 percent of the presidential vote and 75 percent of the legislative vote, holding out the prospect of a consolidation of a true two-party system—an unusual but potentially very constructive outcome in any multiparty democracy. At the very least, the election dispelled fears of continued parliamentary paralysis in the coming years.

Public Policy and the Private Sector

To this point my analysis has emphasized the political party system. However, in recent years a constellation of influential and well-organized economic interest groups and associations has also begun to participate actively in Venezuelan public affairs.[23] As was the case elsewhere in Latin America, the Venezuelan economy expanded and diversified quite rapidly during and after the war, especially in the middle-level service and light manufacturing industries that benefited from the government's import-substitution policies. A handful of wealthy entrepreneurs, already established in food processing, sugar cultivation, and urban real estate (among other things), consolidated their positions in these years; and today their family conglomerates and financial empires wield broad economic influence in the country and play an important part in the organizational and representational affairs of the private sector. A surprising number of Venezuela's economic families are of recent immigrant origin and not of the traditional social aristocracy of the country.

The domestic economy itself is highly oligopolistic, with a very few firms accounting for most of the market in many key sectors. There is also a strong anticompetitive thrust in private economic activity. Effective antitrust laws do not exist, and it is usual for firms to engage in collusion. Prices and shares of the market are often fixed by detailed private agreements, which are sometimes backed by effective informal coercive mechanisms. Nonetheless, there is considerable tension between different sectors of the economy—agriculture versus industry, industry versus commerce, or importers versus exporters—and there is a strong economic regionalism, most notably the rivalry between Maracaibo in the west and the Caracas-dominated central region. Finally, more and more foreign capital is entering Venezuela's nonpetroleum manufacturing and service economy. Much of this has entered in cooperation with domestic capital, but a good portion has come on its own, adding to the diversity of financial and managerial actors in the country.[24]

With the economy's expansion, chambers of commerce and industrial associations proliferated rapidly, and today Venezuela boasts an amazingly dense system of economic interest groups. At the head of this system is the Venezuelan Federation of Chambers and Associations of Commerce and Production (Fedecámaras), which seeks to serve as policymaking body and spokesman for the sector as a whole. Created in 1944, Fedecámaras has almost 200 member associations in nearly every area of the economy, and representatives of the most influential economic families hold important positions in its governing bodies.[25] Since 1958, and particularly since 1965, the organization has taken an increasingly important part in debates over government policy, especially that concerning the private sector as a whole—which of course includes petroleum policy. There are other spokesmen for the private sector, such as the Caracas Chamber of Commerce and the Pro-Venezuela Association, but none are as important as Fedecámaras.

The reasons for this surge of associational activity are the standard ones, if perhaps more powerful than usual: to regulate the internal affairs of the various areas of economic activity (acting as "private governments," to use Robert Scott's term); and to help manage relationships between the private sector and the state.[26] From what I have said about oligopoly and cartelization in Venezuela, the need for institutions to control competition and provide for the exchange of information should be clear; for our purposes, however, the second of these functions is the more interesting.

The private sector in Venezuela is highly dependent on the state, perhaps more so than in any other Latin American country except Cuba. Most enterprises operate behind a wall of complex import restrictions, and the public sector is so important in the overall economy that government policies almost always have extensive and often unanticipated consequences for business. At the same time, because of its oil income the Venezuelan state has been able to remain remarkably independent of the private domestic economy. It has, in a sense, been able to rise above the constraints that affect public institutions in many countries, and can wield great power in the economy without having to support itself by depriving established elites of their income or prerogatives. To be sure, this has affected government policies—in areas directly affecting them private elites have often been able to exercise an effective veto power—but the state's fiscal independence has facilitated rapid bureaucratic expansion and has sustained massive government programs in areas considered less vital by economic interests.

Since 1958 Venezuela's government has been in the hands of political leaders—actually what almost amounts to an entire social sector made up of politicians and administrators—many of whom strongly question the legitimacy of private control of important areas of the economy.[27] Reflecting this, private interests have found it very difficult to gain significant influence within the political parties. No party has served as a vehicle of private interests (with the partial exception of the FND in 1965–66), and AD leaders have always been suspicious of the economic elite, in part because of that group's close identification with the foreign petroleum companies. COPEI has also been unsympathetic, especially since 1970. Christian Democratic ideology, though somewhat ambiguous about economic relationships, nevertheless tends to be anticapitalist, and the COPEI youth wing has been pressing for greater state intervention in the economy in recent years. Many of the smaller parties, of course, are much more aggressively hostile toward the private sector.

Representatives of the private sector have enjoyed considerable *administrative* access to public policy decisions, especially when they have held managerial posts in the government or in one of the many autonomous institutes; and they have obtained *representational* access on a number of special consultative boards, mainly within the planning institutions created to provide channels of communication between the state and private interests. Private-sector influence has been especially strong in the Ministry of Finance, the Ministry of Development and the Central Bank. Here, off and on, leaders with connections to the two largest entrepreneurial families (the Mendozas and the Vollmers) have held top posts since 1958.[28]

Despite this consultative and administrative access, however, economic policymaking in Venezuela has been characterized by chronic tension between economic elites and the government. For a while during the Betancourt administration, when political leaders were especially careful to avoid threatening economic elites, the two sectors seemed to be coming to terms. They faced a common threat from the Left, and leaders on both sides made efforts to compromise their differences; indeed, for a time they toyed with the notion of introducing formal corporate representation in the government. The administration revived the moribund National Economic Council, a consultative institution authorized by the 1936 Constitution, and created several other high-level commissions intended to "advise" the government on economic policy.[29] Little came of these initiatives, however, and most of the new organizations atrophied or disappeared entirely in subsequent years. In practice, neither side was willing to be coopted by the other.

As a result of this structural and ideological cleavage, Venezuela has developed a pattern of "crisis" politics characterized by a constant and sometimes bitter tug-of-war between the government and the economic interests represented by Fedecámaras and other organizations. Made nervous by their inability to dominate the government completely and their vulnerability to public-policy decisions, the private elites have grouped together and assumed a highly defensive posture, relying on their control of the communications media and their ability to influence public opinion. The intensity of government-private clashes has tended to increase over the years, especially since the late 1960's and early 1970's, when the government cautiously began to assert itself in economic policy in ways considered threatening by all or part of the private sector.

As might be expected, the foreign petroleum companies have done their best to take advantage of this pattern of relationships. Although they have always been considered a separate, special group within the private economic sphere, they have sought to enhance their bargaining position by identifying their own interests with those of domestic interest groups, and have worked hard to derive benefits, where possible, from conflicts between the government and the private sector. In fact, since 1958 alliance with domestic economic elites has been a key defensive strategy of the oil companies.

The Doctrinal Basis of Policy

One of the distinctive characteristics of Venezuelan petroleum policy is that it has been shaped by a coherent and explicitly articulated rationale—a rough cluster of assumptions about the proper goals of policy, about the actors involved and their motivations, and about the kinds of alternatives and strategies that make sense within this context. One man, AD's "petroleum philosopher" Juan Pablo Pérez Alfonzo, has been the chief propounder of this underlying doctrine.

Since the earliest years of petroleum exploitation in their country, Venezuelans have been acutely conscious of their dependent pattern of development and their vulnerability to external political and economic events. The phrase *sembrar el petróleo* ("to sow the oil"), now a classic epigram within the community of oil-producing nations, was coined by Arturo Uslar Pietri in the course of a 1936 debate about the uses of oil income. Though originally referring to agricultural development, it has come to mean the generalized use of funds to create an economic infrastructure independent of petroleum. It encapsulates the overall development strategy that has been espoused by virtually every leader and regime since 1936. But it was Pérez Alfonzo who took this idea, added new, conservationist concerns of his own, and fashioned from it a practical doctrine for the formulation of policy alternatives.[30]

Pérez Alfonzo began his career as AD's spokesman on oil matters during the decade of conservative rule that followed Juan Vicente Gómez's death in 1935. A lawyer by profession, he was one of the principal opposition spokesmen in the Chamber during the debate that culminated with the passage of the landmark 1943 Petroleum Code. And when AD came to power in 1945, he took charge of petroleum affairs for the new government. Later, after several years of exile in Mexico during the dictatorship of Pérez Jiménez, he became Minister of Mines and Hydrocarbons* under the government of Rómulo Betancourt.

There are several reasons why Pérez Alfonzo's ideas have had such a powerful and long-lasting impact. To begin with, he was for years the foremost expert on oil matters within AD. While minister he received strong backing from President Betancourt,

---

* This title is commonly shortened to Minister of Mines or Petroleum Minister.

even during difficult times when the government's oil policy was under attack and party ranks were divided over the proper course of action.* With this support, Pérez Alfonzo committed AD and the government to a policy closely tied to his theoretical doctrine; and his successors in the Ministry, Manuel Pérez Guerrero, who took charge of oil policy in 1963, and José Antonio Mayobre, who became Minister in 1967, followed his lead closely. Even the Caldera administration that came to power in 1968 stuck to much the same course although Pérez Alfonzo's influence was felt primarily through his public criticism of policy and his personal ties to individuals and factions within the legislature.

But Pérez Alfonzo's ideas also came at the right time. Convinced of the need to "sow the oil" and all too aware of the detrimental effects of dependence, Venezuelan leaders needed more than nationalistic resentment and the desire for a larger share of the profits to bargain effectively with foreign companies. They needed a doctrine to justify their actions and to answer the persuasive arguments of oil-industry spokesmen. Pérez Alfonzo responded to this need: in a direct and articulate manner he challenged the entire structure and rationale of private control of the oil industry, not only in Venezuela but everywhere, and accused it of leading not only to the despoliation of poor exporting countries but also to the waste of natural resources on a worldwide scale.

A conservationist first and foremost, Pérez Alfonzo believes that oil has a high "intrinsic" value not necessarily reflected in market prices, since it is critically important to modern industrial civilization and since the petroleum resources of the earth are nonrenewable and are rapidly being depleted. He feels, therefore, that the only way to assure a satisfactory price is to place the petroleum industry under government control, not only domestically but internationally. His strongest statements on behalf of

---

* Betancourt himself has always been concerned with petroleum and its role in Venezuelan development. His book *Venezuela: Política y Petróleo* combines a history and justification of AD's role in Venezuelan history with a strident denunciation of the role of foreign oil companies in supporting authoritarian regimes. But as president he had neither the time nor the inclination to become familiar with the technical details of the petroleum industry, and thus allowed Pérez Alfonzo, the acknowledged expert, a great deal of autonomy.

his theory of "intrinsic value" came in 1959 and 1960, when the international market was glutted with oil and prices were steadily dropping. During those years he repeatedly asserted that prices should go up and predicted that they would do so eventually as recognition of the importance of petroleum in the world grew. Of course, he said, enlightened and forceful public policies were needed to assure this recognition.

Pérez Alfonzo is also a strict conservationist in the more technical meaning of the term. As Petroleum Minister he did his best to assure that the companies in Venezuela employed the most advanced conservation techniques known. Here he sought to emulate many practices followed in the United States (he especially admired the regulatory system managed by the Texas Railroad Commission). Personally, he finds waste of any kind abhorrent, whether in the flaring of natural gas from wells or in the misuse of public funds; efficiency, economy, self-discipline, and careful long-range planning are the virtues he most admires. Looking backward from our present "energy crisis" and the currently fashionable concern with environmental issues, most of these ideas seem quite respectable. In their time, however, Pérez Alfonzo's critics considered them both radical and eccentric—especially in Venezuela, where the habit of public thrift has been perhaps less cultivated than anywhere else in the hemisphere.*

On the international level, Pérez Alfonzo believes, a kind of "soft" imperialism is at work, one not so much the product of deterministic laws of history as the natural result of massive political and economic inequality. A belief in the redistributive character of international economic relationships has assumed a more prominent place in his thinking since the concept was elaborated in the work of Argentine Raúl Prebisch and subsequently incorporated as organizational doctrine by the United Nations Economic Commission for Latin America, which Prebisch headed. The heart of this doctrine is that there is a general tendency

---

* Anecdotes illustrating Pérez Alfonzo's obsession with efficiency are a commonplace in Venezuela's petroleum industry. Many of them, along with a comprehensive discussion of Alfonzo's "philosophy," will appear in Clemente Cohen's forthcoming biography.

for the course of trade to turn against less developed countries, forcing them to pay more for imports while receiving less for products sold to developed countries. As Pérez Alfonzo puts it, "This is the key to the power and evil of economic imperialism: buy cheap and sell dear."[31]

As far as the overall role of oil in Venezuelan development is concerned, Pérez Alfonzo long ago concluded that there are clear limits upon the rate at which Venezuela can absorb capital and use it efficiently to generate self-sustaining growth. He has often called this the problem of "economic indigestion," referring to Colin Clark's analysis of the British economy between the World Wars.[32] As a consequence, he has always insisted that oil production should be controlled in such a way that income increases come at a rate compatible with the country's capacity to handle them in a productive manner. Also, since oil is a nonrenewable asset with good prospects for increasing value, he insists that income increments should come from price rises, taxed at the highest possible rate, and not from production increases.

The practical objectives of policy, stemming from this doctrinal framework, may be summarized as follows:

1. Conservation.

2. Taxation at the highest possible levels, to assure a just return to the country from the exploitation of its patrimony.

3. High prices that adequately reflect the "intrinsic" value of petroleum.

4. Controlled production, designed to prolong the lifetime of oil reserves and produce income at a rate that can be used efficiently by the economy.

5. Public regulation and control of the industry at both national and international levels to realize these objectives.

As later chapters will reveal, many people in Venezuela disagreed with Pérez Alfonzo—with his disdain for the market mechanism, his extreme concern for conservation, his belief that the capital influx to underdeveloped Venezuela should be slowed, and his assurance that the intrinsic value of oil would sooner or later be reflected in prices. Especially during the years 1960–67, when prices were plummeting and Venezuela's primacy among oil-exporting countries was slipping away, many felt that policies based on this idealistic framework would irreparably damage the country. To a remarkable degree, however, and despite heavy criticism, the Venezuelan government's strategies in handling petroleum have continued to reflect this outlook.

2. Antecedents

Petroleum Policy to 1958

THE EXPLOITATION of Venezuela's oil by foreign interests began immediately after World War I, when changing patterns of energy consumption in the developed countries stimulated a scramble for control of overseas petroleum. British corporations were the first to make major investments, but American capitalists soon followed, backed energetically by the U.S. government. Once begun, oil development proceeded rapidly. Petroleum appeared in Venezuelan export statistics for the first time in 1918; by 1927 it was the country's principal export; and by 1929 Venezuela was the largest oil exporter in the world.[1]

The Gómez dictatorship did its best to attract foreign investors. The legal codes governing the granting of concessions in Venezuela and stipulating the privileges and obligations of concessionnaires were among the most liberal in the hemisphere, and when necessary Gómez used the army to quash oilworkers' strikes for higher wages and improved working conditions. Government income from oil at this time was derived primarily from royalty payments, and beginning in 1920 these were set at between 8 and 15 percent of the commercial value of the product; commercial value, in turn, was determined by the going price in a principal market, usually New York.[2] Additional funds came from small surface taxes levied on concessionnaires in return for the use of the land itself, and from exploitation taxes required of those wishing to explore for new deposits. Gómez, however, supplemented these modest payments in a number of ways to increase his personal income and that of his supporters and sycophants.[3] Most notorious was his practice of selling concession lands to his friends, who the made their own deals with foreign investors. The oil companies, at this time interested in securing attractive concessions and beginning production as soon as possible, reciprocated in full, using bribery and diplomatic pressure in defense of their interests.

Few Venezuelans knew anything about the petroleum industry; and the government, completely unprepared administratively to cope with the boom, did little to supervise or control company activity during the first decade of development. It was common practice for lawyers and executives representing the larger companies to "assist" the government in drafting its own petroleum codes.

When the Depression struck the petroleum industry, it became apparent how dependent on international events Venezuela's economy had become. Before 1929 the industry expanded almost geometrically, and prices remained quite steady; but after that date prices dropped, and the companies had to curtail their operations. By October 1930, 40 percent of the oilworkers employed in 1929 had been fired, and government income, which had reached a peak of Bs 256 million ($83 million) in 1929,* dropped to Bs 175 million ($57 million) by 1932.[4] In the meantime, domestic criticism of some of the oil companies' more blatant abuses was growing.

In response to these conditions, Gómez allowed his Minister of Development, Gumersindo Torres, to begin putting pressure on the companies. Torres established an Office of Hydrocarbons within his Ministry and began to send inspectors out to the fields to check production meters, leading the companies to complain that incompetent government technicians were interfering with the efficiency of their operations. But he went too far in 1932, when he accused the companies of giving false financial information to

* Bs is the symbol for bolívares, Venezuela's currency. Exchange rates of bolívares to U.S. dollars can be found in Appendix Table F, p. 185. Here and elsewhere the figures given are in actual or undeflated currency unless otherwise indicated. A conversion to constant values can be carried out by using the ratios given in Appendix Table E.

the state for the calculation of royalties and demanded some Bs 56 million ($18 million) in reparations. (He based his computation, incidentally, on United States Tariff Commission figures, not on data gathered by the Venezuelan government itself.) Giving in to industry demands, Gómez fired Torres and suspended government claims for damages.[5]

The Death of Gómez and the 1942–43 Agreements

Public debate over oil policy began within months of Gómez's death in 1935, and it grew steadily in intensity as information about the shady practices of the old regime came to light. Almost immediately the government brought suit against several of the larger oil companies, asking damages and compensation for the illegal advantages they had enjoyed in the bidding for the concessions granted in the 1920's. Some of these cases were settled out of court, but in several instances the Venezuelan Supreme Court ordered companies to make substantial payments to the state. In 1938 and 1939, for example, Mene Grande had to pay more than Bs 30 million ($9.7 million) in fines. In addition, following the earlier initiative of Torres, López Contreras's Minister of Development, Nestor Luis Pérez, presented a bill to Standard of New Jersey's principal subsidiary for having incorrectly reported costs, and the company ended up paying some Bs 4 million ($1.3 million).[6]

The government also renegotiated the basis for calculating royalty payments. Companies operating in Venezuela have always sold a major portion of their oil to their own refineries—in effect, to themselves—and the issue of what selling price should be used to calculate the commercial value of the oil has always been of prime concern. The arrangement that had been used under Gómez was terminated in 1936, and after a period of discussion a new formula was worked out. The companies also consented at this time to recalculate the value of royalty payments for the previous six years, setting an important precedent for the future.[7]

In 1938 Congress passed a new concessions law containing a number of important adjustments that favored the government, including an increase of the royalty rate to 16 percent, and large increases in surface and exploration taxes. The companies strongly opposed this measure and lobbied vigorously against it. In 1940, when the president decided to implement it despite their objections, they announced that they would not enter into any new agreements for further petroleum development while it was in force. The arrangement that finally resolved this unprecedented deadlock was the famous 1942–43 petroleum tax and concessions code, which set the terms for the industry's rapid growth in subsequent years.[8]

Despite their tough stand, the companies were quite anxious to obtain new concessions lands. World demand for petroleum was soaring, and they had had time to make careful surveys of the most promising areas for new oil production. Some of the best Venezuelan concessions were due to expire in approximately a decade and most of the others would lapse shortly after that. In order to justify further investment and ensure the continued expansion of the petroleum industry, the companies needed to obtain a secure control of new reserves. They were also anxious to "clean up" their overall legal position in Venezuela, since they were already facing legal challenges to the validity of concessions obtained during Gómez's rule and anticipated more such difficulties. And they were afraid the example set by Mexico, which expropriated foreign oil companies in 1938, might prove dangerous in view of growing nationalist feelings in Venezuela. In sum, the oil companies were ready and willing to start over again on more solid ground.

After the outbreak of World War II, the United States government was anxious to avoid any decline in oil shipments, and the State Department urged American companies to come to some agreement with the Venezuelan government. According to one student of U.S. foreign policy during these years, there was considerable sympathy among U.S. officials for the Venezuelan position in the matter: "Venezuela was viewed by the [State] Department as being in the process of taking steps to secure social reforms denied to Venezuelan people during Gómez' long dictatorship."[9] Again, fear of a repetition of the Mexican troubles was probably an important motive.

On the Venezuelan side, the government of Medina Angarita, which came to power in 1941, found itself in a difficult position in bargaining with the companies. Medina himself took a strongly nationalistic public posture. He was anxious to rectify the mistakes of previous administrations, and he knew that squeezing the oil industry would help win support from the various parties that were emerging as important political forces during his administration. But, like his predecessor, Medina was afraid of damaging the industry and driving it out of the country; and neither he nor his advisors knew enough about the industry and its operations to judge the technical impact of alternative reform measures. The Venezuelan government already depended on oil for one-third of its revenues, and the economy as a whole was rapidly becoming a creature of the industry (see Table 14, p. 167).

More immediately, Medina faced a growing shortage of funds at a time when demands for public investment in Venezuela's economy were growing and the government was anxious to respond with new programs. The shortage itself can be traced mainly to World War II, which again served notice of how closely the country's welfare had become tied to the international petroleum market. Total government income, which had reached Bs 340 million ($110 million) in 1938, dropped to Bs 277 million ($90 million) in 1942, and did not recover completely until 1944 (figures in adjusted 1938 bolívares). Except in 1941, which was a good year in terms of production, the industry ran into serious difficulties during the war as a result of the closure of the European market, losses to German submarines—seven tankers were torpedoed in February 1942 alone—and equipment shortages. In 1941–42, a critical period in the renegotiation of the oil concessions, production dropped 35 percent, and the government's income fell 22 percent. Medina tried to adjust to the budgetary squeeze by cutting salaries and government programs, and eventually by borrowing,[10] but these measures provided little relief. In the end, he had to come to terms with the foreign companies.

In mid-1942 Medina announced his plans to revise the concessions laws and at the same time asked Congress to pass the country's first income tax law, which included a levy on the net profits of the foreign corporations. In January 1943 the income tax went into effect; and in February, Medina presented Congress with the draft of a completely revised petroleum code, which passed unchanged three weeks later.[11] Throughout this time the petroleum companies had issued statements supporting the government and announcing their willingness to accept the new proposals. In retrospect, this is hardly surprising, since the new code had been drafted in secret by several U.S. oil industry "experts," working closely with Medina and his attorney general.*

The agreement consolidated at this time was a compromise in which the government received more income in return for guaranteeing the companies' old concessions and promising new ones. To be specific, Venezuela received increased revenues from income taxes and larger surface taxes, and the royalty rate went up to 16⅔ percent. Later in 1944 the government once again renegotiated the reference prices by which royalty payments were determined, and as before the new prices were applied retroactively to most of 1943. In return for this the government terminated pending litigation that challenged the validity of past concessions and that asked compensation for fraudulent practices. More important, it agreed to let the companies convert their old concessions to the terms of the new code. This had two effects: the companies were able to completely repair the defects in their legal position stemming from past malpractices; and they were able to obtain an extension of 40 years, the time span of concessions under the new code, on their rights to some of the most lucrative oil lands in the hemisphere. Finally, the government agreed to open up

* Pérez Alfonzo discovered this in 1945, when, as Minister of Development under the revolutionary junta, he found a portfolio containing the correspondence between Medina and the United Geophysical Company of Pasadena, California. During an interview with me in the summer of 1973 he described this discovery and displayed many of the documents he had found. This is an important episode, since the 1943 code has been considered the first real nationalistic self-assertion on the part of the government. See Pérez Alfonzo, *Petróleo y Dependencia*, p. 12.

large new areas of the country to foreign oil investors.[12] As all these points were being settled, members of the opposition in Congress, led by Pérez Alfonzo and other AD leaders, repeatedly charged that the government was being soft on the companies, who ought to pay even more to compensate for their past abuses.[13] To a degree, this criticism probably helped Medina strengthen his bargaining position with the companies. He defended his proposals by stating that his goal was to obtain at least half of the companies' future profits for Venezuela.[14]

The new arrangement cost the companies more money in royalties, but it gave them the chance to consolidate their operations in Venezuela on a much more secure basis and opened the prospect of large-scale expansion of their operations. As far as the government was concerned, the agreement established the conditions for an entirely new phase in the growth of the petroleum industry, a growth that provided the fiscal resources for increased government programs. The companies now moved quickly to consolidate their position: before the end of 1943 they had converted their more desirable concessions to the terms of the new code and had begun negotiating for new territory. In 1944 Medina began a massive round of concessions sales, awarding oil rights to 5.97 million hectares of land during that year alone—more than the total awarded in all previous Venezuelan history. These arrangements brought the government some Bs 54 million ($16 million) in additional payments.* Most of the oil produced in Venezuela up to the mid-1970's has come from concessions revalidated or established under the 1943 code.

The Revolutionary Junta

When the 1945 coup displaced Medina and brought a civil-military junta to power, there was widespread fear among the companies that the government might nationalize the industry, or, at

---

* Before 1938 the area of the concessions had been 4.97 million hectares. Between 1938 and 1943 almost no land was granted because the companies refused to conclude agreements. Pérez Alfonzo, *Venezuela y Su Petróleo*, p. 34.

best, might renounce the hard-won 1943 agreements. This fear increased when it was announced that Pérez Alfonzo, one of the most outspoken critics of government policy in previous years, would be the new Minister of Development.* However, although many of the junta's reforms were quite radical, especially those affecting the political process, the government proved surprisingly cautious in its oil policies. President Betancourt later explained the reasons: "Practically the whole Venezuelan economy and an appreciable portion of government income are based on the petroleum industry. . . . Faced with these realities, it would have been a suicidal leap into space to nationalize the industry by decree."[15] Instead, the junta decided to work within the established legal structure, trying to ensure that the reforms made by the Medina administration were carried out efficiently and honestly, and meanwhile working in piecemeal fashion to establish the framework for a system of petroleum development that would ultimately replace the foreign concessions.

Shortly after the coup the junta announced that income-tax figures had been manipulated by the Medina regime to justify its claim that it had received 50 percent of the oil companies' profits in 1944.[16] The junta then decreed an extraordinary levy of Bs 89 million ($27 million) to bring the figure to 50 percent according to its own calculations. To further consolidate the 50-50 principle, the government in 1948 instituted a measure known as the Additional Tax, which provided for a 50 percent tax on any sum by which a company's net profits for any year exceeded the government's total revenue from that company's activities in Venezuela. This simple formula subsequently spread to other oil-exporting nations: Iran adopted it in 1949, Saudi Arabia in 1950, Kuwait in 1951, and Bahrain and Iraq in 1952.[17] Though upset by these new expenses, the companies took a conciliatory line at this time, hoping to cultivate the government's surprisingly moderate stance on petroleum matters. They complied with govern-

---

* This agency set oil policies until 1950, when the Ministry of Mines and Hydrocarbons was established.

ment demands where necessary and avoided serious confrontations of any kind.*

The junta also sought to increase its income from oil by taking part of its royalty in kind and offering the oil for sale or barter directly on the world market. The law, in fact, had always allowed this, but in the past the government had preferred cash payments. From 1946 to 1948, however, there was a worldwide scarcity of crude oil, and refineries in the consuming countries were paying special premiums to assure a continuing supply. Accordingly, the Venezuelan government signed several contracts agreeing to sell its royalty oil at higher price levels and negotiated trade agreements involving oil with Portugal, Brazil, and Argentina. Relatively little oil was actually involved, but these agreements made the companies so uncomfortable that they quickly agreed to buy back the rest of the royalty oil from the government at prices above the established reference levels.

In order to cushion the impact of international events on the dependent Venezuelan economy, Pérez Alfonzo also began to set up what he then called an "anticyclical fund." Expecting the growth of Venezuela's income to continue accelerating, to the point where the country would be unable to spend this income efficiently on existing projects, he planned a special reserve that would contain the equivalent of at least a year's public budget. This would improve the government's bargaining position vis-à-vis the companies and would allow a more gradual adjustment of the economy to future wars or international depressions.[18]

Of far greater importance, from the companies' perspective, were the steps Pérez Alfonzo took to lay foundations for the eventual replacement of the concessions system. Immediately after the coup the junta announced that it would grant no further concessions whatever. Then, in the spring of 1948, the president appointed a special commission to study the creation of a national

---

* According to Gertrud Edwards (in Mikesell, p. 107), Creole, the company most seriously affected by the 1948 Additional Tax, "voluntarily contributed a sum large enough to make the government's share in profits equal to the companies' share for the years 1946 and 1947, as well as for 1948."

petroleum company, which would participate in the development of the nation's remaining oil reserves. But this commission's report, eagerly anticipated in Venezuela, was never made, since the government was overthrown before its completion.

Oil Policy Under the Military Dictatorship

The military dictatorship that took power in 1948 entirely abandoned the reformist orientation of AD. It ended all discussions of an anticyclical fund or a national company, and before long it agreed to open new areas to concessions. On a personal as well as an administrative level, relationships between company executives and government officials became much more amicable and cooperative. On several occasions, the government even passed up opportunities to increase its share of oil profits and its control of company activities. Especially in the later years of the dictatorship, peculation and corruption in the manipulation of oil income reached major proportions. The overall malperformance of the regime in economic matters has already been mentioned.[19]

Despite its willingness to accommodate the companies by continuing the concession system and allowing a generous return on investments, the dictatorship was anxious to ensure a steady growth in its own oil revenues; accordingly, it kept the Additional Tax on the books. Shortly after the 1948 coup the companies tried to convince the government to ease their tax burden, arguing that Venezuelan oil was losing out in the world market to oil from the Middle East, where production costs were lower and foreign companies were treated more leniently. (This line of argument subsequently became a standard formula in company bargaining, and it will be examined more carefully in Chapter 3.) These complaints did not lead to a revision of the 50-50 formula, but they did inspire a renegotiation of the royalty pricing arrangements in the companies' favor. Under the previous agreement, royalty oil had been valued according to prevailing prices at West Texas ports in the United States. However, much of Venezuela's oil was sold on the East Coast North American market, in which prices were substantially lower. The companies pointed this out, and the government agreed to renegotiate. A new and more involved formula, adopted in 1951, took into account both the quality of the oil involved and the cost of transportation to the United States, reducing the "overvaluation" about which the companies had complained. This pricing system was used until the mid-1970's.[20] In the meantime, the competitiveness of Venezuelan oil in the world market improved somewhat owing to the adoption of the 50-50 standard in the Middle East, and also to the nationalization of Iranian oil, which enhanced the strategic value of Venezuela's more secure production.

The effectiveness of the companies' strategies in reducing their costs in Venezuela can be measured in part by the return on their investments. After reaching a low of 14 percent (as a percentage of net fixed assets) in 1949, this figure gradually increased, leveling off at 30+ percent after 1954 (see Appendix Table A, pp. 179–81). Business was good under Pérez Jiménez. In 1956 and 1957 the government gave in to company pressure and agreed to open still another large portion of the national reserves to concessions. In the end, 821,107 hectares were awarded, in return for some Bs 2.25 billion (about $675 million).[21] Unlike the earlier concessions, these were allocated through competitive bidding. In addition to increasing the government's income on concessions at the time of the award, this method allowed a considerable portion of the new land to go to smaller independent companies, thereby partially transforming the structure of the industry in Venezuela.

During the dictatorship, the government's share of the profits reported by oil companies suffered a gradual erosion, leveling off at approximately 52 percent during 1955–57. This was the first time since the establishment of the income tax that the state's share had actually decreased over an extended period of time. The drop reflected the government's policy of seeking funds through increased production and the sale of new concessions rather than through further taxation of earnings. The dictatorship did provide itself with ample funds from oil, however. In the decade between 1948 and 1957 the foreign companies produced nearly 1.5 times as much oil as had been produced in all the preceding years, and government income, in constant 1938 currency, tripled (see Appendix Table B, p. 182).

By the time Pérez Jiménez was ousted Venezuela had become thoroughly enmeshed in a pattern of dependent development. She had become, as Rómulo Betancourt put it, "a petroleum factory."[22] The traditional agricultural base of the society had atrophied, and Venezuelans imported a large proportion of their food. Much of the country's middle-level commercial and manufacturing activity was financed by the spillover of funds from oil development, and two-thirds of the government budget derived directly from the royalties, income taxes, and other payments made by the companies. Whatever happened to the international oil industry would happen to Venezuela. The government accepted this condition and did little or nothing to change it. As long as the money kept coming in, public officials seemed content with the assumption that what was good for the companies was good for them, and hence for Venezuela.

3. The Betancourt Administration

Assertive Experimentation

WHEN THE GOVERNMENT headed by Rómulo Betancourt came to power in 1959, Venezuela's petroleum policymakers confronted circumstances quite different from those of the middle and late 1940's. The concessions system had become even more firmly implanted as a result of the extensive new territories handed over by the dictatorship. In addition, Pérez Jiménez and the free-spending transitional regime that followed him had left the country in a serious economic bind. Unemployment, capital flight, a desperately poor rural lower class, and a very large budget deficit all made it difficult for the government to do anything that would interrupt the flow of oil funds to the country.

The international petroleum market had also changed in important ways. During the 1950's prices for Venezuelan oil had climbed steadily, reaching a peak in 1957, after the Suez Crisis had created a temporary shortage and given an advantage to Venezuela by closing the Canal to tankers from the Middle East. However, after 1957 prices began a steady decline that continued for more than a decade (see Appendix Table C, p. 183). This was caused partly by a breakdown of self-restraint within the cartel of international oil firms and partly by the entry of many small and medium-sized producers into the market. Somewhat later, Soviet efforts to win a portion of the market outside the Eastern Bloc contributed to the downward trend.

Despite these difficult conditions, Pérez Alfonzo, with the strong support of Betancourt, renewed his campaign to refashion the institutional relationship between the state and the private oil industry. This time, however, he was forced to concentrate less upon taxes and royalties and more upon government control of the companies' traditional marketing prerogatives—the determination of production levels, export destinations, and, above all, prices. The companies, too, had to make rapid adjustments. They already bore the stigma of personal and financial collaboration with the dictatorship, and, although international trends enhanced their bargaining power, they found their political access and influence at a new low. In the past they had relied on informal contacts and persuasion; but now, if they were to maintain their political leverage and defend their interests, it was necessary to try to influence public opinion and to build alliances with the domestic economic community.

The Larrazábal junta, which ruled Venezuela during the year following Pérez Jiménez's ouster, at first avoided taking any stand on petroleum policy. The provisional Minister of Mines, Carlos Pérez de La Cova, declared that the government was too busy with other economic problems to think about the concessions system and the possibilities of a national oil company: it would leave these matters to be decided by the constitutional government that was to be elected in the near future.[1] During the electoral campaign itself, AD leaders said they would not nationalize the industry but would seek the same reforms they had been pursuing when they were ousted from power in 1948.[2] For the most part, the companies felt reassured about their future prospects in Venezuela. However, shortly after the December elections the junta unexpectedly announced that it was raising the corporate income tax for companies at the top of the income bracket, the new rates to be retroactive for the entire year of 1958. The decree also provided that royalty payments would continue to be deducted from gross revenue (i.e. expensed) rather than directly from tax liability.[3] These measures immediately raised the government's share of company profits from 52 percent to 65 percent—the largest single increase since the establishment of the income tax.

The companies, accustomed to quite different treatment in Venezuela, aggressively denounced the new tax law. For them, the 50–50 profits split had become a valuable symbolic threshold; once the line was crossed they had no firm standard by which to gauge their relationship with the state. Their anxiety was compounded by the likely response to Venezuela's actions in other host countries, where the 50–50 arrangement still prevailed. Harold Haight, head of Creole Oil, demanded that the government reconsider its action, complaining in a press conference that the companies had not been consulted before the change was announced, even though the provisional government had promised to do so in matters affecting the oil industry. Eugene Holman, Chairman of the Board for Standard of New Jersey (Creole's parent company), said that for Venezuela the ultimate result would be a decline in income, since this surprise action would seriously affect industry reinvestment policy.[4] Shell quickly joined in, stating that it would be forced to review very carefully its plans for future capital investments.[5] Such blustering fell on hostile ears, to say the least. Venezuelan public and official indignation was so strong, in fact, that the U.S. State Department cautioned company representatives to be more politic in their behavior.*

Underlying the junta's action (which had been taken after only minimum consultation with AD) was an urgent need for additional income. The Larrazábal government had been profligate in its use of funds, for the most part trying to deal with serious economic and social problems by simply handing out money to all claimants. It had outspent even the last year of the dictatorship by nearly 15 percent, and even after the retroactive tax levy it left behind a budget deficit of more than Bs 900 million ($270 million).† It was widely reported in the press that the sudden tax increase just before Betancourt's inauguration was intended to make it easier for the new constitutional government to establish itself without having to confront the oil industry; and it certainly did provide a cushion of this kind. However, it seems to have been designed primarily to cover the fiscal tracks of the junta.

---

* *Wall Street Journal*, 26.xii.58, p. 2. Within a short time Haight—known in industry circles as the Iron Duke—was replaced as head of Creole.

† The largest previous deficit, Bs 560 million ($167 million) had come the year before, traceable chiefly to Péréz Jiménez. Venezuela, [4], 1971, p. 305.

The Betancourt government retained the new law without change. At this time and later, Pérez Alfonzo used as a guideline for equitable taxation the principle that oil companies were entitled to profits of 15 percent on their net fixed assets, a return he judged compatible with the prevailing capital market and appropriate for an enterprise akin to a public utility. If the tax structure had not been changed by the junta, he would almost certainly have proposed reforms of his own, since company earnings had been running over 30 percent for several years. The system he inherited, however, was as rigorous as he considered feasible under the prevailing conditions.[6] (In the event, company profits dropped immediately to 13 percent.)

The new administration announced that it would grant no further concessions and quickly moved to establish a state petroleum company. Early in 1960 the Corporación Venezolana del Petróleo (CVP) began operations as an autonomous government agency under the Ministry of Mines. The plan was to assign oil-rich lands to the new company, which would then negotiate a series of service contracts with foreign interests in order to develop oil production. Ideally, this arrangement would draw upon foreign capital but at the same time centralize administrative control and authority in the hands of the state.[7] As it turned out, the CVP remained a very limited venture during the first decade of its existence. It drilled a few wells on proven land, and in 1964 the government (by statute) granted it one-third of the domestic market as an outlet for its products. But its production remained small, reaching only 2.20 percent of the country's total by 1973.[8]

There were several reasons for this. For one thing, the world petroleum market was oversupplied, and prices were dropping; Pérez Alfonzo was not anxious to make things worse by offering large amounts of additional Venezuelan oil for sale. The foreign oil companies were even less anxious to conclude service contracts with the government and thereby, in effect, help create their own competition. Unless Venezuela's output were to be restricted, the existing concessions system—firmly embedded, thanks to Pérez Jiménez's awards—could easily meet the moderate production targets that Pérez Alfonzo advocated. Aware of these circumstances when he created the CVP, the new minister explained that the company was nevertheless essential: it would help Venezuelans gain admistrative experience in petroleum management; and it would provide the nucleus for a system that would ultimately replace the existing network of concessions.

The deteriorating world market also provided the impetus for policy initiatives of an entirely different kind. The immediate catalyst was a series of large cuts in posted prices for crude oil during the first months of 1959. Pérez Alfonzo denounced the cuts as unjustified, and as detrimental to all producing countries. He was correct on the last point: in Venezuela's case, on an average production of 2.8 million barrels a day, the price drop in 1959 (27¢ per barrel) meant a revenue loss of $276 million a year to the companies operating there, and one of about $105 million to the government.[9] Chiefly because of these price trends, policymakers in Venezuela concluded that the country's interests required direct government intervention in the marketing decisions of the companies, as well as a much more active diplomacy designed to bring underdeveloped oil-producing countries together for self-protection and to give Venezuela a more secure access to her major markets. It was Pérez Alfonzo's hope that this dual strategy, involving both domestic and international measures, might prevent further price deterioration and perhaps actually wrest the power to determine global production levels from the multinational corporations and the consumer governments. It was a grand and ambitious scheme.

Domestic Policy: An Experiment in Active Control

Within Venezuela, the Betancourt administration began by organizing a new agency within the Ministry of Mines called the Coordinating Commission for the Conservation and Commerce of Hydrocarbons, to which they assigned broad powers over the production and marketing of the country's petroleum. Made up of Ministry officials, the Coordinating Commission was from the start a highly pragmatic institution.[10] Few people at the outset had a clear idea of what it proposed to do and how it planned to implement its decisions; but from Pérez Alfonzo's own statements, it is evident that he foresaw two major roles for it. First, it would be a general monitor of the entire industry, working with the rest of the Ministry to keep a close watch on the activities of the companies. Second, it would serve as a kind of control board, which could, on the basis of its own information, make recommendations or give orders to prevent marketing decisions from exceeding the broad limits set by government policy. In this second capacity the Commission would make decisions regarding production levels, the destination of exports, and even prices.

The principal model for the Commission was the oil prorationing system already operating in the United States, in which official boards were empowered to make key decisions about production levels in order to prevent wasteful and destructive competition. Pérez Alfonzo hoped that Venezuela could establish such a system for itself, and even invited a member of the most effective American prorationing board, the Texas Railroad Commission, to come to Venezuela and assist in drawing up plans. The success of any prorationing system, of course, depends on the ability of authorities to control the principal sources of supply to the market; otherwise the system can have only a marginal influence on prices. In the United States, and especially in areas like Texas, this kind of control had largely been established. But Venezuela did not control a sufficient share of the world market to make this possible without the cooperation of other producing countries. Pérez Alfonzo of course hoped that such cooperation could be achieved in time, but it did not exist when the Coordinating Commission was first established. This larger role of the agency, then, remained a kind of latent objective, which influenced its actions but could not be fulfilled without success in other areas of policy—specifically, success in organizing the underdeveloped oil producers of the world.[11]

The Coordinating Commission could and did pursue the broader aims of policy in other ways. To begin with, it began to monitor the oil industry. Before 1959, Venezuelan experts were generally well informed about the technical aspects of oil production within the country, in the sense that they knew the principles of conservation and the best procedures for bringing oil to the surface; but they had very little idea of what went on in the industry as a whole, especially at the international level. After 1959 this changed quickly. Pérez Alfonzo turned the Petroleum Economy Section of the Ministry into a central information-gathering agency and instituted a system for collecting worldwide statistical data (newly formed ties with the Middle East proved a tremendous help in this endeavor). The Section also began to make careful studies of the international petroleum system, and the results were then used by the Coordinating Commission to analyze decisions made by the industry within Venezuela. In early 1960 the Commission began to require the companies to submit detailed reports, in advance, on their expected operations for each six-month period, including sales contracts. In order to placate Venezuela's new Arab friends, the Commission ordered the companies not to sell oil to Israel, a demand to which they acceded without difficulty. And, in support of the government's hostile policy toward the dictatorship of the Dominican Republic, it prohibited the shipment of oil to that country in 1960.

But the Commission's main concern was the price of oil, since any downward shift here would produce a corresponding or larger drop in government income. The term "posted price," in petroleum parlance, refers in theory to the average price at which crude oil is commonly sold by producers to refiners. In recent years, however, posted prices have rarely reflected the actual prices of crudes because of the practice known as "discounting." It has always been customary for companies to give discounts of various amounts to large or steady customers; and since the Suez Crisis discounting has become so prevalent that there has come to be, in effect, a flexible set of "ghost" prices running parallel to but below the officially posted rates. Discounts are rarely made public, of course, but most people familiar with the petroleum business would be able to cite the "real" going rates for crude in various parts of the world. Posted prices have retained their importance, but as a guide to discounts rather than as realizable prices. More important, posted prices also are used to assess oil taxes in most of the major producing countries. But in Venezuela during the Betancourt years taxes were paid on "realized" prices, or those actually paid by oil consumers. Given the prevailing buyer's market for petroleum, there was a natural tendency for the companies, when posted prices could not be cut, to use the discounting system as a functional equivalent to lowering prices.

The members of the Commission, well aware of this practice, began to insist that the companies avoid granting large or "abnormal" discounts in their sales contracts. In meetings with company executives, they discussed selected contracts (either pending or in effect), gave their views on whether or not the companies had granted abnormal discounts, and urged revisions where indicated. The companies, in turn, pressed for specific, concrete guidelines to what the government considered "normal" discounting, so that marketing decisions could be made on this basis. But the Commission would offer only vague estimates, preferring to work, as one member put it, "with a minimum of ground rules and a great deal of 'feel' for the marketplace."[12] Pragmatic, flexible discussions of specific contracts, it felt, were better than rigid rules—which would inevitably contain loopholes. And it defined abnormal as simply "outside the normal limits of trade"—which, of course, is not a definition at all. The relationship that gradually took shape was one in which the government focused on certain cases and assumed that the companies, under pressure, would derive their own lessons from the interaction and apply them across the board. Needless to say, this procedure was far from satisfactory to the companies.

The Commission began its active scrutiny of sales contracts early in 1960; and in spring of that year it announced several times that it had turned up special deals by which Venezuelan oil was being sold at prices lower than those prevailing in the market, and that the matter was under discussion with the companies involved. In these cases adjustments acceptable to the Commission were negotiated, and it was not until August that that body's authority was directly challenged. At that time two small operators, Superior Oil and the Sun Group, refused to modify several contracts as requested by the Commission, and the issue of sanctions was raised for the first time. In essence, the government had to act or abandon its efforts to prevent excessive discounts. The Commission therefore ordered the wells of the offending companies shut down and their other productive activities stopped pending modification of the contracts. It also issued a resolution defending its action and notifying the industry that the shutdown procedure would thereafter be a basic administrative practice in dealing with excessive discounting. Among other things, the resolution declared:

Whereas the Petroleum Code establishes that everything relating to hydrocarbons is a public utility, and in . . . Article 59 imposes the obligation on concessionnaires to carry out their operations in such a manner that waste of these substances does not occur. . . . Whereas abnormal discounts in the sale of hydrocarbons constitute an economic waste contrary to the national interest and could provoke the deterioration of petroleum prices in the international markets. Therefore: this Ministry will order the suspension of production that in the judgment of the Coordinating Commission for Conservation and Marketing of Hydrocarbons is destined by concessionnaires for sale at abnormal discounts. The Commission will make recommendations after analyzing each case.[18]

Within ten days the two companies agreed to modify their contracts and received permission to resume production. As it turned out, this was the only occasion on which the Commission had to resort to such sanctions.

On the whole, the government did obtain partial compliance with its demands during this early period of surveillance. Representatives of the larger corporations admitted that they were avoiding "marginal" discounts—that is, the more extreme ones—when possible in order to minimize conflict with the government. The smaller companies were less conciliatory, and the government clashed with them repeatedly. But any control of the independents gained by these confrontations was mainly a contribution toward stabilizing the international price structure, and a minor one at that; it meant very little to Venezuela in terms of income saved, owing to the small volume of sales involved.

This phase of active control, during which the Commission

pursued a policy of constant intervention in company marketing decisions, continued until the middle of 1962.* But the vigor of government action was declining, for several reasons. A major problem was administrative: the Commission was never able to keep close enough track of the companies' marketing decisions. Its leaders, though highly trained, lacked experience, and the agency itself lacked the staff and facilities needed for the complex job it had taken on. At the height of its activities, it relied heavily on the companies' own reports about their contracts, judging these according to very general estimates of prevailing prices. To do an effective job, it would eventually have had to develop the analytical resources to examine in detail many hundreds of extant and future contracts. Since this was impossible, it found itself on the defensive, with fewer facts at hand than the companies, and was consequently unwilling to provide overall guidelines. The token surveillance actually used relied on the effects of uncertainty and insecurity to keep the companies in line. Thus in practice the government was tagging along after the companies, urging them to do its bidding while fully aware that they knew more about actual market conditions.

It is evident in retrospect that the larger companies were able after a time to adjust their competitive behavior to the new "rules of the game," eventually gaining the upper hand in the process of conflict resolution. They did this through a combination of hard argument and a rather conservative discounting policy. By the end of 1962 the major oil producers, at least, were selling petroleum at roughly the prices they would have chosen without the intervention of the Coordinating Commission. Unlike the independents, they were not inclined to give very large discounts in any case—that is, discounts that clearly crossed the ambiguous government thresholds—and they could more easily manipulate other refining and marketing variables to compensate. Finally, they knew the government would be unlikely to shut down their own production, since the loss of even a few days' output from any

* The last government veto of a contract containing excessive discounts occurred in July 1962. See *El Nacional*, 20.vii.62 and 26.vii.62.

of the major producers would be too large to be recovered by discounting adjustments of any magnitude.

In the end, after three years of experimentation with active control, Venezuelan policymakers began to feel that their goals could probably be realized more easily in some other way. The establishment of a true international prorationing system might easily have justified the approach they had been using, but such a system had not been created. The year and a half following the fall of 1962, therefore, became a period of transition in which they began to search for alternatives.

Oil Diplomacy and the OPEC

At the international level, Venezuela launched a diplomatic offensive as ambitious and idealistic—and, in the short run, as ill-fated—as the campaign to involve the state directly in corporate pricing decisions. Aware that only by controlling the supply of oil entering world trade could Venezuela effectively influence price levels, Pérez Alfonzo set about building, piece by piece, a network of international intergovernmental controls designed to subordinate the private cartel of oil to a public cartel made up of producing governments (and, if possible, of consuming governments as well). Specifically, he sought two concrete objectives: first, an organization of exporting countries capable of controlling and prorationing the supply of oil entering the international market; and second, a comprehensive agreement with the United States and Canada to regulate and stabilize oil trade within the hemisphere, thus assuring Venezuela a degree of control and predictability in her principle market area.

The first formal move to organize the producing countries came early in 1959, when Pérez Alfonzo and a delegation of Venezuelan petroleum experts attended the First Arab Petroleum Congress in Cairo. Recent price cuts by the companies lent a sense of urgency to the meeting, and Venezuela's outspoken denunciation of them, which received widespread publicity in the Middle East, guaranteed a cordial reception for the visitors. In Cairo the Venezuelans lobbied vigorously for the creation of an international producers' organization, and they received strong support from the Saudi representative Abdullah Tariki. Other delegations were hesitant, however, and the best that Pérez Alfonzo and Tariki could achieve was the signing of a secret "gentlemen's agreement," in which the delegates promised to convey to their governments three recommendations: (1) that each producing nation should consider the creation of a formal organization to coordinate policies; (2) that no one producer should take advantage of another's problems with the oil companies to improve its own relative position; and (3) that agreement to changes in prices should be granted only after previous consultation with the other producers.[14]

In the year following the Cairo meeting Pérez Alfonzo and Tariki intensified their efforts to create a producers' organization, using both diplomatic channels and personal contacts to further their cause. Early in 1960 both men attended an international oil conference in Tyler, Texas, where Tariki—to the shock of many corporation delegates—presented a paper outlining a plan to limit total world petroleum production by setting up a prorationing commission, which would estimate worldwide demand and distribute the indicated production quotas among exporting countries. As might be expected, the proposal received little serious attention; but it is worth noting in retrospect that Pérez Alfonzo came out in favor of consumer participation in the prorationing scheme. His overriding objective was an international system of public control that could maintain prices and assure a stable oil supply. At this time, as well as in a later series of specific discussions with the United States government, he repeatedly pointed out that both producers and consumers would benefit from joint cooperation of this kind.[15] Following the Texas meeting, Tariki returned to Caracas with Pérez Alfonzo, and together they drafted a comprehensive plan for prorationing. As Pérez Alfonzo envisioned it, this international system would be a functional complement to the control system then taking form within Venezuela under the supervision of the Coordinating Commission.

The sharp drop in posted oil prices that occurred in August 1960 finally provided the necessary catalyst. Middle Eastern governments faced a loss of many millions in tax dollars and were anxious to avoid any further deterioration. When the drop occurred, Tariki was in Baghdad conferring with Iraqi Petroleum Minister Muhammed Salman about the proposed organization. The two called Pérez Alfonzo in Caracas and agreed to arrange an immediate meeting. On September 10, Iraq, Iran, Kuwait, Saudi Arabia, and Venezuela—which together supplied more than 80 percent of the petroleum moving in international trade—met in Baghdad and established the Organization of Petroleum Exporting Countries (OPEC), pledging to cooperate in restoring prices to their previous levels and to "study and formulate a system to insure the stabilization of prices by, among other means, the regulation of production."[16] The agreement (eventually to be joined by Qatar, Libya, Indonesia, Abu Dhabi, Algeria, Nigeria, Ecuador, and Gabon) was a first not only for the countries involved but for the international economy as a whole, in which self-assertion in trade matters on the part of underdeveloped countries was just emerging as a central policy issue.

The Devolution of OPEC Objectives

The success of the OPEC's constitutive meeting reinforced Pérez Alfonzo's optimism about producer control; but it soon became clear that he had greatly overestimated the ability of his new allies to cooperate. When the Second OPEC Conference opened in Caracas in January 1961, President Betancourt himself addressed the assembled delegates and urged them to go ahead with the establishment of the machinery needed to regulate production.[17] However, when the time came to consider pragmatic collective action toward this end, the initiative quickly petered out. Production control was not even mentioned in the final resolutions of the conference, and the best that could be achieved was an agreement to coordinate the various government positions regarding oil pricing.

For the most part, the Middle Eastern countries* were simply

---

* In most cases, for brevity, I include the North African producing nations in those designated by the term Middle Eastern.

not willing to accept the argument that genuine self-protection required more than simply winning a larger share of profits, that producers must take a direct hand in the operation of the international market itself. Aware that Venezuela was losing ground to the Middle East in percentage of total world oil exports, many feared that her chief object was simply to freeze the relative market positions of the key producers. OPEC cooperation was also impeded by the many bitter rivalries and conflicts between the Middle Eastern nations themselves—rivalry between claimants to leadership of the "Arab Revolution," rivalry between these and the more traditional countries, such as Saudi Arabia, and numerous territorial disputes. (Iraq, for example, claimed jurisdiction over the independent sheikdom of Kuwait and refused to attend a number of subsequent OPEC meetings because of Kuwait's presence.)[18]

At the next OPEC meeting Pérez Alfonzo, though continuing to emphasize the importance of prorationing, focused on the lesser objective of convincing his fellow members that they should at least follow the Venezuelan example and establish coordinating commissions to monitor company activities and assert the state's role in marketing. Since outright prorationing seemed too ambitious, he hoped that some coordination of state policies might nevertheless be achieved through the combined action of the various coordinating commissions. Several of the producing governments were poorly prepared and poorly informed when it came to petroleum policy, and it was unlikely that the OPEC could accomplish much until they stopped depending entirely on the oil corporations for information. But even this more limited effort had little success. The resolutions of the Third OPEC Conference included a vague paragraph noting Venezuela's report on the achievements of her own Coordinating Commission and ordering the OPEC Secretariat to study the subject, and the next conference in fact adopted a resolution favoring the Venezuelan proposal. It was evident, however, that the countries of the Middle East had already rejected the idea, and none of them created coordinating commissions.

Early in 1962 the heads of the OPEC delegations met in Caracas to consider the future of the organization. At this time they decided to forego even indirect production control as a primary objective, and instead to try to force the oil companies to grant host governments a greater share of profits. Consequently, the full OPEC conference later in the year resolved that members should at once begin negotiations with the companies to raise posted prices—the prices upon which taxes were levied in the Middle East—and also recommended that members change the tax status of royalty payments.* Neither decision affected Venezuela directly, since she collected taxes on realized prices and did not treat royalties as an income-tax credit; but any increase in Middle Eastern taxation would benefit her by reducing the disparity, in terms of company profits, between her oil and that of the other OPEC members.†

For a year individual OPEC members negotiated with the various companies but could arrive at no agreements. In the spring of 1963, it was finally decided, upon Venezuelan urging, to appoint a three-man committee that would conduct negotiations on behalf of the entire membership. The oil companies agreed to meet with this committee, but insisted that they were negotiating with representatives of the three countries represented on it rather than with the OPEC itself. The subsequent talks took place in Paris, London, and New York, as well as in several Middle Eastern sites—including, it was reported, a "secret desert hideout."[19]

Conflicts within the OPEC continued to be a major problem during these negotiations. Iran, for example, tried to moderate,

* In the Middle East royalties paid to the governments (usually 12½ percent, as compared to the 16⅔ percent in Venezuela) had always been credited against the income tax, which was itself based on the 50-50 formula. Thus royalties and taxes combined made up the 50 percent of company profits owed to the government. Under the new recommendations royalties would be paid *in addition to* tax: the companies would only be allowed to treat royalties as an operating expense, to be deducted from income before it became subject to the 50-50 tax. Crediting royalties rather than expensing them, of course, had meant that governments were actually receiving no royalties as such.

† The Venezuelan oil from some concessions was more expensive to produce than its Middle Eastern counterpart, and Venezuelan tax rates were already higher than those obtaining in the Middle East. The relative "competitiveness" of Venezuelan oil in the world market is an extremely difficult and controversial problem, and will be examined in much greater detail later in this chapter.

if not actually undermine, any strong stand by the OPEC and repeatedly refused to consent to united legislative action against the companies. And Iraq, whose own bargaining position had been altered by its expropriation of large unused concession areas, continued to boycott meetings because of its dispute with Kuwait.[20] Because of these and similar problems, members abandoned joint bargaining after a year and resumed individual company-government negotiations, merely reporting results to the OPEC. Venezuela's role in this entire process was really only advisory, but her representatives did their best to encourage other members and, upon request, supplied experts to advise on petroleum matters. They carefully monitored conversations, pointing out the flaws and inconsistencies in company arguments. As a result, the companies found it more difficult to play producing countries off against each other in closed bargaining sessions.

The negotiations—as well as the internal disagreements within the OPEC—reached a climax at the Seventh OPEC Conference, held at Jakarta in the fall of 1964. The companies had recently offered an attractive-sounding compromise, and five members (Iran, Saudi Arabia, Libya, Kuwait, and Qatar) announced that they favored accepting it. Indonesia, Venezuela, and Iraq, however, were against doing so. The impasse was broken by an "agreement to disagree" in which the Organization voted to leave the acceptance or rejection of the new offer to the discretion of individual member governments. And those in favor of accepting promptly did so.

The new arrangement offered by the companies may be summed up as follows:

1. The companies would accept the principle of expensing royalties.

2. The producing governments were to abandon the OPEC demand for the restoration of posted prices that had been in effect before the worldwide slump in 1960, and were to recognize, for tax purposes, the substantially lower posted prices obtaining after August 1960. Royalty percentages were to remain the same.

3. For tax purposes, the companies would be allowed to dis-

count 8.5 percent from posted prices in 1964, this figure to be reduced to 7.5 percent in 1965 and to 6.5 percent in 1966. Beyond 1966, the companies agreed to eliminate the discount allowance "at the time and in the event that its elimination is justified by changes in the economic situation of Middle East crudes compared with that situation in 1964 and by other economic factors, that is to say, the competitive and market situation of these crudes compared with that situation in 1964."[21]

According to estimates published in the *Petroleum Press Service* (January 1965), the agreement would increase the collective government revenues by approximately $100 million in 1964, $125 million in 1965, and $160 million in 1966. But it is easy to see the reasons for Venezuela's dismay. Not only had the assenting governments compromised the OPEC's position on the August 1960 cuts, but they had agreed to accept a large discount from even the current posted prices. In effect, they had increased their taxes by making royalties an expense deduction while simultaneously giving up their right to demand restoration of higher prices. As the *Economist* noted, the anticipated increases were "not far off what the governments would have got if their concession terms had been left unchanged but the posted prices had been restored to pre-August-1960 levels."[22] At the final meeting of the Jakarta Conference both Indonesia and Venezuela expressed their deep concern about the effect of the new settlement on the OPEC's basic objectives. And Iraq, grinding her own ax, refused to consider any settlement at all unless the companies first agreed to recognize her earlier expropriation of their concessions territories.[23]

By the end of the Betancourt administration it was clear that at least in the near future the OPEC as an institution would be unable to play the central role envisioned for it by Pérez Alfonzo. Venezuelan policymakers, using their own experience and their own strong commitment as a basis for judgment, had overestimated the range of choice available to them in the international arena. However, thanks to Venezuela's initiative, most OPEC members were rapidly becoming more knowledgeable and sophisticated in petroleum policy matters. The process of collective self-assertion of oil-producing host countries at the international level had begun.

Venezuela and U.S. Import Policy

Venezuelan diplomatic initiatives aimed at bringing the oil market under governmental control were also directed at North America. In essence, Pérez Alfonzo sought to work out an arrangement whereby Venezuela and Canada could fit their production into an expanded version of the prorationing scheme already in operation in the United States.

A large proportion of Venezuela's petroleum exports has always gone to the American market (see Tables 4 and 5; Figure 1). This is especially true of heavy fuel oil, which has gradually displaced other energy sources as a means of heating homes and buildings in the populous Northeast. During the 1950's imports of oil into the United States increased rapidly, primarily owing to the relative cheapness of production in the newer and richer fields overseas. Before this time the official U.S. policy toward oil imports had generally been quite liberal, although there were a number of informal constraints.[24] In the late 1930's, for example, a small tariff was imposed on foreign oil, but this was later reduced; and during World War II, the Korean War, and the Suez Crisis the United States relied heavily on foreign oil (mainly from Canada and Venezuela) to meet increased needs. Even during these times, however, the entry of foreign oil was strongly opposed within the United States by an alliance of coal interests with the Independent Producers Association of America (IPAA), which represented hundreds of the smaller domestic oil producers. As the volume of imports increased, pressure for some form of restriction grew commensurately, and by the mid-1950's the opposition to imports had reached such a pitch that the Eisenhower administration began publicly urging the major oil companies to limit their imports.

In the Trade Agreements Extension Act of 1955, Congress granted the President the right to limit the entry of articles he

TABLE 4

Destination of Venezuelan and Netherlands Antilles Petroleum Exports, 1963–73

(Barrels per day × 1,000)

Product and ultimate destination	1963	1964	1965	1966	1967	1968	1969	1970	1971	1972	1973
Crude oil:[a]											
United States	497	480	456	464	436	462	375	371	403	379	497
Canada	242	281	232	169	248	280	299	329	337	324	300
C. America & Caribbean	143	179	191	223	224	233	313	333	441	392	406
S. America[b]	214	245	260	266	290	327	302	209	78	104	96
European Common Market	181	161	139	137	210	173	196	177	130	133	107
United Kingdom	149	151	175	153	154	168	140	141	170	112	87
Other Europe	84	91	110	98	104	101	118	90	67	49	45
Other destinations	6	9	9	10	8	9	15	13	9	9	10
TOTAL	1,516	1,597	1,572	1,520	1,674	1,753	1,758	1,663	1,635	1,502	1,548
Heavy fuel oil:											
United States	588	676	742	763	764	756	875	987	929	920	1,050
Canada	30	44	69	70	83	64	68	88	55	49	58
C. America & Caribbean	68	68	61	61	63	73	70	82	71	56	73
S. America[b]	18	18	25	24	17	19	25	20	16	17	11
European Common Market	44	34	28	17	17	16	18	7	4	8	7
United Kingdom	74	73	67	27	18	12	14	13	7	6	9
Other Europe	22	32	38	25	38	28	13	18	15	13	20
Other destinations	21	15	14	9	20	21	13	10	5	3	8
TOTAL	865	960	1,044	996	1,020	989	1,096	1,225	1,102	1,072	1,236

TABLE 4 (cont.)

Product and ultimate destination	1963	1964	1965	1966	1967	1968	1969	1970	1971	1972	1973
Other products:											
United States	147	152	162	174	172	161	155	218	200	187	252
Canada	33	37	51	50	61	81	76	62	36	42	17
C. America & Caribbean	49	48	62	66	72	105	120	135	147	149	122
S. America[b]	36	50	36	35	33	38	31	33	32	27	20
European Common Market	114	64	56	55	43	22	12	18	19	13	19
United Kingdom	72	58	50	51	48	42	36	26	31	16	19
Other Europe	72	76	53	60	47	34	29	29	34	22	17
Other destinations	82	90	84	101	114	91	77	59	25	24	33
TOTAL	605	575	554	592	590	574	536	580	524	480	499
Total petroleum exports:											
United States	1,232	1,308	1,360	1,401	1,372	1,379	1,405	1,576	1,532	1,486	1,799
Canada	305	362	352	289	392	425	443	479	428	415	375
C. America & Caribbean	260	295	314	350	359	411	503	550	659	597	601
S. America[b]	268	313	321	325	340	384	358	262	126	148	127
European Common Market	339	259	223	209	270	211	226	202	153	154	133
United Kingdom	295	282	292	231	220	222	190	180	208	134	115
Other Europe	178	199	201	183	189	163	160	137	116	84	82
Other destinations	109	114	107	120	142	121	105	82	39	36	51
TOTAL	2,986	3,182	3,170	3,108	3,284	3,316	3,390	3,468	3,261	3,054	3,283

SOURCE: Creole Corp. Rept., 1972, p. 24; 1973, p. 24.
[a] Excluding crude oil exported to Netherlands Antilles. Since a large proportion of petroleum exports from these islands was of Venezuelan origin, it is treated here as part of the Venezuelan total.
[b] Includes Trinidad and Tobago.

TABLE 5

Petroleum Imports into the United States, 1963–73

(Barrels per day × 1,000)

Imports and sources	1963	1964	1965	1966	1967	1968	1969	1970	1971	1972	1973
Total U.S. imports:											
Crude oil	1,131	1,201	1,238	1,225	1,128	1,290	1,408	1,324	1,681	2,216	3,244
Heavy fuel oil	747	810	946	1,032	1,084	1,152	1,265	1,528	1,582	1,742	1,827
Other products	245	254	284	316	325	395	492	565	502	572	890
TOTAL	2,123	2,265	2,468	2,573	2,537	2,837	3,156	3,417	3,765	4,530	5,961
From Ven./Neth. Antilles:											
Crude oil	497	480	456	464	436	462	375	371	403	379	497
Heavy fuel oil	588	676	742	763	764	756	875	987	929	920	1,050
Other products	147	152	162	174	172	161	155	218	200	187	252
TOTAL	1,232	1,308	1,360	1,401	1,372	1,379	1,405	1,576	1,532	1,486	1,799
Percent of total from Ven./Neth. Antilles	58.0%	57.7%	55.1%	54.5%	54.1%	48.6%	44.4%	46.1%	40.7%	32.8%	30.2%

SOURCES: Total figures for United States from U.S. Bureau of Mines, as presented in Creole Corp. Rept., 1972, p. 26; 1973, p. 26. Figures for imports from Venezuela and Netherlands Antilles from Ministry of Mines, Venezuela, as presented in Creole Corp. Rept., 1972, p. 26; 1973, p. 26.

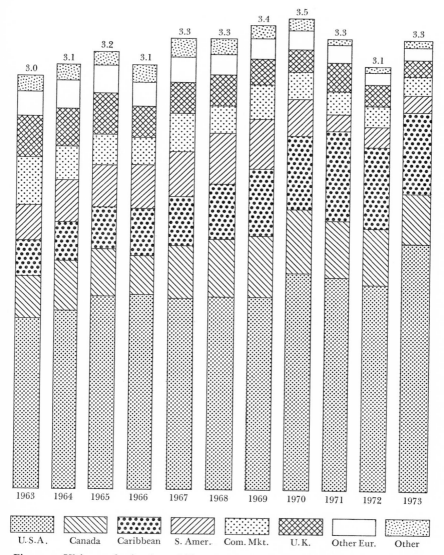

Figure 1. Ultimate destination of Venezuelan and Netherlands Antilles petroleum exports, 1963–73. Figures at top of bars are approximate yearly average production in millions of barrels per day. (SOURCE: Creole Corp. Rept., 1972, p. 25; 1973, p. 25)

considered imported "in such quantities as to threaten to impair the national security."[25] In 1957 the director of the U.S. Office of Defense Mobilization announced that imports of crude oil had reached the point where they posed such a threat, and the government imposed a program of "voluntary restrictions." Importing companies were "requested" to comply with a system of government quotas that kept imports at roughly 12 percent of domestic production. No sanctions were attached to the program, and—to the chagrin of the coal industry—residual fuel and other refined products were not included. Venezuela protested that these restrictions might lead the companies to cut back production in her concessions; Venezuelan oil, she argued, had always been available to the United States, war or peace, and should therefore be considered within the American national-security sphere, not defined as a threat. Canada lodged a similar protest.

As it turned out, the "voluntary" program did nothing to stem the rising tide of imports. The post-Suez production surge and the concurrent weakening of prices at the international level enhanced the attractiveness of the protected, high-priced American market, and crude imports continued to rise. Many companies also took advantage of the lack of even suggested quotas on refined products, importing these at even higher volumes. Since these events coincided with a minor economic recession in the United States, the smaller American producers were hard hit; and many of them, especially in the Southwest, were forced to restrict their output.[26]

In the spring of 1959, just after the Betancourt administration came to office, the United States finally set up an obligatory program of import restrictions, covering both crude oil and refined products. All imports were now brought in under a quota licensing system supervised by the Department of the Interior. Again, the objective was to limit imports to approximately 12 percent of domestic production; and the justification for the measure was once again the national-security clause in the Trade Agreements Extension Act.[27] Anticipating further protests from Venezuela and Canada, President Eisenhower added a qualifier to his announcement of the new restrictions:

The United States recognizes that within the larger sphere of Free World security, we, in common with Canada and with the other American republics, have a joint interest in Hemisphere defense. Informal conversations with Canada and Venezuela looking toward a coordinated approach to the problem of oil as it relates to this matter of common concern have already begun. The United States is hopeful that in the course of future conversations agreement can be reached which can take fully into account the interests of all the oil-producing states.[28]

To the surprise of many observers, Pérez Alfonzo immediately declared that on the whole the new program seemed quite satisfactory. Its main intent, he said, was to make the existing system function well, and it might even benefit Venezuela by raising prices; after all, she had little need for large increases in petroleum exports and would prefer to see prices firm up. Pérez Alfonzo did note, however, that the U.S. decision should be only a first step toward a much more elaborate system involving all the governments of the hemisphere. And, in the light of Eisenhower's reference to future consultations, he was hopeful that such a system could be established.[29]

Several weeks later, however, Caracas learned that the U.S. had issued an additional proclamation exempting all imports coming in "overland by pipeline, motor vehicle, or rail." In effect, this removed all restrictions on oil imports from Canada (and Mexico) while retaining those that affected Venezuela. Pérez Alfonzo denounced the change as discriminatory and unjustified; and he immediately flew to Washington to try to convince the American government to rescind it, but without success.[30] Rather than dwell on the faults of the U.S. program, however, Pérez Alfonzo offered his own proposal for solving the problem of regional petroleum trade: an intergovernmental agreement among the hemisphere's major oil traders (i.e. Venezuela, Canada, and the United States) to control oil shipments, by which the U.S. would grant a preference to its regional suppliers, guaranteeing them a specified proportion of the U.S. market. This differed from the existing import program in that quotas would be granted directly to foreign governments rather than to U.S. companies.[31]

As was the case with the OPEC, the model for Pérez Alfonzo's proposal was the American prorationing system: "Within the different states of the Union, petroleum production is controlled according to the decisions of the respective state organizations. . . . We believe that Venezuela, too, should prorate her production according to her own national interest while she is satisfying the limited demands of the United States." Such a system would have many advantages. It would give the oil traders of the hemisphere a unified energy program and would allow for long-term planning based on continuous, institutionalized discussions. The United States would gain security on a government-to-government basis for a large proportion of her future oil imports and still be able to protect her domestic producers. To be sure, prices would remain high; but the existing system was already forcing American consumers to pay a premium price for "national security" and providing windfall profits for those companies lucky enough to receive import licenses.[32]

One important advantage of Pérez Alfonzo's proposed system was that it would reduce Venezuela's agonizing dependence on the oil companies' decisions regarding her major export market. The United States, of course, would still determine the total amount of petroleum to be imported and the origin of imports; but the producing governments, not the companies, would determine the method of fulfilling quotas, and, more important, their role within the system would be more secure. In terms of Venezuela's overall strategy for managing her dependence, the program would be extremely helpful: oil exports to the United States accounted for more than 40 percent of her external market, and the power to assign quotas for this trade would bring internal prorationing that much closer. The arrangement would also give Venezuela some influence over oil prices and discounts, especially since imports of Middle Eastern oil to the hemisphere would be limited by the preference system. Finally, and most important, Pérez Alfonzo's system could ultimately facilitate the transition to state-managed petroleum development within Venezuela, since an increasing share of the U.S. trade could be allocated to the government-owned CVP as that company expanded its producing capacity, and there would be no risk of damaging international prices in the process.

This was, like the OPEC blueprint, an ambitious but unrealistic plan. In proposing it Pérez Alfonzo clearly overestimated the willingness of the United States to move against the interests of the giant American multinational corporations. Though ambivalent about the mandatory import program, these companies were quick to express their unqualified opposition to the Venezuelan "solution." Hostile to any government involvement in industry affairs outside the United States (and still smarting from the sudden tax increase imposed by the provisional junta only a few months earlier), they were not at all pleased by the prospect of the U.S. government providing Venezuela with the means for greater control of the industry within her borders. The American government, they felt, was not in business to help foreign states regulate the behavior, and perhaps even damage the legal rights, of the most powerful and successful of U.S. corporations. Thus, even though there was considerable dissatisfaction with the mandatory program within the U.S., the acceptance of Pérez Alfonzo's plan was out of the question. American officials listened politely to Venezuela's arguments, but did not even go so far as to rescind the provisions favoring Canadian oil.

In the years following the setting of mandatory import limitation, successive Venezuelan governments repeatedly voiced their dissatisfaction with U.S. policy and advocated programs based on a hemisphere preference with country quotas. President Betancourt, in fact, several times complained personally to President Kennedy about the U.S. system, pointing out that a preferential trade agreement would do more good for Venezuela than any amount of Alliance for Progress aid.[33] The United States did send a number of special missions to Venezuela to discuss the problems involved in the oil trade; and in the years after 1963 restrictions on fuel oil imports were gradually eased (although the quotas for crude oil were actually tightened by about 10 percent in 1962). But there was no structural change in the system. In the meantime, the quota-allocation system itself gradually bogged down in an enormously complex interest-group muddle; and any kind of decisive action by the U.S. government became less and less possible, despite repeated inquiries, task force reports, and congressional investigations. It was not until 1973, under the threat of a major energy crisis, that the U.S. made any substantive changes in the system.

Petroleum Policy and Domestic Politics

As the preceding pages suggest, the Betancourt administration, and Pérez Alfonzo personally, maintained a tight control of petroleum policy. Unlike later regimes, it was able to secure an unusual degree of independence and freedom of action relative to the newly awakened political forces in the country. One reason for this was the enormous personal authority of both Betancourt and Pérez Alfonzo in petroleum matters, which stemmed from their leading roles as the architects of Venezuela's nationalist policies during the 1945–48 period, as well as from their outspoken criticism of the Pérez Jiménez dictatorship. In addition, the AD government had a strong electoral and parliamentary position, especially during its first three years, having won nearly half the total votes cast in 1958. Supported by COPEI, its coalition partner, AD had a working majority in both legislative houses until 1962; and even after that, though weakened by schisms, the party could still block opposing legislation. Finally, the most forceful opposition to government petroleum policy in this period came from groups on the political Right, and these had little or no representation in the legislature.

President Betancourt granted his Minister of Mines considerable freedom of action and generally backed him up whenever there was disagreement within their party. At one point in 1961, for example, a group of AD legislative leaders began to press for still another increase in oil taxes as a means of offsetting budgetary deficits and providing funds to cope with the ongoing economic recession. Pérez Alfonzo strongly opposed the idea; at a special session of the Chamber of Deputies he pointed out that company profits on net fixed assets had already fallen well below the 15 percent he considered necessary if the industry were to remain healthy. With Betancourt's support, his position finally prevailed—much to the satisfaction of the companies—and the administration instead had to control the recession with the politically unrewarding expedient of an austerity program.[34]

Although the administration held tight control over all decisions regarding petroleum, it did try to justify its policy in detail and to gain the cooperation of the economic and political interests concerned. Pérez Alfonzo held weekly press conferences and appeared frequently before the legislature to explain his actions and plans. Under his direction, the Ministry of Mines bulletin, *Carta Semanal*, lost its dry, technical character and began to explain and justify policy. Pérez Alfonzo also sought the active cooperation of the other parties in AD's coalition, appointing their members to positions in his Ministry and including them in missions sent to represent Venezuela in the Middle East and elsewhere. As a result, both COPEI and URD (the latter while it remained in the coalition) supported the government position on oil. And even those groups favoring more radical changes cooperated, at least as long as they were committed to working within the democratic framework.*

The oil companies themselves strongly opposed Venezuela's new policy, but after their tangle with the provisional junta over the tax increase they realized that the new political environment called for an entirely different approach. Accordingly, led by Creole and Shell, they adopted a two-pronged strategy designed to bring indirect economic and political pressure to bear on the government. To begin with, following up on their threats, the majors embarked on a program of graduated disinvestment in the Venezuelan petroleum economy and simultaneously began drawing increases in production from other areas under their control (notably Canada and the Middle East). Investment, exploration and drilling activity, and even employment declined—the last by some 28 percent between 1960 and 1966 (see Tables 6 and 7). The govern-

---

* For example, Domingo Alberto Rangel, later an outspoken radical critic of government policy, represented Venezuela at OPEC meetings.

TABLE 6
Employment in the Venezuelan Petroleum Industry, 1950–72

Year	Salaried employees			Workers			Total		
	Venezuelan nationals	Foreigners	Total	Venezuelan nationals	Foreigners	Total	Venezuelan nationals	Foreigners	All employees
1956	13,438	4,270	17,708	25,424	971	26,395	38,862	5,241	44,103
1957	14,100	4,603	18,703	25,990	959	26,949	40,090	5,562	45,652
1958	14,325	4,672	18,997	24,866	857	25,723	39,191	5,529	44,720
1959	14,501	4,400	18,901	23,725	705	24,430	38,226	5,105	43,331
1960	14,496	3,646	18,142	22,004	544	22,548	36,500	4,190	40,690
1961	13,741	2,730	16,471	20,451	402	20,853	34,192	3,132	37,324
1962	12,935	2,189	15,124	19,399	295	19,694	32,334	2,484	34,818
1963	12,809	1,923	14,732	18,778	232	19,010	31,587	2,155	33,742
1964	13,055	1,780	14,835	18,240	187	18,427	31,295	1,967	33,262
1965	12,852	1,660	14,512	17,180	146	17,326	30,032	1,806	31,838
1966	12,091	1,469	13,560	15,776	112	15,888	27,867	1,581	29,448
1967	11,519	1,279	12,798	14,194	80	14,274	25,713	1,359	27,072
1968	11,132	1,187	12,319	13,030	70	13,100	24,162	1,257	25,419
1969	11,053	1,125	12,178	12,285	58	12,343	23,338	1,183	24,521
1970	11,150	1,030	12,180	11,766	47	11,813	22,916	1,077	23,993
1971	11,348	937	12,285	11,387	42	11,429	22,735	979	23,714
1972	11,681	819	12,500	10,791	37	10,828	22,472	856	23,328

SOURCE: Venezuela, [9], 1971, p. 139; 1972, p. 145.

TABLE 7

Exploration for Petroleum Resources in Venezuela, 1958–73

Year	Exploratory wells	Field parties[a]	Year	Exploratory wells	Field parties[a]
1958	598	363	1966	90	14
1959	341	173	1967	75	10
1960	276	42	1968	100	13
1961	279	13	1969	102	17
1962	197	13	1970	102	20
1963	170	19	1971	165	24
1964	179	8	1972	169	36
1965	181	16	1973	148	29

SOURCE: Creole Corp. Rept., 1972, p. 9; 1973, p. 9.

[a] Activity of geological and geophysical field parties, in party-months.

ment had expected production levels to increase so rapidly that it had planned to limit them to an optimum expansion of 4 percent per year; but the average growth was well below this figure. Fiscal income from oil leveled off, and in 1966 even declined.

The companies justified their measures by explaining that the general "climate of investment" in Venezuela was unfavorable. With the concessions system terminated and no "viable" alternative to replace it, the future of their operations was in question, and they had no incentive to do further exploration or increase their investment. They also pointed out that the petroleum of the Middle East and North Africa had become more "competitive" than the Venezuelan product, and that the capital diverted from Venezuela was going to these more "promising" areas.[35] When the scale of the companies' disinvestment and leveling of production rates became apparent, others began to echo these views, predicting a dismal future for the oil industry in Venezuela. The *New York Times*, for example, noted with alarm: "New investments by the companies that ran to several hundred million dollars a year have been slashed to minimums required for maintenance. Some 3,000 U.S. and other foreign oil technicians have left the country in the last two years."[36]

A second thrust of company strategy was to build an alliance with the domestic private sector in Venezuela. Aware of the long-standing hostility between AD and the economic elites of the country, the companies felt confident of convincing the private sector to bring pressure to bear on the administration. To consolidate this alliance, the companies in August 1959 established their own Chamber of the Petroleum Industry, which immediately gained admission to Fedecámaras, the powerful peak association of the private sector, and quickly became an important source of "technical advice" for the preparation of studies attacking government policy.

In addition, the companies began to provide generous financial support for Fedecámaras. (In a recent year, for example, they pledged more than Bs 200,000 to the organization—over 10 percent of the total pledged by its nearly 200 members.) Gifts from the petroleum industry far surpassed those of any other single contributor, including the well-heeled banking industry.* Beyond this, the companies provided large-scale support in both manpower and money to private-sector publicity and propaganda campaigns. The close ties of the major Venezuelan newspapers, *El Nacional* and *El Universal*, to private economic interests facilitated this.

At the ideological level, the petroleum companies repeatedly pointed out that the prosperity of Venezuela's economic elites had always been closely tied to the welfare of the oil industry, and that government policies damaging to the oil industry would damage the private sector. The companies also argued that the future of private enterprise itself was being challenged by the new socialist government. They stressed that the world of private capitalism was a unified whole, and if the foreign companies went down, domestic capitalists would ultimately go under as well. These arguments fell on fertile ground. The private sector in Venezuela has always been conscious of the close ties between petroleum income

---

* Information about these, as might be expected, is difficult to obtain. According to informed observers, Fedecámaras draws income from several sources. There is an openly acknowledged dues assessment on all members, levied monthly; in 1972 the Petroleum Chamber's share of this was a mere Bs 400 ($91). In addition, the family conglomerates and larger business concerns customarily donate substantial sums to the organization when each new Fedecámaras director begins his two-year term. The petroleum companies' most recent biennial pledge was some Bs 400,000 ($91,000)—twice that of the next largest contributor. And individual oil companies or company executives often make ad hoc contributions to support particular publicity campaigns.

(derived from direct purchases by the companies as well as large-scale government spending) and the welfare of the private economy, especially in such areas as services, construction, food processing, transport, and manufacturing. The ongoing recession was the best evidence of this.

With an identity of interests and firm institutional ties thus established, the foreign companies and leaders of the domestic private sector began a united assault on government policies. Fedecámaras itself led the attack, joined later by other individuals and groups committed to the free-enterprise ideal and strongly concerned about the "crisis in the industry," or simply interested in weakening the political position of AD.[37] The most prominent of these allies was Arturo Uslar Pietri, a well-known writer and orator with close ties to the private sector, who held a Senate seat as an "independent" (running on the URD ticket).[38] Another critic was the National Economic Council, a consultative body that included representatives of the private sector. The URD party also joined in after it left the governing coalition in 1962.

Most critics of the government repeated the basic argument of the oil companies: that the government, by overtaxing, refusing to grant new concessions, and interfering with company activities, was causing the decline of the private oil industry and was doing little or nothing to replace it with a viable alternative. They also argued that Pérez Alfonzo's assumptions about "economic indigestion" and about the increasing future value of oil—this at a time when prices were actually dropping—were probably mistaken and in any case dangerously speculative. Stressing the declining rates of production, investment, and exploration, they pointed out that Venezuela was losing out to more "competitive" producing areas even in her traditional markets.

Comparative Costs and "Competitiveness"

The question of the "competitiveness" of Venezuelan petroleum, so important in this and later debates over government policy, is worth examining in greater detail. Regarding the basic cost of extraction, industry lore has it that Venezuelan petroleum

TABLE 8
*Costs per Barrel of Middle Eastern
and Venezuelan Petroleum, 1966*
(U.S. dollars)

Cost	Middle East	Venezuela
Production cost	.10	.34
Depreciation	.05	.20
Taxes	.80	.91
Total cost (FOB)	0.95	1.45

SOURCE: Adapted from Mikesell, p. 113; published originally in *The Daily Journal Supplement* (Caracas), 23.ix.66, p. 36. The figures check closely with Adelman, p. 76, and with publications comparing host-government receipts in both areas.

is more expensive on the average than its counterpart in the Middle East, and that this, combined with higher taxation levels, has made it less attractive in the world market.* Although estimating costs and tax levels is difficult because of a lack of complete and unbiased data, the available evidence roughly confirms this contention.[39] During the 1960's Venezuelan oil *was* more expensive to produce, and more highly taxed (see Table 8). This said, however, it should be added that oil companies can to some extent determine average production costs by manipulating their offtake from different fields, some high-cost and some low-cost. Indeed, after a careful examination of the available data, M.I.T. economist M. A. Adelman has concluded that average cost figures for Venezuelan oil have been as high as they have in part because the companies have chosen an expensive "mix" of producing areas.

However rough the calculations, one conclusion is plain: national averages understate the real competitive strength of Venezuelan crude oil. . . . The bulk of Venezuelan output would appear to be cheaper to produce and deliver to the United States than is oil from the Big Four of the Persian Gulf, and some considerable fraction can compete even at Rotterdam. . . . Even in 1968 . . . there was plenty of Venezuelan crude to compete with Persian Gulf on the basis of comparative costs. In the 1950's, with tanker rates far higher, the proportion must have been much larger. . . . *But comparative cost does not seem to be at work inside Venezuela either*, since high-cost crude continues to be produced when lower-cost crude is available.[40]

---

* As we have seen, this argument was used in the late 1940's and early 1950's to persuade the dictatorship to renegotiate the royalty formula.

The relative attractiveness of different oil sources is also determined by transport charges—primarily tanker rates—and here Venezuela has a geographical advantage, especially in the U.S. market. Tanker rates have fluctuated considerably in recent years, declining slowly from 1960 to 1967, increasing after the closure of the Suez Canal, and reaching very high levels in 1970, when an important Middle Eastern pipeline was also closed off. They have since remained generally high, despite the appearance of some very large supertankers. And high freight charges, of course, have tended to favor Venezuela, compensating somewhat for production-cost disparities.

Perhaps the most important variable in this already complex equation is what is often called the "strategic" or "security" factor. In effect, the companies have been willing to pay a continuing premium (of undetermined size) in order to control a production capacity in an area relatively free from threats of war or sudden expropriation. Because of the presumptive political instability of the Middle East and that region's history of abrupt interruption of oil operations, Venezuela has always been considered a more secure production zone, likely to be available in times of crisis or scarcity—as in fact it has been during the last decade and a half.

Finally, though less profitable than that of the Middle East, the Venezuelan oil industry has not been *un*profitable by any means, and the high corporate profits in the Middle East are hardly something that Venezuelans could be expected to emulate.*

A careful examination of past company bargaining reveals clearly that the petroleum companies in Venezuela have always been anxious to consolidate their position in the country despite high costs. In the short run, of course, reducing costs has been important because of the companies' fear that Venezuela's policy of

---

* According to Mikdashi, p. 141, an unpublished study prepared for the OPEC by Arthur D. Little, Inc., estimated that average net earnings for the major producing concessions ran as follows during the 1950–60 decade: Iran, 71%; Iraq, 62%; Qatar, 114%; Saudi Arabia, 62%; Venezuela, 20%. Mikdashi himself estimates the rate for Kuwait as 150+%. Actually, profit comparisons of this kind can be misleading, since they involve the profits of affiliates rather than those of the parent multinationals and hence are subject to considerable manipulation by central management.

high taxation and bothersome controls would spread to other producing countries—as in fact it has. But reducing costs has been far less significant as a long-run objective than winning an assured place in the country's production future, though in company calculations the two have been closely linked. As we shall see, during the Leoni administration, several years later, the companies agreed to abandon their squeeze on the Venezuelan economy and government, accepting increased costs in return for what they believed would be greater security.

By itself, then, Venezuela's lack of competitive strength owing to high production costs cannot explain the stagnation of her oil industry during the early 1960's. Oil companies were not simply responding automatically to immediate market imperatives, but were pursuing a strategy designed to reverse the trend of government policy and improve their long-range prospects.

Government Response

The key problem facing the government in responding to the economic and political offensive mounted by the industry and Fedecámaras was to decide how to assess company actions and intentions. How much were the companies willing to pay as their "security premium"? Were the average cost figures provided by the companies a true reflection of the relative attractiveness of Venezuelan oil? Would tanker rates increase or decline in the future? In sum, to what extent were the companies bluffing, that is, underrepresenting the competitive strength of Venezuelan petroleum in order to put economic pressure on the government and undermine its domestic political standing? From what has been said, it should be evident that any true calculation of Venezuela's relative position in the marketplace was complicated enough, and allowed enough freedom of action to the companies, to make this a strong possibility; it should also be clear that it would have been difficult for the policymakers to know for sure.

In the end, the government decided to sit it out, stick to its policies, and see what happened. In response to his critics, Pérez Alfonzo openly charged the companies with complicating matters by undertaking economic reprisals. In view of the regime's overall position on oil and its determination to reduce Venezuela's dependence on the industry, this action was understandable. But calling the companies' bluff was unquestionably risky, and the stakes were high indeed. The country had become accustomed to a pattern of rapid growth—a kind of income joyride—and showed little inclination to stop it. Since Venezuela had no currency reserves or "anticyclical fund" and was in addition struggling to recover from a recession, the government could do little to protect itself and the economy from the consequences of dependence.

The debate about petroleum policy continued more or less in the same vein until the end of the Betancourt administration. Although the companies were able to deprive the government of resources, they and their domestic allies failed to force a change in policy. They had almost no leverage within the domestic political arena: Uslar was a senator without a party, and Fedecámaras represented private elites who had few political ties and a long tradition of hostility toward AD. The government's position was strong enough politically that it could continue on the path it felt was right, despite a reduction in income and even though the policy initiatives themselves, both domestic and international, were faring quite badly.

4. The Leoni Administration

Political Conflict and the 1966 Tax Reform Crisis

THE LEONI administration inherited intact the unresolved conflicts and problems of its predecessor's petroleum policy. Company-government relationships were cool, reflecting the standoff on issues of key importance to the industry. Neither diplomatic initiatives nor the experiment in direct control of industry marketing prerogatives had proved successful, and the new government was forced to take up the search for policy alternatives begun by Pérez Alfonzo during his last year in office. The overall orientation of policy remained unchanged, however, at least at the outset. The new Minister of Mines, Manuel Pérez Guerrero, made it clear he intended to follow the objectives established by the previous regime; and Pérez Alfonzo, though retired, remained a close adviser to the administration. Also, most of Venezuela's new professional petroleum administrators stayed on in their positions.

As indicated in Chapter 1, the 1963 election left AD severely weakened and the party system as a whole quite fragmented. COPEI, reassured by its enlarged mandate, decided to stay out of the government, and for a while it seemed that Leoni would have to try ruling the country without a coalition. After half a year of negotiations, however, he succeeded in patching together a new coalition that included URD, now purged of most of its revolutionary cadre, and Uslar Pietri's new party, the Frente Nacional Democrático (FND). Uslar later explained that he had joined the government under the mistaken assumption that the new Minister of Mines was prepared to reorient petroleum policy.[1]

At the international level, the new administration continued along the same lines as its predecessor. In her relations with the United States Venezuela pressed repeatedly for a hemisphere preference and for equality of treatment with Canada, but to no avail. Within the OPEC she continued to urge greater attention to prorationing and production control. As we have seen, however, little could be accomplished on this front either, although the OPEC countries did increase their tax income by disallowing the write-off of royalties.

Within Venezuela the government made three important changes in petroleum policy during 1964–65. First, in an effort to fulfill AD's campaign pledge to promote the growth of the state oil company, Leoni sponsored a law entitling the company to take one-third of the domestic petroleum market by 1968 as an outlet for its production. Second, the government sent a note—subsequently known as the "Fuel Oil Letter"—to the companies informing them that discounts of more than 10 percent on fuel oil sales would not be permitted. This caused a stir, since heavy fuel oil accounted for nearly one-third of the country's total exports. The government subsequently explained that the limitation did not apply to the companies' realized prices but instead would serve as an artificial reference price for taxation purposes; and later the permitted discount was increased to 15 percent for the most important of the heavy fuels ("Bunker C").[2] The object here was to establish a tax floor for the product and thereby discourage large discounts. This method, similar to the one used to fix the value of royalty oil, later became the government's chief means of controlling company pricing behavior.

The third major thrust of government policy proved the most important—and controversial—of all. This was the attempt to use retroactive taxation as a means of influencing company marketing decisions. Instead of trying to take up individual contracts and force revisions in them, as in the past, the administration set to work reviewing past prices and claiming back taxes on sales it felt had been made at artificially low prices. By 1965 the total amount of these claims, covering only the years up to 1960, had reached more than $110 million.

The claims had two purposes. First, when paid, they would bring a substantial amount of money into the treasury. This was important, since the Leoni government, like its predecessor, was suffering from a lack of funds caused by the falling-off of petroleum-generated income. In 1965, in fact, total government income decreased by 0.7 percent from the previous year—quite serious in a country accustomed to an annual budgetary growth (in constant Bs) of more than 10 percent. As important as the prospect of greater income, however, was the policymakers' hope that the threat of retroactive taxes would force the companies to keep their prices at the highest possible levels to avoid future claims.

As might be expected, the companies firmly resisted the new policy. They grudgingly accepted the loss of part of Venezuela's internal market, but they challenged the legality of the Fuel Oil Letter and steadfastly refused to pay the new tax claims. By the end of 1965 it became clear that companies and government were trapped in a bitter and dangerous deadlock. In order to avoid a major confrontation, which might threaten oil production itself, they agreed to begin high-level negotiations in search of a solution.

The Tax Reform Crisis

At this juncture, early in 1966, petroleum policy became deeply intermixed in a political crisis that shook the country. The trouble began when the government, still in need of funds, decided to overhaul the tax system, increasing the overall level of taxation in the process. This decision, together with the deadlock in company-government negotiations, prompted Uslar Pietri, who had been chafing for months over his lack of influence within the coalition, to take his party out of the government and resume his attack on AD policies. Fedecámaras quickly joined him, making petroleum policy the principal topic at its annual convention in May and subsequently publishing a highly critical analysis of the state of the industry.[3] As with previous Fedecámaras projects, the petroleum companies supported this effort with funds and extensive technical assistance, and the resulting document faithfully reflected their position.

The crisis came to a head in July, when President Leoni announced his new tax proposals and called an extraordinary session of Congress to consider them. The reform package, designed to achieve an increase of nearly 7 percent in receipts, increased taxes on personal and corporate incomes in top brackets, as well as on cigarettes, liquor, and automobiles. More than half the new funds (approximately Bs 300 million, or $67 million) were destined to come from the petroleum companies through an increase in income taxes and the application of a special "selective tax" on profits in excess of 15 percent of net fixed assets. This last proposal, by far the most threatening part of the reform from the perspective of the companies, was the brainchild of Pérez Alfonzo. Company profits had climbed steadily from their record low in 1958–60 and by 1964 had reached more than 30 percent, double the figure he considered a "just" return on investment. Consequently, he had lobbied strongly for a mechanism that would automatically adjust profits to the levels he thought appropriate; and this was to be done by the selective tax.

The proposed increases in personal and corporate income taxes were both modest and progressive.* The reform envisaged an average increase in personal income taxes of approximately 1.8 percent of reported income, affecting only those in the top 6.6 percent of the income scale, and increases in corporate taxes of 4 percent of reported income, affecting only corporations in the top 17 percent of the scale. The new tax load, in other words, would rest primarily on the economic elites of the country—and very lightly, at that.[4]

An overhaul of the tax system, it should be pointed out, was long overdue in Venezuela. Owing in part to the availability of petroleum income and in part to the success of private interests in preventing increases, the level of taxation on these income "streams" was one of the lowest in the world for countries at equivalent development levels; nor did it serve to equalize income distribution to a significant degree. It was, as one careful analysis

---

* They were expected to bring in Bs 52 million and Bs 22 million, respectively. The rest of the added income, excluding that from oil, was to come from the new luxury taxes.

concluded, "little more than a token levy."[5] A study completed just before the 1966 reform controversy compared taxes as they affected "typical" individuals of the upper-middle class ($12,000 a year income) and medium-sized corporate entities (owner's equity of $2 million) in Mexico and in Venezuela. The effective tax rates on the Mexican examples were 8.5 percent and 44.7 percent, respectively; the comparable rates on the Venezuelan examples were 2.2 percent and 16.3 percent. Clearly, there was plenty of room for an increase.*

From the moment Leoni made public the proposed reform, it was evident the government had made a serious tactical error in undertaking to increase taxes on domestic individuals and corporations at the same time it increased them on the petroleum companies. Not only did this cement the alliance of domestic and foreign economic elites, but it provided an opportunity for opposition parties, in this case both COPEI and FND, to join the attack on a weakened AD government. Following Leoni's announcement the opposition exploded into vitriolic denunciations of the regime, making the selective tax on the petroleum industry the central focus of attack. This was logical, in view of the state of the industry and the deadlock in government-company relations. The selective tax was the most vulnerable part of the reform, and seemed to offer opponents of the domestic tax increase a means of distracting attention from the low, nonprogressive tax rates they sought to preserve.

Uslar Pietri, Fedecámaras, the Caracas Chamber of Commerce, and numerous party spokesmen mounted an enormous publicity barrage aimed at the government proposals.[6] Headlines screamed "Liquidation of Venezuelan Petroleum Industry in Progress!"[7] Even the petroleum companies abandoned their cautious, behind-the-scenes stance to attack the proposed reform. Leo Lowry, the president of Creole, complained publicly about the damaging ef-

---

* These calculations, by economist Raynard M. Sommerfeld, refer to corporations with a net taxable income of $500,000 per annum, and to individuals who are resident citizens, earn salaries as employees, and are married with two dependent children. Sommerfeld, pp. 93–102. Both tax rates are far higher in most countries of North America and Europe. As Shoup puts it (p. 11): "By comparison with other countries ... Venezuela is not close to any economic limits, whatever they may be, on taxation."

fects of the new law, adding—not surprisingly—"The most accurate appraisal of the tax reform is contained in the analysis and conclusions of the Fedecámaras document."[8] And shortly afterward Creole presented an extensive position paper to the Congress arguing that the new taxes would only further damage the already declining industry in the country.[9] In the meantime industry executives slowed production to the lowest rate in nearly a decade; and by the end of 1966 production had dropped nearly 3 percent from the previous year. COPEI spokesmen asserted that the government was totally unjustified in asking for more income from any source, in view of the inept and corrupt way it was spending the money it already had, and stated that the party opposed every aspect of the proposed reform.[10]

An entirely new group calling itself the Committee of the Middle Class appeared from nowhere to join the attack on the government. The Committee, chaired by a man with close ties to the oil industry, took an even more conservative position on the reform. As one spokesman put it: "The conclusion is clear: the laws submitted to Congress will take Venezuela directly into Communism."[11]

When the extraordinary session of Congress met to vote on the government's proposals, the opposition parties boycotted it, preventing a quorum. Faced with parliamentary immobilism, the administration had no recourse but negotiation with the united opposition. After extended discussions, COPEI, FND, and the other opposition parties agreed to return to Congress, but only after AD agreed to postpone consideration of the tax reform until the completion of a multipartisan investigation of the government's conduct in the use of public funds, and until the government produced a plan showing exactly how it intended to use its increased income. This was a major setback for AD and an unprecedented victory for the private sector.

The Compromise Solution

Throughout the dispute over the tax reform, the Leoni government continued its discussions (begun early in 1966) with representatives of the companies. In the middle of September, as the outcry against the government reached its peak, Minister of Mines Pérez Guerrero and Minister of Finance Eddie Morales Crespo held a number of urgent, top-secret meetings with representatives of the largest companies operating in Venezuela, Creole and Shell. At the conclusion of these meetings, President Leoni surprised and shocked the opposition by announcing that the negotiators had come to a comprehensive agreement that would eliminate the sources of friction in company-government relations and provide a basis for the future growth and development of the industry in Venezuela. The "solution" he described, which Pérez Guerrero elaborated on in later speeches, dealt with five basic problems: back taxes, pricing, production levels, future taxation, and Venezuela's own participation in the exploitation of her resources.[12]

Retroactive tax claims. The issue of back taxes was resolved by a compromise in which the companies agreed to pay Bs 700 million ($155 million), the major portion in installments spread over five years and the rest in the form of public works to be performed by the companies for the government. The government, in return, agreed to consider all taxes for the years up to and including 1965 already paid. Since even the claims through 1960 totaled some $110 million, the government, in theory at least, was giving up to a considerable sum. However, because the companies refused to accept the legality of the claims, the governmnt was faced with the prospect of placing the issue before Venezuela's Supreme Court and proving its contentions about company sales; and there was considerable doubt that it could do so in any clear fashion. The year 1966 was not covered by the agreement, which was scheduled to go into effect at the beginning of 1967; but the companies agreed to pay taxes for that year on prices no lower than those prevailing in 1965, thereby ensuring that the administration would not be forced to accept any drop in prices, for tax purposes, during the intervening period.

Prices. The long and bitter controversy over oil prices—the central concern of the Coordinating Commission and the reason behind the retroactive tax claims—was the most important problem resolved by the 1966 compromise. The companies and the government agreed that for a period of five years (1967–71) all crude oil and petroleum products exported from Venezuela would be assigned "reference prices" for the purpose of taxation. These would be negotiated in advance for the whole period; and the companies would be free to sell at whatever actual prices they wished but would always pay taxes according to the reference schedule. Should realized prices rise above the reference levels, however, taxes would be paid according to the higher prices. A list of reference figures somewhat above current realized prices had already been agreed to by the companies, and these were to increase annually over the five-year period.

This system, more than any other part of the agreement, was a significant modification of petroleum policy; for the government, implicitly but clearly, was abandoning its intention to intervene directly in day-to-day marketing decisions. Depending on future market conditions, the companies would now be free to give very large discounts, perhaps even weakening world prices. The change was hardly a radical departure, since the Coordinating Commission had already abandoned most of its efforts at direct control of pricing decisions, and since the government would still be able to review the course of prices every five years, when the time came to negotiate a new reference schedule. Meanwhile, the administration expected substantial short-term benefits from the compromise. As Pérez Guerrero pointed out, the country had been suffering for years from a steady deprivation of income caused by the decline in realized prices. For the next five years this trend would be reversed, and prices, at least for tax purposes, would steadily increase.

Production levels. The government had also sought a firm agreement on future petroleum output in Venezuela, but the companies refused to bind themselves legally on this point. However, though this was not announced publicly, they did offer a "gentlemen's agreement" to increase production between 3 and 4 percent for the coming year, and to continue this rate of expansion in subsequent years if conditions allowed.

Future taxation. In return for the partial back-tax payment and the new price reference system, the government agreed to modify the tax reform proposal by eliminating the selective tax (much to Pérez Alfonzo's chagrin) and by reducing the new levies on company income. The companies would still have to face a tax hike—roughly, from 65 percent to 68 percent of profits—but the new system would include incentives to promote reinvestment, exploration, drilling, and secondary recovery. In explaining the changes in the tax proposal, Pérez Guerrero stated that he had been instructed by Leoni to compromise on company income taxes if the overall results of the agreement would provide the same increase in government revenues. This goal, he said, had been achieved: the 1966 agreement would add approximately Bs 850 million ($190 million) to the country's treasury for each of the five years the agreement was to last.*

Conditions of exploitation. President Leoni also announced that the Ministry of Mines and the nationalized CVP had been working on a series of formulas for service contracts, and that the present "climate of mutual understanding" between the government and the companies would facilitate an eventual agreement on this point as well. Late in October Pérez Guerrero presented the companies with a detailed sketch of the general conditions the government felt to be acceptable for service contracts. The variations suggested included mixed companies (private-public) limited to extraction; integrated mixed companies (exploring, extracting, refining, marketing); and service contracts in the full sense of the term (i.e. contracts between the CVP and private companies for oil development directed by the state agency). All contracts were to be under the supervision and control of the CVP. The purpose of the new arrangements, the Minister explained, was to ensure "a broad, operative participation of the Venezuelan State through the CVP, along with a greater financial benefit to the nation."[13]

The agreement with the companies put an abrupt end to the

---

* C. C. Pocock, who headed Shell of Venezuela, estimated that the government's share of company profits would rise immediately to about 72 percent and would reach 75 percent by the end of the five-year period. (*El Universal*, 8.i.67, p. D1; compare this projection with the actual split in Appendix Table A.)

tax reform dispute. Shell and Creole announced that it had dispelled much of the companies' uncertainty, and that they could now plan for the future with more confidence. The leaders of the domestic opposition, however, found themselves in a very embarrassing position indeed. One commentator in *El Nacional* charged them with doing nothing but hindering the government in its attempt to "transfer earnings from the strongboxes of the international cartel to the treasury of their country."[14] The very outcome of the negotiations, as other observers began to point out, put the lie to the companies' previous contention, so loudly repeated by their domestic allies, that they could not stand further taxation if their Venezuelan operations were to continue in a healthy condition.

The president of Fedecámaras, Concepción Quijada, grudgingly announced that the change might possibly improve the economic future of the country.[15] But Uslar Pietri quickly returned to the attack, charging that the agreement was unsatisfactory because it had been concluded "under pressure"—quite true, though hardly appropriate coming from a major source of that pressure.[16] A COPEI spokesman said that his party was not happy with the way the government had concluded the agreement "behind the nation's back," adding his personal opinion that more income might have been gained from the tax claims.[17] (Actually, the government had announced several times—to the extent that it was a matter of general knowledge—that it was negotiating with the companies.)

The modified law passed with little fanfare. Once having concentrated their attack on the petroleum tax provisions of the law, the domestic elites could hardly mount still another offensive against the tax increases particularly affecting themselves. This would have been difficult in any case, given their very light current tax burden. The initiative had been lost. Few people, in fact, even bothered to consider at length the investment plan the government had prepared as part of its "treaty" with the opposition in July. The rather superficial investigation of public expenditures also attracted little attention.[18]

The Tax Reform Solution: A Balance Sheet

When measured against the previous objectives of government policy the 1966 agreement was a significant admission of failure. However, it did contain some benefits. One of these, of course, was the increased income from back taxes, new taxes, and reference pricing. Another was the government's acquisition of an acknowledged role in pricing matters, partly as a result of company agreements to pay back taxes but mainly as a result of the reference-pricing system, which would prove to be a more satisfactory instrument of policy than either direct intervention or retroactive claims. In addition, the government gained valuable information, for the agreement was a tacit admission by the companies that Venezuela was still a going concern in terms of oil earnings—so much so that they agreed to a substantial and immediate tax hike and some loss of freedom in return for small and, as it turned out, very short-term gains in security.

The crisis was also important in another way: it revealed that the process of political change in Venezuela was, in a way, catching up with the AD leaders and their petroleum policy. By 1965–66 the freedom of action obtaining during the Betancourt administration had been circumscribed by the progressive fragmentation of the party system, the partial dissolution of the coalition mechanism, and the willingness of the domestic private sector to ally with the petroleum industry against the state. The kind of independent experimentation with alternatives that Pérez Alfonzo had used in his search for an effective means of controlling the industry and reducing the country's dependence upon oil was no longer possible without political repercussions.

Still another consequence of the agreement was that it drove a wedge between the government and Pérez Alfonzo himself. Even after retiring from his official post, Pérez Alfonzo had continued to devote most of his time to petroleum matters and had regularly met with AD petroleum experts to discuss important policy issues. He also held periodic press conferences and published papers assessing the state of the industry and the effectiveness of government policies. Beginning in 1964 he had pressed the government to implement a tax mechanism that would limit rising profits and also provide an incentive for the companies to maintain their investment levels in the country. He estimated that Creole had been making more than 50 percent profit on its net fixed assets during the two years preceding the reform crisis. In view of such excesses, he considered the government's agreement to abandon the all-important selective tax a near-total capitulation to the companies.[19] And he said so. In subsequent years Pérez Alfonzo pointed out rather bitterly that industry profits were soaring even higher than they had under the Jiménez dictatorship, something he found intolerable under a democratic government: "During a democratic regime ... the anomaly [of overdependence on oil] grows because public liberties allow the most powerful economic sectors ... to use all the methods at their disposal to contribute less and less to the satisfaction of collective needs."[20]

The Desulfurization Agreement

The years immediately following the compromise of 1966 were marked by an absence of major conflict in company-government relationships, and even by some degree of cooperation and goodwill. Such lulls are common in interdependent bargaining of this kind. Contacts between the industry and the Ministry of Mines increased, and company officials felt more able to "communicate" with the government regarding their needs and problems. For their part, the government officials were satisfied with their recent political victory, a victory that had provided needed income and at the same time cleared the air of hostility. There was considerable hope, too, that the proposed service contract system, in which the companies were showing increasing interest, would soon provide a viable alternative to concessions.

Nonetheless, there was still much anxiety in Venezuela about the world petroleum market and about the place of Venezuelan oil—now even more costly—within it. Prices continued their steady decline, and oil from the Middle East continued to encroach upon traditional Venezuelan markets in the United States,

Canada, and Latin America. There was considerable fear, too, that the launching of even larger supertankers then under construction in Japanese shipyards would reduce transport costs and further damage Venezuela's position. The government had successfully called the companies' bluff on the current value of Venezuelan oil; but since no one in the Ministry knew the exact margins of cost and profit involved, no one could anticipate the effects of a further weakening of the market.

Taking advantage of both the generally cooperative ambience and the government's continuing apprehensions about the market, Creole requested, and was granted in January 1968, a number of special incentives in return for its agreement to install a large desulfurization facility within the country. For several years the petroleum companies had been conducting a campaign to focus attention on the marketing difficulties caused by the high sulfur content of most Venezuelan crude oil. In private conversations with the government Creole had expressed willingness to invest in desulfurization, but had stressed that because the sums involved were in excess of $100 million, the project would only be possible if the government provided "favorable" conditions. This was a rather classic example of the use of control over investment to extract beneficial treatment from the state.

Just at this time, Venezuela's concern about the salability of her exports was heightened by the passage of the first environmental regulations on the U.S. East Coast, which put strict limits on the sulfur content of heating oil.[21] After extensive negotiations with Creole, the government agreed, in a special memorandum signed by Creole and the Ministers of Mines and Finance, to modify existing regulations in several ways in order to secure the necessary investment for desulfurization. The major concession was an arrangement allowing the company to accelerate the rate of tax depreciation on the new equipment.* Creole went ahead with the project, and by 1971 was exporting low-sulfur oil in quantity.

The desulfurization agreement met with little legislative re-

---

* Among the other adjustments was a special customs exemption for the desulfurization equipment. It was also agreed that desulfurized oil could be

sistance; but it did have political repercussions, since it, too, was strongly opposed by Pérez Alfonzo, who felt it was not only un-justified economically but also of doubtful legality. He subse-quently published a lengthy criticism, claiming that the companies had hoodwinked the government by overstating the amount of new investment required and charging that as a result Venezuela would lose more than Bs 300 million ($67 million) in income. Coming as it did after the government's agreement to abandon the selective tax, the desulfurization agreement confirmed Pérez Al-fonzo's belief that the government was no longer willing or able to oppose the united private economic interests operating within Venezuela.[22] The rift between petroleum policymakers in the AD government and the country's most articulate and outspoken *émi-nence grise* in oil thus became firmly established; it would later have a major impact on petroleum policymaking.

Taken together, the tax reform and the desulfurization agree-ments bespoke a considerable "taming" of government petroleum policy. Though still holding to the premises and objectives estab-lished under Betancourt, the Leoni administration had been forced to adapt to a much more complex and constraining political environment; and the adaptation had been painful, producing a growing disunity within AD itself. Still, as the Leoni years came to an end, problems that had been worsening for nearly a decade seemed to have been resolved, for the time being, by a forced ac-commodation between an industry and a government both newly conscious of the facts of interdependence. And there was consider-able hope within Venezuela that the uncertainty of the past would soon be replaced by a new and more satisfactory working arrange-ment.

---

sold on long-term contracts—which would, in effect, extend the current refer-ence-price schedule for that oil beyond the time when a new schedule might be negotiated for other petroleum products.

5. The Caldera Administration, I

Political Immobilism and Fiscal Distress

THE ELECTION of Rafael Caldera in 1968 set the stage for one of the most tumultuous and divisive periods in the history of Venezuelan democratic politics. The ensuing half-decade of COPEI government was also a critical period in the devolution of the concessions system. The government passed enabling legislation—the now-famous Hydrocarbons Reversion Law—with the end of concessions clearly in mind, and the petroleum companies began to think seriously about either writing off their interests or finding some mixed-enterprise arrangement that would be politically viable. Then prices soared to levels beyond even the fondest dreams of Pérez Alfonzo as the world oil market suddenly tightened under the combined impact of growing self-assertion among the Middle Eastern governments, an unexpected growth in world demand, and the outbreak of still another Arab-Israeli war. A lot happened in a short time.

Caldera's victory at first brought considerable satisfaction to the oil industry. Although the companies refrained from overt gestures in favor of any candidate, it was understood that they supported COPEI during the 1968 campaign, anticipating a more moderate oil policy under that party's rule. At first all signs indicated that this would be the case. In a speech before the Chamber of the Petroleum Industry during the campaign Caldera seemed very conciliatory, among other things criticizing recent suggestions that the government take control of the entire domestic market for petroleum products. And after the election he received a team of top Creole executives and listened with apparent sympathy to a lengthy exposition, generously illustrated with charts and graphs, of the grave problems facing the industry in the future.*

The early months of 1969 seemed to confirm the government's adherence to a conciliatory posture. The new administration unveiled no new initiatives in petroleum policy; indeed, it seemed rather uninterested in the subject. The new Minister of Mines, Hugo Pérez de la Salvia, though a skilled politician, was no petroleum expert and seemed to have few ideas of his own about the basic issues involved. To the extent that the administration did commit itself, it did so in incremental rather than innovative ways; policymakers continued negotiations leading toward service contracts; spokesmen again pressed the United States for a hemisphere preference, and were again rejected; and the government, despite a lukewarm attitude toward OPEC, kept on advocating an international prorationing system.

Before the end of Caldera's first year in office, however, petroleum policy became the central issue in a series of intense political struggles. These, in turn, worsened company-government relations and accelerated the enlargement of government controls over the industry. This reversal stemmed not from the formulation of a new strategy toward oil, but rather from important changes in the political process itself, changes that shifted the focus of policy initiatives quite suddenly from the executive to the legislature and stimulated the emergence of competitive nationalism among the political parties. Changes in the international oil market reinforced the trend.

In terms of doctrine, the Caldera administration associated itself closely with previous democratic governments. However, as was the case toward the end of the Leoni administration, the government was less concerned with conservation, the defense of inter-

---

* More recently, Caldera reflected on that meeting. "Everything seemed to be against us—the supertankers, Libya, Nigeria, sulfur, Alaska, the reopening of Suez, and any other circumstance that would convince Venezuelans that the goose with the golden eggs was dying. . . . The outlook was so pessimistic that we should both have ended the meeting in tears, he [Leo E. Lowry, president of Creole] over managing an oil company doomed to failure, and myself over leading a country that was soon to be without petroleum." *El Nacional*, 8.v.73, p. 1.

national prices, and large-scale international agreements than with ensuring a steady growth of its oil income. For this reason, Caldera became increasingly preoccupied with production levels and showed little sympathy for Pérez Alfonzo's policy of holding back Venezuelan output to strengthen prices and conserve petroleum resources for later years. Until late in 1971, at least, he operated on the assumption that low prices would continue for the foreseeable future, as Creole and other companies repeatedly assured him they would.

Caldera's administrative style was also quite different. Despite his very limited mandate (only 29 percent of the vote and a margin of some 30,000 votes over the AD candidate, Gonzalo Barrios), Caldera was not inclined to compromise. Nor did he encourage extensive intraparty discussions of policy, preferring to hold decisionmaking rather tightly in his own hands.* At the outset he chose to do without the multiparty coalition that previous regimes, with more substantial electoral mandates, had considered necessary; and as a result bureaucrats and technicians affiliated with other parties were turned out in large numbers, depriving the government of much of the expertise accumulated over the preceding decade. Since the new Minister of Mines was not a petroleum expert himself, this housecleaning created serious problems. Indeed, throughout Caldera's term the level of technical competence in

---

* The two major parties in Venezuela have had somewhat different styles of operation. Since 1958, AD has consistently encouraged intraparty discussion, and Adecos in the government have always been available for consultation with each other, with rank-and-file party members, and with representatives of the country's important interest groups. President Betancourt, for example, several times drove across town for informal talks at the home of his Petroleum Minister; and Pérez Alfonzo was always willing to talk things over with the technical people in his ministry. Once a decision has been made, however, AD party discipline tends to be strict—which may explain the AD's tendency toward fragmentation in the past. COPEI government, in contrast, has been characterized by a presidential aloofness reminiscent of Charles De Gaulle, and even important cabinet members have had very limited access to the chief executive. But COPEI seems to tolerate many differences of opinion even when the party line on a question is clear. Much of the party's style can probably be attributed to Caldera himself: formal and aloof, though an excellent orator, he seems more a father figure than a down-to-earth politician in the AD style, and is apparently very conscious of his public image and place in history.

government was markedly inferior to that of earlier regimes, a circumstance that led to several embarrassing mistakes and an overall decline in the prestige of the Ministry of Mines.

The Political Imbroglio

Although Caldera won the presidential contest, AD emerged with a stronger position than the president's own party in both the Chamber of Deputies and the Senate. The AD leaders, as might be expected, were quite bitter about their defeat. On a national level, their party had never lost an election, and many Adecos had come to view themselves as the only authentic representatives of the Venezuelan people. Their hostility increased when so many AD officials were ousted to make room for loyal Christian Democrats, and they quickly took advantage of Caldera's legislative weakness to form a majority opposition coalition in the legislature. They then proceeded to foment one of the worst episodes of parliamentary paralysis since 1958.

Led by AD, congressional opponents assailed the presidency at every opportunity: they removed the executive's right to appoint members of the judiciary (except on the Supreme Court) and placed it in the hands of a special panel dominated by opposition parties; they limited government borrowing to two-year periods; and they passed a law forcing all autonomous institutes and corporations with a majority of shares held by the government to appoint union representatives to their boards (AD's strength in the union movement surpassed that of COPEI). AD tried briefly to persuade Congress to make Venezuela's state governors elective rather than appointed officials, and at one point seriously discussed the possibility of changing the constitution itself to a parliamentary system. Because of the standoff between the legislature and the executive, Venezuelan politics deteriorated into petty wrangling. Bitterness, fragmentation, and empty rhetoric became the rule, while the country drifted. Things got so bad that there were rumors of "restlessness" in the military. Even Fedecámaras attempted to reconcile the antagonists, inviting COPEI and AD leaders to meet at its own headquarters (they declined).

Not until early 1970 did the situation improve. The AD leaders then agreed, after lengthy negotiations and strong pressure from the party's experienced "old guard," to arrange a modus vivendi with COPEI and to support the government in predefined "areas of coincidence." Though far from a coalition—since COPEI refused to share posts in the administration itself—this detente did allow the passage of essential legislation and halted boycotts and procedural quarrels for a time. However, despite a dramatic lecture to party members by Leoni on the virtues of loyal opposition in sustaining a democratic polity, AD hostility continued to run strong, and the party's legislative caucus continued to promote its own programs and modify government bills to suit its wishes.

This political quandary affected petroleum policy in important ways. For one thing, the initiative in oil policy formulation gradually shifted to Congress. This was caused partly by the relative inactivity of the administration, but also by the "availability" of petroleum policy issues—really for the first time—to individuals and party factions in the legislature. AD's leaders, for the most part, were quite reluctant to take up oil matters. After all, COPEI was following the path established by the earlier AD governments, though less aggressively. Also, there has always been an understanding in Venezuela that executive initiative is essential to the conduct of petroleum affairs; the lessons of the recent tax-reform crisis were only too clear in this respect. But AD, like most parties, had its factions, and one group, led by Congressman Arturo Hernández Grisanti, strongly favored congressional intervention in oil policy. And Hernández Grisanti was fortunate in having the collaboration and support of none other than Pérez Alfonzo. The former minister, still in retirement, was only too pleased to reassert his own conceptions of oil strategy, and it soon became clear that Hernández Grisanti and his associates had chosen to follow this strategy within Congress and within the party.

These new political circumstances, taken together, set the conditions for a sudden and rather extreme politicization of Venezuela's petroleum policy. The pattern of government-company bargaining continued, but within a new framework, a fragmented political context of great complexity.

Service Contracts

The first item on the agenda, as far as petroleum was concerned, was the implementation of the new service contract system.[1] Leoni had begun negotiations to establish standardized conditions and terms for the contracts; and most knowledgeable observers felt that setting up a new system of exploitation was the last and most important step in reestablishing an equilibrium in oil, a process begun with the tax reform and desulfurization agreements. Industry representatives urged the government to move ahead on this, and administration officials were anxious to comply, since production, despite the "gentlemen's agreement" of 1966, had increased very slowly (see Table B, p. 182). Accordingly, after receiving preliminary bids from several companies, in the fall of 1969 the government submitted to Congress its proposals for the overall terms it was prepared to offer the companies. The proposals then went to a special joint Senate-Chamber committee for review.

The moment chosen for this was hardly auspicious. Executive-legislative infighting was intense, and the opposition was busy delaying the passage of Caldera's first budget proposal. To make matters worse, Pérez Alfonzo, always sensitive to timing, reaffirmed that he strongly opposed service contracts, as he had first stated publicly in 1967. Although he himself had originated the idea of offering such contracts, he charged that now they would only place the country further under the control of foreign companies, suggesting instead that the government simply freeze production levels and meet further budgetary needs by improving income tax collection and increasing taxes. In fact, he still favored a selective tax on profits over 15 percent.

Within Congress, the AD leadership was divided over the proposals. One group favored a rapid approval, noting that this had been an AD idea in the first place. Another favored delaying approval and making extensive revisions in the terms to be offered the companies; this faction included followers of Pérez Alfonzo, and others who resented Caldera's style and wanted to deny him any legislative success. In the meantime, AD began discussions with COPEI on the "areas of coincidence" within which the parties might work together and thus restore public (and military) confidence in the democratic process. When the two finally agreed on a program of limited cooperation early in 1970, they began to work out their differences on service contracts. But final agreement here had to wait until AD resolved its own internal divisions on the question. At this point the formation of a "third force" in Congress further complicated matters. This was made up of URD, MEP, and FDP, all parties who resented AD's detente with COPEI and had decided to take an independent line as critics of the government. Led by MEP's Jesús Angel Paz Galarraga, the Third Force denounced all service contracts as "disguised concessions."

In April 1970 the AD leaders finally reconciled their differences, and the party's parliamentary caucus voted to support the service contract system, but with modifications designed to increase the benefits received by the government. This decision assured passage of the measure, since the combined AD and COPEI vote constituted a majority in both houses. The struggle dragged on, however, as the joint committee went over the terms of the contracts clause by clause. Meanwhile Pérez Alfonzo and the Third Force continued to attack the system. At one point URD's Jóvito Villalba even called for public demonstrations to protest congressional approval.

It was not until fall 1970 that Congress finally voted to approve Venezuela's final terms for contracts, which by this time had stiffened considerably. The revisions included additional payments to the CVP to be based on the contractors' net profits per barrel —in effect, a selective tax—as well as greater power for the CVP in administering the program.[2]

The whole episode was a major defeat for Caldera, the first in what became a long string of frustrations in petroleum policy. Although more than 25 companies had expressed interest in the new system at the outset, only Occidental, Shell, and Mobil proved willing to sign up under the revised terms. The area offered in this "first round," the south of Lake Maracaibo, was considered by the industry to be a good risk owing to its proximity to Venezuela's most productive traditional fields: estimates of reserves *in situ* ran from 1.2 to 3 billion barrels of oil, and the government hoped to see a production of 300,000 or more barrels per day within a few years.[3] Occidental was the most enthusiastic bidder, hoping to establish its first foothold in Venezuela. Creole, whose executives were openly hostile to Occidental, declined to participate in the bidding at all, explaining that the financial contributions demanded of the companies were incommensurate with their decisionmaking power under the contracts.

The lack of company enthusiasm disappointed the administration, but it was unwilling to send the terms of the contract back to Congress for softening. To make matters worse, even after the government had received final bids from the companies the signing of contracts was delayed by another tax reform controversy and a series of abrupt changes in the international price structure, which led both parties to hold off in order to assess the impact of new conditions. The contracts were not actually signed until late summer 1971, nearly 30 months after Caldera had begun to promote them.[4]

Thus congressional opposition, though it did not prevent the service contract system from coming into existence, severely impaired its prospects as an alternative means of petroleum development. The final terms, given existing tax levels, seemed unlikely to attract many companies. Of course, the willingness of some companies to sign up despite the increased costs indirectly revealed that the state retained a measure of bargaining power; indeed, this explains Creole's hostility toward Occidental, which did not disguise its eagerness to "get into" Venezuelan petroleum.[5]

But the most damaging aspect of the long congressional debate was its effect on the companies' sense of security. In the end, Congress had politicized the service contracts to the point where many companies were rightly skeptical of the state's long-run ability to abide by the new system. Once the issue of "disguised concessions" appeared in public discussions, it did not take a sophisticated political forecaster to conclude that the whole arrangement was insecure. Geophysical misfortunes subsequently compounded this political damage: the agreements signed, the companies moved ahead with exploration and drilling activities; but to the time of this writing they have been able to find only small quantities of commercially exploitable oil in the new fields.

Tax Reform and Unilateral Reference-Price Control

Once the revised service contract provisions had passed out of Congress, political attention quickly shifted to the government's budget. When Caldera came to power, Venezuela had already been suffering an economic slump for several years. Between 1964 and 1968 the yearly growth of per capita gross domestic product (GDP) had slowed to an average of less than 1 percent, and in 1968 it actually declined by 1.5 percent (see Table 9). Caldera hoped to restore the country's economic health in part by starting important new public works projects, such as the Caracas subway and low-income housing developments. But these required large-scale government spending. Fiscal receipts had increased, though erratically, by more than 25 percent (in constant bolívares) during the Leoni administration, and policymakers in the new government counted on similar increases—in fact, they demanded them. As we have seen, Venezuelan society had become reliant on a rapidly expanding public sector to sustain economic growth, and COPEI had no desire to reverse this trend.

Unfortunately, the forces that had sustained fiscal expansion in previous years were weakening even before Caldera entered office. Indeed, AD left nearly Bs 1.5 billion ($335 million) in debts, arising chiefly from unpaid commitments to various domestic construction companies. The major reason for the deficit, of course, was the reduced growth of oil income owing to sluggish production, continued price weakness, and, somewhat later, the end of the back-tax payments begun in 1966. Caldera, like Leoni, faced a difficult choice: he could again increase taxes on the domestic pri-

TABLE 9

Gross Domestic Product and GDP per Capita, 1950–71

(1958 bolívares)

Year	Population (thousands)	GDP (millions)	Change	GDP per capita	Change
1950	5,035	11,994	–	2,382	–
1951	5,179	12,665	5.6%	2,445	2.6%
1952	5,422	12,665	8.9	2,543	4.0
1953	5,665	15,077	9.3	2,662	4.7
1954	5,908	16,377	8.6	2,772	4.2
1955	6,150	17,698	8.1	2,877	3.8
1956	6,393	20,299	14.7	3,175	10.3
1957	6,636	24,284	19.6	3,659	15.2
1958	6,879	24,585	1.2	3,573	−2.3
1959	7,122	25,405	3.3	3,567	−0.2
1960	7,364	25,852	1.8	3,511	−1.6
1961	7,612	26,730	3.4	3,512	0.03
1962	7,872	29,555	10.6	3,754	6.9
1963	8,144	31,804	7.6	3,905	4.0
1964	8,427	33,940	6.7	4,028	3.1
1965	8,722	35,148	3.6	4,030	0.05
1966	9,030	35,924	2.2	3,978	−1.3
1967	9,352	38,506	7.2	4,117	3.5
1968	9,686	37,268	2.0	4,054	−1.5
1969	10,035	40,528	3.2	4,039	−0.4
1970	10,399	43,793	8.1	4,211	4.3
1971	10,617	48,216	10.1	4,541	7.1
1972	10,970	52,575	9.0	4,793	5.5

SOURCE: Venezuela, [9], 1964, p. 2; 1973, pp. 2–4.

vate sector and/or the foreign oil industry; or he could let the budget itself respond both to company decisions about production and to "natural" increases in domestic tax income, that is, increases roughly paralleling the growth of the economy as a whole. Closing the vicious circle, of course, was the close tie between the performance of Venezuela's public sector and that of her economy as a whole. In the short run, oil remained pivotal.

At the very outset Caldera was forced to ask Congress for special credits to reduce his government's indebtedness. Notwithstanding its partial responsibility for the problem, AD refused to grant the Bs 2 billion requested, in the end approving only some Bs 780 million ($174 million).* When Minister of Finance Pedro Tinoco

---

* This was eventually borrowed from a group of New York banks.

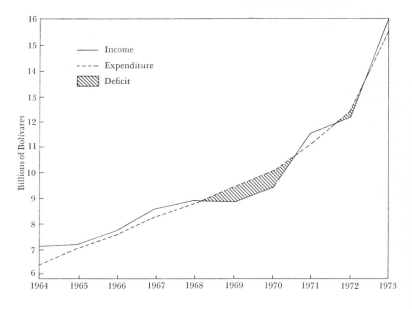

Figure 2. Venezuelan government income and expenditure, 1964–73. The figures for 1973 are estimated. (SOURCE: Venezuela, [6], 1962, App. p. 6)

submitted Caldera's first budget to Congress in the fall of 1969, the opposition attacked that as well, demanding a full accounting of where the government planned to obtain the funds, especially for its large and politically glamorous public works. Tinoco opposed any increase in taxes, but indicated the government would remain solvent by improving collection procedures and drawing on an anticipated increase in petroleum revenues.

Tinoco's optimism proved unjustified. As 1970 wore on it became evident not only that the government would be unable to avoid a large deficit in the current year, but that it would have to increase its income somehow in order to prevent budget cuts in the coming year (see Figure 2). Despite continuing pleas from the government, the oil companies increased production only some 3 percent over 1969—hardly enough to cover the desired 10–12 percent increase in fiscal revenues. And it was clear that the hoped-for production from the new service contracts would not materialize in the immediate future.

The fall of 1970 was in many ways a low point for Caldera. Teachers' and steelworkers' strikes, a restless military, and an aggressive legislative opposition all contributed to the worsening political climate. It was hardly an auspicious time to propose still another tax reform, but Caldera and his Minister of Finance concluded that they had no alternative. In October, along with the budget for 1971, Tinoco presented a package of reform proposals to Congress. The new measures, intended to increase income by approximately 9 percent over 1970, included: a graduated sales tax; a 10 percent increase in nonpetroleum profits taxes; increased taxes on liquor, cigarettes, and gasoline; a lottery tax; and the elimination of a divided tax credit in the income tax. Of these, the sales tax was the most controversial, since such taxes are generally regressive in character; however, the proposed system exempted staples and concentrated the highest rates on luxury items of all kinds. Most notable in the reform was the complete absence of any income tax increases affecting the oil companies. This reflected both the administration's desire to avoid any deterrent to production growth and Tinoco's personal conviction that higher taxes would damage the industry. (Tinoco had been coordinator of the 1965–66 Fedecámaras analysis of AD's tax reform, and even then had strongly opposed any new taxes on the industry.)

The proposal set off a political struggle that eventually produced another partial defeat for the administration and another major defeat for the petroleum companies.[6] As might be expected, AD immediately attacked the proposal as regressive, pointing to the sales tax and the taxes on liquor and cigarettes. Fedecámaras and the business community in general also opposed the new measures, and a series of personal briefings by Tinoco failed to change their attitudes.[7] Meanwhile, Pérez Alfonzo, Hernández Grisanti, and their congressional allies decided to derail the new reform entirely and replace it with increased taxes on the petroleum companies.

Watching the international situation closely throughout 1970, Pérez Alfonzo decided that the government, preoccupied with production, was missing an opportunity to increase its income and enlarge its control of the oil industry. In the spring Syria had blocked the Trans-Arabian Pipeline to obtain higher transit payments; and shortly afterward Libya, led by the revolutionary government of Colonel Qaddafi, had cut back production to force the companies operating there to pay higher taxes, which they soon agreed to do. (This set off a spiral of demands for increased tax payments that would transform the entire character of the oil market within a few years and would eventually bring on the infamous oil "crisis" of the early 1970's.) For Venezuela, these were important events. To begin with, they created a mild production shortfall and placed a heavy strain on existing tanker capacity. Oil prices in the Middle East and tanker rates worldwide began to rise, the latter precipitously. Venezuelan oil became a more attractive commodity as a result, a condition reflected in the prices for heavy fuel oil in the eastern United States.[8] However, these changes did not immediately affect prices and government tax receipts within Venezuela. The companies' failure to assure an immediate Venezuelan benefit from the improved world market provided powerful ammunition for Pérez Alfonzo and the congressional opposition.

International events also prompted Pérez Alfonzo and Hernández Grisanti to push for a decisive Venezuelan contribution to the worldwide drive for higher prices and higher taxes. As it happened, the next OPEC meeting was to be held in Venezuela in December 1970, just two weeks after the most decisive phase of the tax reform controversy. Events in the Middle East had taken OPEC by surprise, and at this meeting the organization would have to respond to, and perhaps take charge of, the new movement. Pérez Alfonzo saw this as an opportunity for Venezuela to again demonstrate her leadership in international oil affairs, something he felt Caldera had neglected entirely. For more than a decade he had been waiting for a chance to break the paralysis of the oil-producing countries, and this might be it.[9]

Thus international and domestic trends combined to enhance the strategic importance of a legislative blow at the companies. Accordingly, Hernández Grisanti launched a series of widely publicized attacks on the industry in mid-November, charging the companies with making "excessive profits" and asking Congress to investigate the discrepancy between prices in the Middle East and those reported by Venezuelan producers. A number of other opposition spokesmen, among them URD's Leonardo Montiel Ortega, joined the attack, demanding increases in taxes and a revision of the reference-price schedule. As these critics began to press the issue, they encountered some resistance from AD. But the political appeal of the more nationalistic strategy soon overcame objections, and by early December the debate within Congress had shifted from Tinoco's reform package to the new opposition proposal for a straight increase in petroleum taxes, from the current 52 percent to 60 percent. The substitute reform also contained a clause giving Venezuela the right to set oil reference prices unilaterally at any time, rather than through negotiation with the companies every five years, as stipulated in the 1966 agreement.*

Events in Congress caught Caldera by surprise, and he tried to head off the opposition. He and Tinoco met with legislative leaders to reassure them that the government would protect the country's interests under the new market conditions. They also stressed the damage the substitute tax measure would do to the new service contracts, negotiated but still not operational. At the same time, the Ministry of Mines let it be known that it was studying the market and was urging the companies to bring Venezuelan prices in line with international prices; it also raised the possibility of new retroactive tax claims when the 1970 tax declarations were presented in March 1971.†

If the government was surprised, the petroleum companies were stunned by the sudden change in Venezuelan attitudes, and they quickly launched an intensive publicity campaign to defend themselves. Both Creole and Shell pointed out that they had supplied complete pricing figures to the government, and that these data were entirely in line with earlier agreements on prices. The Pres-

* The 1966 agreement in fact provided for taxes to be paid on income calculated at realized prices rather than reference prices, should the realized prices rise above the established reference prices. But most Venezuelan critics felt that reference prices should remain substantially higher than realized prices, as they had been in the past—and as they no longer were for key products late in 1970.

† The government had apparently been planning to use this method to make up part of its deficit if the Tinoco reforms did not get past Congress.

ident of Creole, Leo Lowry, formally requested permission to present his company's case before Congress. Privately, Shell executives conveyed grave warnings to government and legislative leaders about the effect of the new tax on service contracts. The companies also sought the support of their allies in the last tax reform conflict. In a special meeting, the Chamber of the Petroleum Industry told Fedecámaras that the existing "artificial climate of tension and antagonism" was not benefiting the nation, and rejected accusations against the industry as unfounded, "as is proved by statements of the Petroleum Ministry and other government spokesmen."[10] Few missed the irony in the industry's relying on government authority to defend itself.

In sharp contrast to the 1966 conflict, however, the companies now seemed almost powerless. Lowry's request to appear before Congress, repeated several times, was eventually granted. But there was no sudden outpouring of support from the domestic private sector, although Fedecámaras did issue a few very mild statements of concern about the industry. There was no great publicity campaign, no intensive person-to-person lobbying; there was, in short, no apparent desire to force a confrontation over the matter. Several things account for this. In part, private interests were forestalled by the speed with which the substitute measure moved through Congress. Also, the contending reform proposals cast domestic and foreign private elites as opponents: assuming some tax change were inevitable, each would gain by the other's loss, at least in the short run. Of course tax increases were not necessarily inevitable, and the two could possibly have joined to oppose any reform; but this time they found no ready allies among the politicians, since both the government and the opposition favored some sort of tax increase. The pattern of cross-cutting interests was such as to exert a maximum strain on the decade-old partnership of private interests.

Actually, the partnership had been crumbling since 1966. Many leaders of the Venezuelan private sector had emerged from that earlier battle with a sense of resentment and a conviction that they had been "used" by the foreign companies, that they had been left stranded, with their taxes increased, while the companies negotiated a separate arrangement with the government. Moreover, many concluded that the companies had actually lied to them about conditions within the oil industry and about the consequences of increased taxation. It was one thing for the companies to "cry wolf" as a bargaining move; it was another for them to damage the standing and credibility of their domestic allies while doing so. As the rift between private interests grew wider, the companies, despite repeated appeals, could no longer count on domestic groups for significant tactical support. Of course, Venezuela's economic elites were still deeply concerned about the fortunes of the petroleum industry, since their prosperity, like that of the government, was closely tied to that industry. However, they no longer accepted uncritically the companies' argument that private property, capitalism, and limitations on state power were parts of a whole and must stand or fall together.[11] In a sense, the companies were now paying the long-term costs of the short-term benefits gained from their separate bargain in 1966.

On December 7, 1970, the congressional subcommittee in charge (chaired by Hernández Grisanti) unanimously approved the substitute tax proposal and the unilateral determination of reference prices.* The opposition parties now backed the bill enthusiastically, since its success enabled them to claim credit for nationalist vigilance and at the same time fault the government for passivity. Once it became clear that his own reform was doomed, Caldera wavered and then announced that he accepted the substitute bill as the best available alternative. Although a tactical defeat for him personally, it would nevertheless bring in a badly needed Bs 600–800 million ($135–180 million), and was all the more valuable because it applied retroactively to the fiscal year in progress. Caldera was joined by a growing number of COPEI *técnicos* in the Ministry of Mines and by many COPEI legislators who were anxious

---

* There would now be a flat tax of 60 percent on oil-derived income, and the executive would be able, without negotiation, to fix the reference prices on crude oil and petroleum products as much as three years in advance. The bill did provide some relief for companies whose profits fell below 15 percent of net fixed assets after costs, royalties, and income tax had been deducted.

to avoid having to go down in the record as voting against a major nationalistic measure. Tinoco, almost alone, opposed the substitute measure to the end, but his influence waned rapidly. He spread the word that if it passed he would resign in the near future, which he did.

The substitute reform passed the lower house (where all fiscal measures must originate) by a unanimous vote on December 13, 1970. COPEI whip Pedro Pablo Aguilar attempted to amend the bill to give the President discretionary power to apply a lower rate to companies operating on service contracts, but with no success. Within two days the Senate approved the bill and sent it to Caldera for his signature. Pérez Alfonzo immediately called a press conference to express his approval and "explain the reasons for the increase." As one reporter put it: "He could hardly conceal his glee over the turn of events, and accepted reporters' speculations that he had been the *éminence grise* in the reform with a smile."[12] The oil industry was gloomy, complaining that the measure seemed to assume a permanent increase in world oil prices. Spokesmen also lamented the unilateral character of the move, expressing fear that it signaled the end of negotiated agreements in Venezuela.[13] Three months later, in March 1971, the government unilaterally raised reference prices (now called "tax reference values," or "TRV's") an average of 59¢ per barrel.

6. The Caldera Administration, II

Concessions Reversion, Nationalism, and the 1973 Bonanza

WHILE VENEZUELA'S Congress grappled with the 1970 tax reform, still another conflict over petroleum was brewing behind the scenes. This time the issues were the deterioration of oil production facilities and the depletion of proven reserves. Events followed a familiar sequence: the initiative began with Pérez Alfonzo, took center stage despite the reluctance of moderate AD leaders and the administration, and subsequently moved through the legislature, with little opposition, as an essentially unchallengeable nationalist gesture.

In the absence of guarantees that they would continue making satisfactory profits in Venezuela, it was only to be expected that the petroleum companies would avoid further investments in the country, and would instead stretch the lifetime of old equipment and expand production only to the amounts extractable before concessions expired.* Refusal to invest was also an important bargaining card in the hands of the companies: to a degree, at least, they could hold the industry itself captive in order to extract guarantees of security from the state. The oil companies, in fact, had begun a program of graduated disinvestment during the Betan-

---

* Another, less publicized, problem associated with a write-off spiral of this kind is the tendency for companies to become less concerned with conservation measures designed to maximize long-term production from existing wells. Rapid pumping, for example, can cause water seepage into petroleum fields; but it may be justified in profit calculations by the desire to pull out as much oil as possible before access to the field is cut off. Similarly, it is possible to reinject the natural gas found in association with crude oil, but it may simply be flared off when time is short and investment incentives are lacking.

court and Leoni administrations (see Chapter 3). After the desulfurization agreement and the government's commitment to service
contracts, however, many Venezuelans hoped that the companies
would abandon this strategy in the near future. But when it became evident that the service contract system had been debilitated
in the legislature, the specter of a rapid deterioration of the industry reappeared. Informed observers feared that given current
trends, by the early 1980's Venezuela might inherit rusting, dilap-
idated equipment and run-down, depleted oilfields.

A closely connected problem, of growing concern to policymakers, was deciding what would happen when the existing concessions
expired. Would Venezuela automatically acquire the equipment
and facilities installed by the companies, on and off concession
sites, or would the state have to buy these from private industry?*
Just what would revert, and in what condition, was intensely de-
bated in Venezuela toward the end of 1970. At a special conference
held in December several Venezuelan and foreign analysts re-
viewed the issues involved; and although there was considerable
disagreement on ways of reversing the write-off trend and the gradual decline of the industry, it was generally acknowledged that
Venezuelan laws were far too vague about the ultimate ownership
of facilities and the constitutionality of government restrictions
on the companies' administration of fixed assets.[1]

In March 1971 opposition leader Alvaro Silva Calderon (MEP)
introduced a bill designed to "resolve" the issues in the reversion
debate by enormously extending state control of the industry. In
general terms, this Hydrocarbons Reversion Law had the following provisions: (1) all concessions and other properties owned by
the companies in Venezuela would revert to state ownership when
existing concessions expired in the early 1980's; (2) unexploited
concessions land (about 70 percent of the total) would be returned
to state control during the three years following enactment of the
law; (3) all companies would be required to post a form of "bond"
with the government amounting to 10 percent of the value of their
installations, to guarantee that these would be turned over to the

---

* Many refining, transport, and port facilities are located off concession sites.

state in good condition; (4) company operations within Venezuela would be under government control in the sense that any changes in operations would have to be approved, and the government would have the power to tell the companies where and when to explore or drill new wells.[2]

Although a member of MEP, Silva Calderon had worked in the Ministry of Mines under Pérez Alfonzo; and, to no one's surprise, it turned out that the former minister had assisted in the final drafting of the proposed legislation. From the outset, the bill was vigorously promoted by a nationalist coalition that included, in addition to its authors, AD's Arturo Hernández Grisanti, and COPEI's Jesús Bernardoni.

AD once again had difficulty deciding what to do. With an eye on the 1973 elections, several of the most important moderate party leaders were worried about antagonizing Venezuelan business interests. Others doubted the constitutionality of the bill. There was also considerable resentment of the way Pérez Alfonzo and Hernández Grisanti were pushing the issue to decision before AD's Central Executive Committee could take a position on it. After much discussion, however, AD's legislative caucus decided to support the measure. It would have been difficult to oppose politically, and in any case COPEI would have to live with it for the first two years.

Caldera and the COPEI legislators also had reservations about the bill, especially regarding its constitutionality. COPEI Secretary General Aristides Beaujon even proposed, unsuccessfully, the formation of a special commission of jurists to improve the bill. And Caldera himself complained about the unwillingness of opposition congressmen to consult him about the bill's wording. This time, however, the President was much more cautious in his criticism; and when forced to either accept the existing bill or fight it, he chose not only to support it but to strike an aggressively nationalistic posture on oil while doing so. As it turned out, this decision marked an important turning point in administration strategy. Thereafter, the government grew more willing to take a nationalistic attitude toward the companies, to bait industry spokesmen, and to challenge their explanations of actions and decisions.

There are several reasons for this major reorientation. For one thing, AD had broken the unwritten understanding that petroleum policy must be insulated from partisan struggles. If someone were to reap a reward for being the "dragon slayer," it might as well be the COPEI government. Willingly or not, Pérez Alfonzo and the AD had made competitive nationalism in oil policy politically irresistible. Moreover, Caldera and his policymakers blamed the oil industry for exposing their government to the opposition tactics. The administration had accepted the companies' assurances that prices were weakening, only to be embarrassed by Pérez Alfonzo and his supporters. In piecemeal fashion, Caldera and the Ministry of Mines were receiving an education in the politics of oil—an education apparently available only to those responsible for policy.

Fedecámaras, too, was concerned about reversion, but remained discreet on the subject, reflecting its changed orientation toward the companies. At one meeting there was outspoken criticism of the "upsurge of nationalism," but despite a denunciation by the Chamber of the Petroleum Industry, which attacked the proposed law as "confiscatory" and "de facto nationalization," the Fedecámaras leadership opted for a milder stance.[3]

The companies, just recovering from the shock of a tax hike, were positively horrified, not so much by the bill's reversion provisions as by its extension of government control over company operations. At first they adopted a low profile, perhaps hoping that AD and COPEI would resolve their uncertainty in the industry's favor. In June, when the bill issued from its subcommittee hearing intact and began its course through the legislature, Shell President J. J. Liefde suggested that a negotiated settlement of the issue might be preferable. The nationalist leaders in Congress, however, denounced the possibility of any nonlegislative accord. At the urging of oil lobbies, three U.S. Senators—Stevens of Alaska, Bellmon of Oklahoma, and Hansen of Wyoming—introduced legislation to prohibit U.S. petroleum imports from Venezuela if the reversion bill passed; but this attempt made no headway.[4] In fact, there was little the companies could do, so extensive was their loss of political influence in Venezuela. The reversion bill became law on July 30, 1971.*

It is hard to assess the impact of the Hydrocarbons Reversion Law. To the time of this writing (1975), the government has been very light-handed in exerting its new power over the industry except in the matter of production and pricing. The hypothetical cost to the companies of the deposits required by the Law, over a ten-year period, has been projected at roughly $500 million.[5] In theory, the companies can expect to reclaim whatever part of this they have paid at the time of reversion; but in private company officials concede that they are treating the deposit as a loss for planning purposes, the implication being that they will do little to keep their facilities in a condition to justify the return of the deposit. Thus the guarantee payment, rather than providing an incentive to maintain oil facilities, has become just another cost of operation.

When the Hydrocarbons Reversion Law was first passed, there was considerable anxiety within the industry that the government would place impossible managerial strains on the companies. So broad were the provisions of the law that in theory permission might be required to move a typewriter from one office to another. These fears seemed justified when, shortly after the law was passed, Venezuelan border police arrested an American engineer, one Erskine P. Fillingim (Colombia manager for Core Laboratories International, a drilling firm), as he tried to cross into Colombia at the border city of San Antonio del Táchira. Searching him, the police found laboratory equipment and a few documents, and charged him with trying to carry away equipment belonging to the state and data vital to the industry. Although he was cleared

---

* Shortly afterward several companies, including Shell, Creole, Gulf, Texaco, and Mobil, asked the Venezuelan Supreme Court to nullify part or all of the Reversion Law on the ground that it was unconstitutional. However, company officials had little real hope that they could dispose of the Law in this way: as Silva Calderon pointed out, Venezuela's legislature would simply amend the Constitution, if necessary. By early 1974 the Court had still not acted on the request.

six weeks later by a panel of judges, many oil executives viewed the incident as a confirmation of their worst fears. But with this exception the government proved relatively cooperative. Even the new Office of Hydrocarbons Reversion, established to administer the Law, refrained from unnecessary harassment.

The companies were also afraid the government would require extensive—and costly—exploration and drilling that they would not otherwise undertake. Legally, it could now order additional activities of this kind on pain of loss of concessionary rights. Here also, the administration has been restrained. Company officials admit to a degree of activity they might not otherwise have undertaken, in order to retain concessions for a longer period, but also indicate that the government has approved their proposed programs with few significant changes.* Presumably, Venezuelan policymakers are aware that they can exact only limited compliance in this area, in view of the large investments needed, before forcing the companies to close up shop altogether. This issue has become even more sensitive since early 1974, when the government announced that it would nationalize the industry completely in the near future.

Production Control and Price Increases

Actually, the state drew upon its new powers in only two areas, production and prices, and it did so only after a precipitous decline in output and still another budgetary crisis.

The first warning about production problems came from the oil fields, where union leaders complained that the companies had suddenly cut output by nearly half a million barrels a day, threatening several thousand jobs.[6] Production averaged 3.7 million barrels a day (MBD) in 1970 and climbed to 3.8 MBD during the first quarter of 1971; then, just as the reversion proposal was introduced as a bill in Congress, production dropped off. For 1971 as a whole, production averaged 3.55 MBD, a 4.3 percent drop

---

* Decree 832 (17.xii.71) requires the oil companies to submit for approval their plans for exploration, investment, and production each year; and any subsequent changes in plan must be formally approved in advance. Venezuela, [9], 1971, pp. xvii–xviii.

over the previous year, and in 1972 it declined an additional 9.3 percent, to 3.22 MBD. This was the lowest figure since that reached under the Betancourt administration a decade earlier (see Appendix Table B).

As with previous production cuts, it is impossible to determine the degree to which the companies were boycotting Venezuelan oil as a means of pressuring the government. Costs actually had risen in Venezuela as a result of the tax reform, and tanker rates had dropped off during part of 1971. But the government concluded firmly that the production drop was indeed a reprisal tactic. Early in 1972 Pérez La Salvia announced that on the basis of extensive studies of the market Oil Ministry experts had concluded that there were no "valid reasons" for such large cuts in Venezuelan production.[7] President Caldera himself stated that the decline in production could not be explained by "rational economics" and labeled company assessments "phantoms."[8] There could be no agreement here while uncertainty and mistrust were so great—and mistrust, especially, increased as production fell.

Reduced oil income meant a new budgetary squeeze, and government policymakers began to search for some means of compensation. Thanks to the Reversion Law and the bill granting authority to fix reference prices (now termed Tax Reference Values, or TRV's), they could legally manipulate taxes as well as production levels. The problem was determining how they should do so and how far they could safely go. In the budget for 1972, announced in the fall of 1971, the administration revealed that it was counting on a 2 percent production increase and an average boost of some 6¢ per barrel in TRV's to see the country through. Simultaneously, the Minister of Mines began pressing the companies to increase production. Pérez Alfonzo now stepped in, claiming that average TRV's should go up a full 40¢ per barrel to compensate for anticipated increases in Middle Eastern taxes and for the recent devaluation of the U.S. dollar. He also criticized the government for pushing production, suggesting instead a cut in output of half a million barrels a day. Shortly thereafter, the opposition parties began vying to see which could ask for the highest TRV's.

In the midst of this controversy, Caldera surprised everyone
with two quick moves. First, in a special decree, he required the
companies to submit in advance their programs for exploration,
production, sales, and investment, and to report bimonthly on
fulfillment.[9] Second, and more important, he established a system
of special export-volume penalties to force the companies to either
produce as nearly as possible at the record high levels of 1970 or
compensate the government for failure to do so.* The object of
the penalties, of course, was to assure a steady government income
despite variations in production; but they were also intended to
deprive the companies of one more means of pressuring the government. After establishing the penalty system, Caldera raised the
basic TRV's an average of 32¢ per barrel for the coming year, a
compromise between the much higher level now being demanded
by the opposition and the 6¢ per barrel he had originally contem-
plated.

Few outside the government had anything good to say about
these measures. The companies, of course, were unhappy, and they
subsequently challenged the legality of the production penalties
and unilateral price control—without success.[10] Pérez Alfonzo and
several others in the opposition were also displeased, despite their
own role in the matter. This attitude stemmed partly from a series
of unfortunate administrative errors by the government. For example, the Ministry at first set extraordinarily severe penalties for
export deficiencies, but revised them five days later after an outcry of indignant disbelief from the industry and a subsequent consultation with U.S. government representatives. The Ministry did

---

* In general, companies were allowed a quarterly variation of 2 percent
above and 2 percent below the 1970 levels, after which they would be assessed
a penalty calculated as a percentage increase in their TRV's. The penalties
became more severe as exports fell further below the allowable level, reaching
a maximum of 10 percent additional TRV when the deficiency was more than
8.9 percent (that is, more than 10.9 percent below the 1970 figure). In the case
of export deficiencies the penalty was levied on all the exports of the company.
The maximum penalty for overproduction was a doubling of TRV's for production 20 percent over the allowable limit (i.e. 22 percent over 1970), but this
applied only to the quantities actually exported beyond the allowable limit.
See Fuad, "Oil Penalties" and "The Haunting Prospect."

not admit its mistake, however, but simply announced the revision as the correction of a typographical error.[11] Also, the export regulation itself contained important loopholes and ambiguities. CVP officials, for example, assumed that their state-owned company was covered by it and wondered aloud whether they would have to abandon their plans for a rapid expansion of output. Also, there was no provision covering a company that exported nothing but instead sold its production to other companies to allow them to meet the export requirement.[12] Finally, Pérez Alfonzo criticized the system because it was designed to keep production levels at the 1970 record high, whereas he felt they should be allowed to drop.

All this grumbling from the opposition, however, also stemmed from a simple resentment that Caldera had—really for the first time—taken the initiative away from Congress in petroleum policy matters, if only to exercise powers granted him by the legislature itself. Hernández Grisanti indignantly declared that he thought the application of the Hydrocarbons Reversion Law was "Congress's business."[13] From the government's own perspective, the system was flawed because it did not relate to actual production closely enough to automatically meet government income needs. Following the creation of the export penalty system and the setting of new TRV's, the companies actually accelerated their production cutback. By February 1972 daily output had fallen to a scant 3 MBD, a drop of 13 percent in two months. Government-company hostility grew apace and Caldera's charges of economic reprisal became more strident as it became obvious that he would face another deficit despite his drastic measures. Government policymakers had simply not anticipated a cutback as radical as the one the companies carried out.*

In midsummer the administration achieved a stopgap solution by changing the sequence of tax payments to bring in more money

---

* Shell and Creole were primarily responsible for the magnitude of this decrease: their cutbacks in the months from May 1971 to February 1972 were greater—25 percent and 17 percent, respectively—than those of the most important smaller producers.

during fiscal 1972. Normally, the companies paid taxes monthly or quarterly on the basis of realized prices, making up the difference between these and the TRV's in March of the following year. But in June 1972 the government decreed that payments during the tax year could not be less than 90 percent of the amount indicated by the TRV's. This of course depleted the income expected for 1973, but it was vital in saving the government during the 1972 production crisis. As it turned out, in fiscal 1972 the government registered a deficit of Bs 202 million ($46 million), less than a third of those experienced in 1969 and 1970.*

As the time for setting the 1973 budget drew near, Venezuelan policymakers were determined not to let the companies force them to trim expenditures. Elections were coming up in that year, and it was no time for an incumbent government to ask constituents to tighten their belts. The accelerated tax payments had already pulled down the projected resource base for the coming year, exacerbating the problem.

Events in the Middle East helped out. Following its Teheran meeting in 1971 the OPEC group had won the companies' agreement to an immediate tax increase and an additional escalation of taxes until 1975. In view of these changes, Venezuela decided to raise the TRV schedule for 1973 once more, this time using a more complicated formula that would allow the TRV's to parallel changes in Middle Eastern taxes. Among other things, there was to be a special freight adjustment to offset changes in the relative cost of shipping Venezuelan oil. As before, Pérez Alfonzo and other critics demanded a much greater boost than the 12¢ to 17¢ TRV increases chosen by the government. But this time the administration stuck to its more moderate figure. (Shell, among others, had warned that any higher tax demand "would literally close us down.")[14] However, it did revise the penalty system for 1973, adding much stiffer penalties for production deficiencies and extending the range of cases covered by the system.[15]

---

* As a result of production decreases in 1972 Creole and Shell ended up facing some Bs 220 million ($50 million) in export penalties. Fuad, "The Haunting Prospect," p. 15.

In the event, the budgetary difficulties stemming from low production soon disappeared entirely. A sudden wave of price increases and a surge in world demand for oil followed the outbreak of the 1973 war in the Middle East, and the Arab members of the OPEC soon decided to place an embargo on shipments to the United States and to start a graduated squeeze on world oil supplies. In January 1973 the average TRV in Venezuela was just over $3 per barrel; during the year the government boosted this figure six times, and by December the average reached $14.08. Since international prices then surpassed those of the U.S. domestic market—the basis for calculating Venezuela's royalty payments—the government also pressured the companies into repurchasing royalty oil at the higher TRV rate.* Although estimates vary, at the time of this writing it appears that the government received nearly Bs 2.2 billion ($514 million) in extra income for 1973 alone—a surplus equalling nearly one-sixth of the entire budget.

After years of worry and scheming over income, Venezuela had once again received a sudden bonanza that solved all immediate budgetary problems and completely recast the bargaining relationship between the government and the companies, heading off the impending confrontation over production levels. Before we examine the impact of this latest bonanza, however, it is important to review some other dimensions of Caldera's petroleum policy: specifically, his natural-gas export scheme and his oil diplomacy.

Gas "Nationalization"

In 1969 and early 1970 Venezuela received inquiries from several buyers about the country's liquified natural gas (LNG) reserves. Wishing to maintain a steady and increasing government income, Caldera followed up these leads; and early in 1970 he unveiled plans for building a large LNG export capability. The plan involved the construction of expensive gas liquefaction

---

* When Venezuelan officials learned that Nigerian oil was selling at more than $19 a barrel on the open market, they briefly considered collecting royalty oil in kind and marketing it themselves; but this scheme was abandoned, apparently because of the administrative burden involved.

plants and transmission lines in eastern (Puerto la Cruz) and western Venezuela, and a new, Venezuelan-controlled tanker fleet for shipping the gas to eastern U.S. markets. The gas exported would be that already produced in association with oil (associated gas) and that contained in the country's extensive natural-gas fields (nonassociated gas), which were mostly in the eastern part of the country. Overall, planners estimated that the project would require nearly a billion dollars of new capital investment and would bring in an additional $200 million annually from a total daily production of 1.2–1.3 billion cubic feet.[16] There would also be important political benefits. Caldera was anxious to live up to campaign promises to the two regions involved; the eastern region was quite depressed economically, and the residents of Zulia state, in the west, harbored considerable resentment over Caracas's monopolization of the benefits from Maracaibo oil. The new program, it was hoped, would improve conditions and help to win the votes of these regions for COPEI in the next election.

At first Caldera expected to finance the gas project by working out joint ventures between the CVP and the two original proponents of the idea, Creole Oil and the Philadelphia Gas Works. After feeling out the opposition, however, he decided to keep the system wholly Venezuelan, allowing foreign equity capital only in the tanker fleet and relying for the rest of the project on government borrowing and any available domestic funds.

The LNG project suffered a fate by now depressingly familiar. To justify his intention to utilize associated gas currently produced from the concessions, and to lay the foundations for an exclusively national development of nonassociated reserves, Caldera was forced to seek congressional approval. And like its predecessors, the gas bill, entitled "A Law Reserving the Natural-Gas Industry to the State," would have to run the gauntlet. As expected, Pérez Alfonzo swiftly attacked the bill, stating that if the government needed more revenue it should try to sell oil at a better price, not drain Venezuela's gas reserves. Gas liquefaction and transport were both expensive and risky, he said, and Venezuela would receive less per BTU of gas than she was receiving for oil.

He agreed with the idea of "nationalizing" gas, and argued that the gas associated with existing fields should be reinjected rather than being flared off, as was the case with a large proportion of current production.

AD and other congressional factions soon joined the attack, and the Mines Committee proceeded to make some important changes in the bill. Minister Pérez La Salvia tried to save the day, but his denunciations were so bitter they only served to rally the opposition. The companies, of course, opposed the whole bill, but had little influence on the outcome. When the dust had settled, President Caldera had his bill, but it was so restrictive as to effectively block his project. Approved in August 1971, the bill asserted state ownership of all natural gas, associated and nonassociated. However, the amended legislation limited exports to associated gas only, reserving the vast, untapped gas fields in the east for domestic use. The Committee also eliminated a provision that the government compensate the companies for the associated gas it took, providing instead for government payment of the costs incurred in collecting and delivering gas to the CVP. Finally, there was to be no private capital, Venezuelan or foreign, in the new industry, making it a complete state monopoly.

Government experts studied the revised bill carefully to see if they could still carry out the export scheme under its provisions, but concluded in the end that they could not. Once again, the congressional opposition, sparked by Pérez Alfonzo, had twisted the government plan in such a way as to turn it into a defeat for Caldera and, simultaneously, a further extension of state authority over the industry. Caldera and Pérez La Salvia subsequently went on to speak with pride and nationalistic fervor of their success in "nationalizing" the country's natural gas and dealing a blow to the exploiting foreign companies.[17]

Petroleum Diplomacy Under Caldera

Although the Caldera administration at first displayed little enthusiasm for the OPEC, it continued urging the other members to adopt a production prorationing scheme in order to consolidate the Organization's control of the market. However, anxiety about Venezuela's slipping position in the market had more to do with this than conservationist idealism. In January 1970 Venezuela lost her place as the world's foremost petroleum exporter, being passed by both Iran and Saudi Arabia. The OPEC Secretariat did experiment in 1965–66 with a preliminary, self-enforced prorationing schedule; but this was a failure, and a second attempt the following year was stillborn. Production programming in oil is actually enormously complex and politically difficult, requiring sophisticated market analysis and an exacting regulation of private companies, as well as general willingness to compromise. And its difficulty has been increased by the strident opposition of both private companies and consuming governments.[18] Therefore, it is not surprising that Venezuela's appeals met with little more than verbal agreement about the importance of the subject.

Venezuela did contribute to the buildup of determination among producers that led, during and after the Caracas OPEC meeting of December 1970, to a round of substantial price increases. She did so by passing the tax reform and unilateral reference-pricing bills, thus dramatizing the trend begun by Libya and imitated in the Persian Gulf. And at the Caracas meeting OPEC members agreed on "concerted and simultaneous action by all countries" to push forward on the tax front. At a later meeting, OPEC set a deadline for the companies' cooperation and attached the sanction of complete embargo for failure to comply. This, in turn, led to the Teheran agreements and the subsequent price increases. For the most part, however, Venezuela was at this stage a passive beneficiary of OPEC efforts. This was also true of the next thrust of OPEC policy, the "participation" demands that led to the Riyadh Agreements of 1972. These agreements provided for gradual increases in host-government ownership of company assets, to culminate in 1982 with a 51 percent share of all petroleum operations. Such an arrangement reflected the rather distinctive objectives of the Middle Eastern governments and had little applicability in Venezuela, whose own approach, roughly parallel, was reversion.*

At the regional level, the Caldera administration continued the effort, begun by Pérez Alfonzo, to open channels of communication between Latin American governments on energy policy matters.† In 1972 and 1973, acting on Venezuela's suggestion, the region's ministers of energy and petroleum met on an informal basis to exchange views and discuss their energy policies; and at the second of these meetings, held in Quito in April 1973, the delegates agreed to create the Latin American Energy Organization (Organización Latinoamericana de Energía, OLADE). Venezuela's representatives at OLADE meetings promoted the idea of a regional self-sufficiency in oil, hoping to halt the incursion of Middle Eastern oil in the hemisphere's markets and to increase sales to important state companies, such as Petrobrás of Brazil.‡ Venezuela also proposed, on several occasions, a regional fund to finance energy projects. The OLADE members generally agreed on the need for better communications; but the cleavage between the majority of the importing countries, who naturally wanted lower prices, and the continent's two chief exporters (Venezuela and Ecuador), who wanted higher prices, remained a constant source of friction.

* Pérez Alfonzo repeatedly criticized Venezuela's decline in leadership and influence within the OPEC, complaining on several occasions that Venezuelan delegates to the Organization's meetings were poorly prepared, and that the Arab producers were somewhat contemptuous of Venezuela's lack of firmness with the companies. The government began to pay more attention to OPEC after 1971, however; and in mid-1973 Pérez La Salvia himself called a special meeting of the Organization's Board of Governors in order to discuss ways in which the producing countries could take advantage of the impending energy crisis in the United States.

† In 1961 executives of the various Latin American state-owned oil companies had met in Caracas, at the invitation of the CVP. And in 1966, after several more meetings, they created the Asociación de Asistencia Recíproca Petrolera Estatal Latinoamericana (ARPEL), which was to act as an information exchange and also work to gain a greater percentage of the regional market for state companies.

‡ See *Petroleum Intelligence Weekly*, 4.viii.72. In 1968 Venezuela had exported an average of 384,000 barrels a day to other South American nations, or 11.6 percent of her total oil exports. But by 1971 the average was only

TABLE 10
Venezuelan Crude Oil Reserves, 1953–73
(Millions of barrels)

Year	Gross increase in reserves	Production	Net increase in reserves	Reserves, year-end	Theoretical life of reserves (years)
1953	1,572	644	928	10,154	15.8
1954	1,472	692	780	10,934	15.8
1955	2,283	787	1,496	12,430	15.8
1956	2,466	899	1,567	13,997	15.6
1957	2,610	1,014	1,596	15,593	15.4
1958	2,139	951	1,188	16,781	17.7
1959	1,233	1,011	222	17,003	16.8
1960	1,446	1,044	402	17,405	16.7
1961	541	1,063	−522	16,883	15.8
1962	1,094	1,170	−76	16,807	14.4
1963	1,390	1,182	208	17,015	14.4
1964	1,421	1,239	182	17,197	13.9
1965	1,321	1,271	50	17,247	13.6
1966	855	1,232	−377	16,870	13.7
1967	384	1,296	−912	15,958	12.3
1968	1,031	1,321	−290	15,668	11.9
1969	560	1,315	−755	14,913	11.3
1970	478	1,352	−874	14,039	10.4
1971	1,019	1,296	−277	13,762	10.6
1972	1,289	1,176	113	13,875	11.8
1973	1,251	1,226	25	13,944	11.4

SOURCE: Creole Corp. Rept., 1972, p. 13; 1973, p. 13.

Government-to-Government Deals

As time passed with no defined plan for providing the investments necessary to increase production capacity, Caldera became increasingly concerned that within a few years, perhaps even in the next presidential term, oil production would begin to fall off rapidly. The theoretical lifetime of Venezuela's proven reserves, at current production rates, stood at just over 10 years, down from nearly 18 in 1958 (see Table 10). Industry spokesmen did their best to draw attention to this figure and its implications.

126,000 barrels a day, or 3.9 percent. The decline was mainly caused by the region's increasing reliance on Middle Eastern oil: in 1972, for example, the Latin American nations were importing 1.11 million barrels a day from that area (Venezuela, [9], 1973, p. 195).

Caldera accordingly began to look for alternative means of securing needed capital, and the method he favored—once the service contract proposal had been crippled by Congress—was a series of direct agreements between the CVP and the state oil corporations of other countries. This had the appeal of both helping to displace private multinationals and reducing Venezuela's dependence on the U.S. market. For several years the country's representatives carried on discussions with Germany's Deminex, Italy's ENI, and Spain's Hispanoil, among others; and late in 1972 they came close to signing an agreement with Deminex under which the Germans would provide venture capital to the CVP in return for guaranteed access to a portion of whatever oil was found. When the plan became public, however, opposition leaders criticized it as economically wasteful. Pérez Alfonzo and others noted the extra transport distances involved, and claimed that Venezuelan oil could find an ample market within its own hemisphere, allowing the government to receive a greater income. Simultaneously, Deminex demanded price discounts for the oil to be purchased under the arrangement, which would have made the arrangement an even greater political liability for Caldera. Thus by early 1973 it was clear that this strategy, too, was unworkable, given the volatile and fragmented Venezuelan political milieu. It took its place on the shelf, alongside the service contracts and the LNG plan.[19]

Venezuela and the United States

In dealing with the United States Caldera continued to press for some form of preferential treatment in the American oil market. When President Nixon named a special task force on oil policy early in 1969, Pérez La Salvia went to Washington and presented a long and rather forceful statement in favor of Venezuela's "solution," demanding, at the very least, equal treatment with Canada and Mexico. Subsequently, Venezuelan representatives lobbied for favorable changes in U.S. policy in a series of meetings with American oil administrators; and Caldera took the matter up with Nixon during a state visit to Washington in the summer of 1970. As might have been expected, the Nixon administration rejected Venezuela's petitions, despite the recommendation of the Cabinet task force that the existing quota system was inefficient and should be replaced by a tariff system with a built-in hemisphere preference in order to reduce the risks of a growing American dependence on oil from the Middle East.*

Not only did the United States turn down Venezuelan requests, but, responding to company demands for assistance, she began to use the quota system itself as a lever to win better treatment for U.S. companies. The marginal manipulation of quotas, and hints about possible preferential treatment, closely paralleled petroleum policy trends within Venezuela, accompanied by unsubtle warnings about the future implications of any further nationalist measures. After a small reduction in quotas early in 1970, the United States raised quotas slightly for those areas of the country traditionally supplied by Venezuela.† This was while Caldera was actively promoting a pro-company position on service contracts. But U.S. officials warned that the change was conditional—that future increases would depend on Venezuela's productive capacity, which could be assessed by the success of the service-contract system.[20] Given the mood of the Venezuelan Congress at the time (the service-contract formula was still in subcommittee), this pressure probably only damaged the chances of contracts favorable to the companies.

American pressure continued as new threats to corporate profits surfaced in Venezuela. In January 1971 U.S. officials informed Venezuela that any hopes for special preference were "fruitless" in view of the country's recent tax increases.[21] And early in 1972,

---

* U.S. Cabinet, *The Oil Import Question*, p. 129. Relations between Nixon and Caldera had begun on a sour note when Nixon nominated a Texas oilman prominent in the protectionist IPAA as his new ambassador to Caracas. Protests in Venezuela and rumblings in the U.S. Senate led to a withdrawal of the nomination, but the episode did little to inspire confidence in the good intentions of the new American administration.

† The 1970 reduction actually had little effect on Venezuela, since the U.S. also increased the quota of imports to Puerto Rico, justifying them as economic aid to the island, and these imports did have to come from hemisphere sources. U.S. Cabinet, *The Oil Import Question*, pp. 10–12; see also *Latin America*, 9.i.70, pp. 10, 12.

after the passage of the Reversion Law and the gas nationalization measure, U.S. spokesmen reportedly "let it be known unofficially that the U.S. would be looking towards Canada rather than Venezuela in the future to meet its demand for oil."[22] Except as a bargaining posture, these comments seem incredible in view of the proximity of the world's worst energy crisis and the fact that within a year the Canadian government, worried about its own supplies, would begin to place restrictions on the flow of oil to the United States. The explanation, of course, is that the United States, like Venezuela, was ignorant of the real world oil situation.

In an effort to bring the United States around, Caldera tried to take advantage of the lapsing, in June 1972, of the twenty-year commercial treaty between the United States and Venezuela. As the date for termination neared, Caldera "denounced" the treaty, adding nationalist rhetoric to his decision not to renew it on the old terms. The treaty had provided favorable access to Venezuela for American products in return for low tariffs on crude and fuel oil entering the U.S. Its lapsing, without compensatory arrangements, would have caused a loss of $100–200 million to U.S. oil importers, according to one study, but would also have damaged the standing of Venezuelan oil in the U.S. market.* In the end, with both countries facing a loss (Venezuela's might have been the greater amount, and would certainly have been larger in proportion to the country's economy), neither was able to exact a

---

* The conditions surrounding the treaty negotiations were extremely complex, owing to the piggybacking of earlier legislative measures. The U.S.-Venezuelan trade treaty of 1952 placed U.S. import duties on crude oil and a number of petroleum products that were one-half to one-fourth lower than the amounts specified in the 1932 Revenue Act, which had first established duties on oil products and was still legally in force. Under subsequent GATT (General Agreement on Trade and Tariffs) provisions, concessions to Venezuela were extended automatically to all countries outside the "Communist bloc" who sent oil to the United States. Thus the lapsing of the U.S.-Venezuela treaty in 1972, according to most experts, would force the United States to resume higher tariff rates on all imported oil. The study referred to here, a report prepared by the Petroleum Institute Research Foundation, estimated that U.S. importers would lose about $165 million per year if this happened. (See *Petroleum Intelligence Weekly*, 3.vii.72; *Journal of Commerce*, 26.i.72 and 28.i.72.) My own analysis here is chiefly derived from discussions with U.S. and Venezuelan officials involved in the negotiations concerning the treaty.

price for agreement. Finally, in an exchange of notes—Caldera's nationalist stance had made a treaty as such too sensitive politically—the United States reaffirmed her tariff preference for Venezuelan oil, and Venezuela continued a "most favored nation" treatment of U.S. imports.* Thus, as far as oil and the U.S. market were concerned, Venezuela gained no ground with this tactic.

The denial of Venezuela's request for hemisphere preference and country quotas placed her oil in unavoidable competition with oil from the Middle East and North Africa for import quotas in the lucrative U.S. market. Venezuela argued that such competition was unfair because of the "security factor," which made U.S. dependence on Venezuelan oil less objectionable on national security grounds. Since crudes coming from Canada were not included in the quotas allowable, Venezuela was also vulnerable to company decisions to increase imports from there—which they quickly proceeded to do, despite a commitment on the part of the Canadian government to prevent any such expansion.[23] Between 1963 and 1972 the oil corporations reduced their Venezuelan imports, as a percentage of all imports, from 58 percent to 33 percent (see Table 5, p. 70). Had Venezuelan crude and petroleum products (other than fuel oil) been granted country-specific quotas or been allowed unrestricted entry, they would have been competing with much more expensive American production, and companies would have had an incentive to import as much as possible.

Of course, this did not apply to residual fuel oil. Owing to the high quotas in effect since 1966, this had been entering the eastern U.S. market without effective restrictions. Residual fuel oil is a low-priced product, and American refineries prefer to produce as little of it as possible, instead turning their crude into valuable commodities such as gasoline and using imported fuel oil to meet the U.S. demand. In 1963–72, Venezuelan fuel oil exports to the United States increased from 48 percent of the total (by volume) to 62 percent.[24]

---

* Venezuela's note provided a special exemption if that country were to enter the Andean Pact. This was necessary to prevent the United States from automatically receiving all of the additional trade benefits granted to the other countries in the Pact. Shortly thereafter Venezuela did indeed enter the Pact.

The control of crude and the decontrol of residual fuel oil left Venezuela with a relatively unprofitable product mix, which in turn affected earnings and government income. The elimination of crude quotas for Venezuela would have changed this, providing an incentive for importing crude rather than fuel oil and allowing higher profits for Venezuelan output. Thus, in terms of production, prices, and government income, Venezuela would have benefited greatly from some kind of commodity agreement in oil, or even preferential treatment, in return for the guarantee of supply. This would also have eliminated the justification— and perhaps even the need—for the production decline that the Venezuelan government so resented.

To those familiar with oil affairs the U.S. response to Venezuelan proposals is hardly surprising. What served as energy policy in the United States was really an enormously complex compromise, worked out under pressure from numerous powerful interests—multinational corporations, American independent producers, coal interests, Eastern state governments, foreign governments, and environmentalists, to name but a few. And this compromise gradually became frozen in place in the years after 1958. Within this framework, Venezuela was only one small contender asking for important special favors. To refashion the American energy regulation system would inevitably have damaged key domestic groups, and this the government was simply not going to do in the absence of a major crisis, despite the finding of repeated special task forces—themselves decision-avoidance mechanisms of great popularity—that the existing system served none of the public policy objectives in whose name it had been created.

A decision favoring Venezuela was especially improbable because it would face major opposition from the oil multinationals. Their reasons were many: a stake in Middle Eastern oil and thus a "nonhemispheric preference," despite the resulting security problems for the United States; well-established fuel oil supply and refining patterns that would have been costly to rearrange; a fierce disapproval of anything smacking of government-to-government arrangements that bypassed the companies; and an ongoing conflict with the Venezuelan state that they viewed as their own major security problem. Clearly, U.S.-Venezuelan cooperation along the lines requested by Caldera and his predecessors would have been exceedingly difficult for any American government, and it was next to impossible for the Nixon administration, with its close ties to large business.

The irony here is that when the crisis did come the tables turned so quickly that policy losses by the United States in Venezuela could not be recouped. From the published debate, it is clear that the State Department—unfortunately sidelined within the Nixon administration—foresaw the implications of America's failure to refashion her inherited energy policy. U.S. refining capacity and regional oil supply were closing with demand rapidly, and State Department forecasts, along with others by private groups and government agencies, pointed to massive increases in U.S. dependence on the Middle East.[25] Although the quantities needed for the mid-1970's and later could not be obtained entirely within the hemisphere, it was clear that any additional supply from there would be terribly valuable in offsetting the growing U.S. dependence on the Middle East and North Africa. This became evident to all in the early 1970's, after the Libyan squeeze, the successful OPEC ultimatums, the Riyadh "participation" formula, and, finally, the Arab embargo itself.

The Faja Bituminosa

To the more farsighted U.S. analysts, Venezuela also offered a possible long-term source of oil. In 1969 and 1970 news circulated in Venezuela of the presence of an enormous deposit of very heavy oil—tar, almost—in the eastern part of the country. According to the most widely circulated estimates, this deposit contains some 700 billion barrels of petroleum. Using a relatively low hypothetical recovery figure of 10 percent—the standard for fields of regular oil in Venezuela is 18.5 percent—this leaves some 70 billion barrels of oil recoverable. This would sustain a daily production of 3.7 million barrels, the record production rate for 1970, for more than fifty years. Given existing technology and the then low prices of more conventional oil, no one knew whether this oil could be extracted commercially; but it took very little foresight to anticipate high enough prices in the future to make the *faja bituminosa,* as it was called (government spokesmen now refer to it by the more optimistic name of *faja petrólifera*), an attractive venture with important strategic implications for the United States.

Actually, information about the faja has been poor up to the time of this writing. The companies have known of the deposits for years, but have considered them unimportant because they are not commercially viable. Estimates of the amount of oil in them have appeared in scores of publications and government documents in Venezuela, but apparently these can all be traced back to one serious geological study.[26] On the basis of this study, and considering company drilling histories, it seems clear that there is indeed an enormous deposit; but its exact boundaries and size, the investment and technological developments needed to bring it into production, and the probable cost per barrel of its output have not been established.

As strategic circumstances changed, and as it became clear that the United States faced a serious energy crunch and a growing problem of dependence on the Middle East and North Africa, American policy toward Venezuela began to thaw. James Akins, then the highest level "energy diplomat" in the Nixon administration, visited Venezuela and made the rounds of key leaders (including Pérez Alfonzo) to sound out the possibility of some kind of agreement for the development of the faja and a guaranteed U.S. access to its oil. In September 1972 serious discussions of the matter began between the two governments, at the initiative of the United States. Caldera acknowledged the discussions in December of that year, noting that Venezuela might be interested in a government-to-government agreement by which she could gain needed investment capital, a guaranteed market, and high oil prices for her product.

The American position, however, doomed this possibility from the outset. U.S. representatives acted as if they were surrogate company spokesmen, as if world trends had not convinced them of the futility of trying to salvage private multinational control of mineral resources in developing countries. In brief, the United States asked for long-term guarantees of security, amortization, and profits for the private companies in return for company investment capital and a possible guaranteed market access to the United States. To be sure, Caldera was looking eagerly for capital, since he and his advisers were concerned about recent production decreases and the budgetary consequences of these. And under different political circumstances he might have been willing to consider new accommodations, properly disguised, along the lines of the service contracts and the old desulfurization agreement. Secretary of State Rogers, in a brief stopover in Venezuela in May 1973, attempted to play on these concerns and urged the Venezuelan government to work out an agreement.[27]

But Venezuela had changed. Caldera's announcement of the discussions and the subsequent mention of a possible agreement in a *Foreign Affairs* article by James Akins (which, widely reported in Venezuela, raised the suspicion that some kind of a special "deal" was in the works) brought a great outcry of indignation in Venezuela, with charges that the government was negotiating behind the back of the country and the Congress, compromising Venezuelan sovereignty.[28] Montiel Ortega, a URD senator and an articulate critic of government oil policy, proposed a special congressional investigation of government dealings, and editorials flooded the newspapers, criticizing the suggestion of any foreign involvement in the development of the faja.[29] The outcry reached such a level that the administration again found it necessary to launch a series of defensive, nationalistic counterattacks, declaring: "Venezuela will not turn over the heavy crude petroleum belt to exploitation by foreign companies, since we are determined to maintain our sovereignty."[30]

It was simply too late for the kind of deal the United States was suggesting. Within Venezuela, elections were near, and any gesture that even implied concessions to the private companies would be an instant liability. More important, in the United

States the energy crunch was on. By midwinter of 1972–73 fuel shortages were commonplace in the American Midwest, and in early spring of 1973 the U.S. raised import quotas to the point where the control system existed in name only. In April, in his long awaited energy message, President Nixon finally abandoned the mandatory oil import program, with its quotas and tariffs, substituting a license-fee system.

More than anything else, this change symbolized the opening of a new era in oil. The holders of the old quotas would now be able to import up to the level of their quotas without additional fees (thus continuing the discrimination against Venezuelan oil, if only for a short time), and imports beyond those levels would be uncontrolled, though subject to a fee. Quota-based exemptions from fees, however, would be phased out over several years, thus placing all imported oil on the same footing. As an incentive for the construction of new refining capacity, the President indicated that crude oil in amounts up to 75 percent of new refining capacity could be imported with no fees.[31] It had taken a large-scale crisis and the prospect of serious damage to the American economy, but the old system had finally given way to an arrangement recognizing that in the short run, at least, the U.S. needed all the oil it could get. The temporary exemption of quota holders from fees was simply intended to smooth the transition for those refiners who would suffer the loss of their windfall earnings.

The tables had turned: the sloping curves of supply and demand had shifted sharply, fundamentally altering the bargaining position of producers and consumers, of governments and companies. As one consequence, the idea of hemisphere preferences and country quotas, a Venezuelan policy objective for a decade and a half, lost much of its meaning. As Caldera put it:

If the United States didn't have the intelligence to offer us a hemisphere preference ... for so long, it now makes little difference to us. ... Now it is impossible to hide the fact that we have a very precious commodity ... the need for which is increasing daily at an astonishing rate in every country. What we cannot understand, and must therefore attribute to dissembling manipulations, is the fact that during the last ten years oil prices have gone down in our chief markets. Why down? Were people consuming less? Was oil less important? Or was it because we became the victims of manipulation on the part of those who held control of the valves, could open here and close there, and thus could cheat the people of those countries with oil resources?[32]

Subsequent discussions between Venezuela and the United States have focused not on hemisphere preference arrangements but on the broader picture of trade relationships in general. With supply and price conditions so clearly in Venezuela's favor, and with little immediate prospect of a reversal in these conditions, the capital for further development of resources, including the faja, seems secure; and the formal guarantee of a U.S. market hardly seems vital now that dependence on the Arabs has become a recognized security problem for the United States. Understandably, therefore, Venezuelans have come to think of oil policy as an instrument to dismantle existing tariff barriers and obtain trade concessions of many kinds. Ironically, these are much more difficult for the United States to grant, since, unlike the oil quota system, they necessarily involve the entire network of U.S. trade relationships. For the time being, it would seem, there is very little to bargain about.

From Caldera to Carlos Andrés

As the 1973 election campaign gathered momentum, the major parties chose, as in the past, to maintain a low profile on petroleum issues, at least in public debate. COPEI's Lorenzo Fernández spoke vaguely several times of "accelerating" the reversion process; and AD's Carlos Andrés Pérez agreed, in somewhat more moderate terms, that Venezuela was not likely to "wait until 1983." However, neither candidate showed interest in stirring up a debate that might launch a spate of unrealistic nationalistic promises, which would commit him in advance to policies more radical than he might otherwise prefer.*

Official reticence notwithstanding, the future of the industry,

---

* In midsummer 1973 both major parties cooperated in passing a law that would reserve to the CVP, by 1975, the entire domestic market for the sale of petroleum products. This supplanted the 1964 law that had allowed the CVP to take over one-third of that market by 1968. In reality, the state company was far behind schedule in this process (by 1971 it had taken over only 22

especially the need to ensure future production, remained an important undercurrent in informed discussions about the country's development. The companies did their best to foment anxiety about this in numerous small meetings with Venezuelan leaders and in private forums such as the annual Fedecámaras meeting, but they remained in the background as much as possible. Privately, company representatives did little to hide their strong preference for an AD victory in the coming election, apparently hoping for a return to the kind of easy cooperation that had marked the last two years of the Leoni government. The Venezuelan Left repeatedly charged that AD's campaign was being subsidized by the petroleum interests, and it seems likely that this was the case. Beyond this, it became apparent that the oil companies had decided on a strategy of quietly maximizing profits and minimizing new investments, meanwhile hoping that after the election economic trends and Ministry forecasts would prompt the government to offer them a new and more secure role in the nation's petroleum economy.

Immediately following Carlos Andrés's landslide victory in December 1973, which gave AD control of both houses of the legislature, Venezuela's leaders, reflecting the optimism stimulated by the improved oil market and the consequent flood of government income, abandoned their restraint. In his last address to Congress Caldera urged his successors to nationalize the petroleum industry posthaste. More significantly, Carlos Andrés adopted an unexpectedly strident and aggressive posture in his first postelection comments:

The private companies are maintaining their exploratory activities at minimal levels, and we run the risk that our industry, owing to the failure to incorporate new techniques in the absence of appropriate investment and maintenance, will rapidly deteriorate, so that when the concessions are given up, we will find ourselves with outworn equipment and an obsolete technology. For these reasons, it appears impossible to

---

percent of the market), but CVP officials and the Mining Ministry hoped to move along more rapidly in the future. If necessary, they intended to make up any deficit in the production of products available for sale in Venezuela by purchasing them from the foreign companies and reselling them—as they were already doing to meet their share. See *Petroleum Intelligence Weekly*, 12.vi.72.

wait until 1983 before the state assumes the full management of the petroleum industry. It would be prudent, as an alternative, that we proceed in the immediate future to nationalize—which ensures our sovereignty in the industry—and that we arrive at new formulas for the participation of the foreign companies in those areas where we need their technical resources, their financing, or their marketing ability.[33]

Subsequently, he indicated that Venezuela would nationalize foreign holdings "within two years." He also made it clear that Venezuela would immediately begin using oil as a lever to win more favorable trade relations with the developed countries:

As gold disappears as the governing pattern in world monetary arrangements, petroleum is tending to take its place.... The oil is not in Fort Knox, nor in the London exchange, nor in Germany, nor in Japan. It is here in Venezuela, in the Arab countries and elsewhere in the developing world. It will be our great weapon for achieving our position in the world as well as in an international division of labor and more just participation in world markets.... We say to the developed countries: "You have the technology, but this technology cannot work without petroleum energy." We would say to them: "You give us the technology in a just fashion, and we in the same framework of justice will give you our petroleum."[34]

7. Conclusion

IT IS NOW TIME to return to the broader questions raised at the beginning of this book. On the basis of a careful review of the conduct of petroleum policy, what can we conclude about how Venezuela handled it? About the interdependence of politics and public policy? About what these mean for the country's future as it enters a new era in oil management?

At the outset, it is useful to reiterate the importance of an accurate grasp of the complex and evolving bargaining relationship between the government and the companies, which was so critical in shaping policy. The key to this relationship, of course, is its degenerative instability. This is partly a result of the shift in bargaining power to the state that occurs as foreign companies sink their capital in extractive enterprise and become more vulnerable to government demands for a greater share of profits. Its main source, however, is the mistrust and uncertainty built into the concessionary system itself. Thus, although the two parties are interdependent—the host country needs capital, technology, and managerial skills; the companies crave profits and access to raw materials—the relationship nevertheless contains the seeds of its own demise. The government can never be sure that profit calculations are made in such a way as to benefit the host country; nor can it be sure that foreign decisionmakers are not manipulating downstream variables to punish it for seeking to maximize its own income. But uncertainty and mistrust cut both ways. If the government becomes certain that the companies are unable to tell the truth, instead crying wolf whenever threatened, the companies grow insecure about the longevity of any agreement with the state. The resulting conflicts, as the state seeks greater income and control and as corporate policymakers seek guarantees in return for new investments, tend to increase mistrust and uncertainty. This manifests itself not only in growing animosity, but also in a physical deterioration of the industry itself—the "write-off spiral" described in Chapters 3 and 6.

The rate of change and the relative distribution of bargaining power in the relationship at any one time depend on many factors, the most important being the willingness and ability of the state to assert itself. This, in turn, may be expected to vary with leadership, domestic politics, and conditions in the international market. If the Venezuelan case can be taken as a guide, it is likely that a similar degenerative instability is a latent tendency to be anticipated whenever similar conditions occur in massive, foreign-controlled export dependency.

Bargaining and Learning: The Strategy of Assertive Experimentation

Some of the most interesting aspects of Venezuela's experience relate to what might be called the cybernetics of dependence management—i.e., to how information and learning affect the bargaining process, and how available options can be identified and tested in practice. If uncertainty was a pervasive characteristic of the relationship, information and the ability to "read" and learn from interaction was a precondition for success. The kind of criticism that has been directed against policymakers attempting to work with problems of this kind indicates that there is little understanding of the magnitude of this task.[1]

The fact is that until very recently no Venezuelans knew how the oil industry worked insofar as its large-scale decisions were concerned.* The notorious "policy of silence" and the general secretiveness of multinational corporations contributed significantly

---

* Adalberto Pinelo diagnoses this problem in almost the same terms in his study of the International Petroleum Corporation in Peru (p. 155): "The fact was the Peruvian government did not have the expertise necessary to deal with an organization as sophisticated as IPC."

to this. Pérez Alfonzo and his Middle Eastern counterparts complained frequently that the companies "treated them like children." However, as they became more determined to shape the impact of the industry upon their country, Venezuelan policymakers found several ways of improving their informational stand. The acquisition of new data became a prime occupation of the Petroleum Economy Section of the Ministry of Mines. Data on the companies' domestic operations were extracted—practically subpoenaed—by formal demands, and the OPEC proved invaluable in facilitating the accumulation and transfer of data about company operations at the international level.

Playing the producing countries off against each other now became noticeably more difficult for the companies. Indeed, the change in the whole international bargaining climate, which proved so beneficial to Venezuela in handling her own problems, can be attributed as much to a rising level of understanding about international oil as to the growing assertiveness of host governments. Because of this, Venezuela's petroleum diplomacy stands as one of the most creative parts of her overall policy, despite her failure to win agreement to an international prorationing system, and despite the relatively minor role she played in OPEC affairs between 1969 and 1974.

Ultimately, however, the most reliable source of information and understanding was the bargaining process itself. Herein lies one of the most important conclusions of this study. The nature of the relationship between the government and the foreign corporations was such that only forceful and admittedly experimental initiatives seemed to provide policymakers with an accurate sense of the range of choice available to them. How much income could they extract? How much control could they impose? What were the best ways to force government priorities upon the corporations? These questions could only be answered by continuous experimentation.

The series of experiments that ended in the TRV system, first negotiated and then unilateral, are especially instructive in this regard. Although a reference-price system of a different kind had been used for years to calculate royalties, policymakers discovered its attractiveness as a means of assuring income and influencing company pricing behavior only after failing with two more direct and comprehensive arrangements: active control through the Coordinating Commission, and retroactive taxation. Either of these, or both together, would have allowed the government to squeeze out every available penny while forcing the companies to price according to government wishes. But they were unmanageable. The government simply could not, at acceptable costs, supply itself with the knowledge and expertise required for this kind of direct intervention. Venezuela's problem in this respect is similar to that voiced by the Federal Communications Commission in the United States when it announced that it simply did not have the resources to determine the fairness of Bell Telephone rates. Organizationally, in both cases, the regulated and the regulators were so unequal that direct control of this kind was impossible. The Venezuelan government needed a better instrument, one that did not require it to remake company sales decisions (Coordinating Commission), or even to reconstruct them in retrospect (retroactive taxation), but one that was flexible and sensitive enough to extend state influence beyond the crude weapon of tax statutes and permit an easy assessment of results.

To a considerable extent, policy advances since 1958 can be measured by the gradual sophistication of the government's policy instruments, instruments that in the end allowed a calculated intervention in company decisions about prices, production levels, and even exploration and drilling. To be sure, these instruments did not completely eliminate the bargaining power of the companies, nor were they fully utilized—petroleum administrators, especially during Caldera's term, were worried that at some point the companies might decide to close up shop altogether rather than comply—but they increased Venezuela's access to the entire range of company behavior, something that became increasingly critical as the time for reversion approached.

It has been characteristic of Venezuelan policy, from the initial steps of the Coordinating Commission to the recent establish-

ment of the tax-penalty system, that efforts to control have proceeded well ahead of the government's ability to implement its
new powers or fully anticipate the consequences of its actions. But
the efforts themselves have forced the government to acquire new
competence, which has then led to a more informed and skillful
implementation.

The stress here upon conflict, experimentation, and bargaining
as means of eliciting information and helping shape adequate
policies will be recognized immediately by those familiar with
Charles Lindblom's work as an example of "muddling through."
It will also be familiar to those acquainted with the orientation
toward development decisionmaking that has been so persuasively
expounded by Albert O. Hirschman.[2] In particular, the case of
Venezuelan petroleum seems to provide an example of what
Hirschman has called the principal of the "hiding hand."[3] By this
he means that there is usually more creativity and problem-solving
ability around than we realize, and that this creativity is activated
by going ahead with projects even if we aren't sure of our ability
to handle them. Indeed, our inability to grasp the full range of
difficulties that will arise may be viewed as a blessing in disguise,
since we might not have undertaken a project if we were aware
of what we were getting into. What Hirschman is stressing is that
new efforts to control a portion of the world often generate commitment, thought, and learning that otherwise would have remained unused. Responsibility, education, and competence can
grow together and reinforce each other.

These thoughts suggest that an aggressive and openly experimental strategy is likely to be the best for dealing with foreign
companies, at least during the middle stages of dependence management; and that uncertainty and the absence of a "sure" technical program for maximizing measurable goals ought not to deter
such experimentation. On the contrary, a measure of self-assertion
may well be necessary to clearly define one's self-interest and help
discover ways of promoting it. And in fact, Venezuela did fairly
well in capturing a stream of income from the petroleum companies, both absolutely and in comparison with other oil-producing

TABLE 11

Payments by Companies to the Government and Profits Split in
Venezuela and the Eastern Hemisphere, 1957–71

(U.S. dollars)

Year	Venezuela			Eastern Hemisphere	
	Total paid to govt. (millions)	Govt. income per bbl.	Profits split, govt./comp.	Govt. income per bbl.	Profits split, govt./comp.
1957	968	.95	52/48	.78	50/50
1958	993	1.04	65/35	.76	56/44
1959	926	.92	68/32	.76	57/43
1960	877	.84	68/32	.71	56/44
1961	938	.88	66/34	.70	56/44
1962	1,044	.89	66/34	.71	57/43
1963	1,078	.91	66/34	.75	57/43
1964	1,105	.89	66/34	.75	64/36
1965	1,122	.89	65/35	.76	65/35
1966	1,099	.89	66/34	.77	65/35
1967	1,241	.96	68/32	.80	68/32
1968	1,253	.95	68/32	.83	68/32
1969	1,256	.96	71/29	.84	70/30
1970	1,409	1.04	78/22	.86	72/28
1971	1,755	1.35	77/23	–	–

SOURCE: For Venezuela: see Appendix Tables A and E, pp. 179–81, 184. For Eastern Hemisphere: Mikdashi, p. 139. The data obtained by Mikdashi (from the First National Bank, New York) cover the whole of the Eastern Hemisphere (excluding the socialist bloc) and pertain to the seven "majors"—Exxon, Shell, Texaco, Mobil, BP, Standard of California, and Gulf. For other limitations on the data, see Mikdashi, p. 140.

countries. The major difficulty here was that income increments tended to come in spurts, reflecting the moves and countermoves of the government and the companies, as well as changing market conditions.

Venezuela's success can be measured in several ways. One can simply go by the division of profits between the state and the foreign companies, or by total payments made to the state. A more refined measure, however, is the economist's concept of "retained value," a formula designed to express benefits retained by the host country from economic activity stimulated by foreign investment. In addition to payments to the state, retained value measures such things as domestic wage payments and purchases of goods and services (see Tables 11–13). Between 1959 and 1972 company payments to the government (in constant 1958 bolívares) increased

TABLE 12

Payments to the Venezuelan Government by Oil Companies, 1959–73

(Millions of 1958 bolívares)

Year	Payments to govt.	Annual change	Year	Payments to govt.	Annual change
1959	2,843	–	1967	5,051	14.9%
1960	2,730	−4.0%	1968	4,967	−1.7
1961	2,870	5.1	1969	4,890	−1.6
1962	3,228	12.5	1970	5,487	12.2
1963	3,292	2.0	1971	6,533	19.1
1964	4,630	40.6	1972	7,098	8.6
1965	4,576	−1.2	1973	10,172	43.3
1966	4,396	−3.9			

SOURCE: See Appendix Tables A and E, pp. 179–81, 184.

annually at an average rate of 7.9 percent. Inclusion of the sudden increases registered in 1973 brings this figure to an average of 10.4 percent over the 14 years. This is well above the 4 percent increase generally recommended in the government's National Plans during this period. Between 1959 and 1971, retained value from the oil industry increased at an annual rate of 5 percent, a lower figure, as might be expected, but still respectable.

Venezuela not only captured an increasing portion of available oil income, but did so without significantly hampering the production process at any point. There were periods of very real fiscal distress, especially by Venezuelan standards, after 1959, notably in 1960, 1965–66, and 1969. But the flow of oil-derived benefits increased over time, both in total quantity and, more fundamentally, in payment for each barrel of the country's resources sold. Meanwhile, the government pushed ahead in its search for more effective direct controls of company activity and prepared for the eventual nationalization of the entire industry.

Ideology—and Luck

In implementing a strategy like Venezuela's, the role of doctrine or ideology seems to be critical: it provides a filter for information, a source of new bargaining positions, and a guide and justification for policy as a whole. Just such a doctrine, a coherent and endur-

TABLE 13

Retained Value from Venezuelan Petroleum Industry, 1950–71

(Millions of 1958 bolívares)

Year	Total retained value	Annual change	Retained value per bbl.	Year	Total retained value	Annual change	Retained value per bbl.
1950	1,853	–	3.39	1961	5,241	1.4%	4.92
1951	2,189	18.1%	3.52	1962	5,439	3.8	4.66
1952	2,448	11.8	3.71	1963	5,955	9.5	5.02
1953	2,717	11.0	4.22	1964	6,428	7.9	5.18
1954	2,655	−2.3	3.84	1965	6,091	−5.2	4.81
1955	3,170	19.4	4.03	1966	6,135	0.7	4.99
1956	4,611	45.5	5.14	1967	7,033	14.6	5.44
1957	6,191[a]	34.3	6.10[a]	1968	7,044	0.2	5.34
1958	4,933	−20.3	5.19	1969	6,958	−1.2	5.30
1959	5,416	9.8	5.35	1970	7,442	7.0	5.50
1960	5,168	−4.6	4.96	1971	9,081	22.0	7.01

SOURCE: Data for 1950–64 from William Harris, "The Impact of the Petroleum Export Industry on the Pattern of Venezuelan Economic Development," in Mikesell, p. 130, Table 22. Data for 1964–71 based on my own calculations, using Harris's formula as described in Appendix A of his article (pp. 151–55). Figures for these years obtained from: Venezuela, [1], [6], and [9], various years. Data converted to constant bolívares using the government's composite price index published in Venezuela, [4], 1970, p. 213; 1971 estimate based on data in *International Monetary Statistics*, Dec. 1972, p. 285, line 64, adjusted. Retained value = recurring taxes + nonrecurring payments to government + foreign exchange profits + domestic wage payments and benefits + domestic purchases.

[a] Abnormally high retained value for 1957 and generally for 1956–59 was due to the combined impact of the Suez Crisis price increases and the Pérez Jiménez "round" of concessions sales.

ing interpretation of the international petroleum system and of the proper role of petroleum in the country's development, has been the backbone of Venezuela's policy initiatives for nearly fifteen years. It is an invaluable and unusual asset. Most of the "accepted" analyses of development problems originate in developed countries and reflect the views of those countries on the international economic system, of which they have been the chief beneficiaries. It is actually very difficult for policymakers in less developed countries to generate a coherent but "dissenting" understanding of these problems and hold to it in the presence of the extensive and technically elegant literature that justifies existing relationships.

The role of a strong and consistent doctrine in Venezuela's petroleum policy adds support to Nathaniel Leff's argument (based on his work in Brazil) that the form and content of elite ideology can be of central importance in determining the quality of development policy.[4] In the management of dependence, it would seem especially important in determining whether a moderate, incremental, and experimental approach is possible or whether policymakers will turn to a more extreme response, either submissiveness or xenophobic reaction.

But doctrine can also be a liability. One of the great dangers of a strategy of assertive experimentation is that the government will make a mistake so costly that the society as a whole will suffer unnecessarily as a result. A coherent sense of purpose and justification may be necessary for action, but it can also produce inflexible attitudes and obscure the range of choice rather than clarifying it. This very situation was the target of the critics who periodically charged the Venezuelan government with irreparably damaging the oil industry. They feared, each time, that the government had finally gone too far, that the companies were telling the truth about the disastrous consequences of policy.

As it turned out, two factors saved Venezuela from any real calamity. The first was flexibility, a trait essential to bargaining of this kind. The government frequently came to an accommodation with the companies when this seemed advisable because of a mistaken experiment or an unfavorable turn in the international system. There are many examples: the avoidance of shutdown orders for larger companies and the shift away from active control; the 1966–67 compromise on selective taxation and desulfurization; the implementation in practice of the Hydrocarbons Reversion Law and the production penalty system. Venezuelan democratic governments have been willing to adjust and learn, and for much of the time they have been able to avoid nationalistic posturing, an activity that in most circumstances serves only to reduce flexibility and adaptability. Doctrine is important as a legitimizer of policy and a guide to long-range goals; but it becomes dysfunctional when it introduces rigidity into the day-to-day conduct of policy, impairing the policymakers' ability to learn from their mistakes and successes.[5] Striking a balance between righteousness and adaptability, however, is obviously very difficult.

The second key to Venezuela's success was, quite simply, luck. An oil-company executive once told this writer that the president of his firm, upon hearing of an international price rise that saved Venezuela from the dangers of its most recent tax increase, slapped his forehead and exclaimed: "How can they luck out every time?" The story holds an important truth; for it is clear that things might not have turned out as well as they have, especially regarding capital investment and government earnings. In the late 1960's it seemed as though Pérez Alfonzo's doctrine might be bringing Venezuela to a sudden and unwanted cutback in the benefits received from the oil industry. His search in previous years for international control, higher prices, and prorationing had begun to appear starkly unrealistic, and his belief in the ultimate triumph of the underdeveloped countries over the multinational corporations a specious act of faith. The companies' forecasts about decreasing prices and a loss of markets for Venezuelan oil seemed to be correct, and U.S. intransigence had eroded faith in the idea that Venezuelan oil benefited from a "strategic factor," allowing prices higher than those obtaining elsewhere. Leoni's desulfurization agreement and the conciliatory atmosphere of the early Caldera years reflected these growing fears (and, it may be added, demonstrated Venezuela's adaptability, Pérez Alfonzo's bitterness notwithstanding).

In retrospect, it appears that Venezuela had pretty much reached the limit in testing its bargaining strength against the companies by this time. During the first years of Caldera's government, in fact, owing to the unprecedented political enmeshment of policy and the diffusion of control over it, both of which caused a marked loss of flexibility, policy almost surely exceeded that limit. Then came the international energy crisis of the 1970's, and Venezuela's troubles receded. The crisis debased the companies' most important remaining bargaining card, their control of the capital investments needed to maintain the industry and extend the lifetime of production.

Venezuelan diplomacy, of course, had been instrumental in laying the foundation for the international events themselves. But the changes in the world market might nonetheless have taken place later or in a different way, and Venezuela might then have been forced to accept a drastic decline in income, or, more important, a disastrous confrontation with the companies. She might then have had to pay dearly for further production or new investment commitments, which would have enormously complicated her plans for the peaceful nationalization of the petroleum industry.

In sum, there were very real risks and costs involved in the conduct of bargaining during the 1960's, and many in Venezuela felt uncomfortable with them. In 1969–70, especially, this discomfort was probably justified, in the sense that the risk at that time was incommensurate with policy objectives. As it was, the country accepted two very real short-term losses in order to pursue its strategy. The first was in deferred investment—an acceleration of the write-off spiral already mentioned. The second was a periodic reduction in total (rather than per-barrel) government revenues and other retained value; and since the entire Venezuelan economy was so dependent on oil, each reduction was accompanied by a lag in general economic growth (cf. Table 9, p. 109, and Table 12, p. 151). The persistent lack of vitality and independence in the non-oil areas of the economy made the loss more noticeable than it would otherwise have been. But Venezuela was lucky. As in any case of successful interdependent bargaining, she benefited from a combination of skill and circumstance; and in her case a change of circumstance came when it was most desperately needed.

Petroleum Policy and Domestic Politics

Obviously, petroleum policy has been highly sensitive to changing political conditions in Venezuela. But across regimes, it is easy to see a considerable historical continuity—more so, perhaps, than has been emphasized by past writers—most notably in that each government viewed itself as an adversary of the oil industry and sought to obtain a greater income from oil. However, regimes differed quite strikingly in their perceptions of the range of alternatives available to them, reflecting in large measure their diverse

opinions about the legitimacy of the existing international petroleum system.

As Venezuela's polity evolved from traditional dictatorship to a
relatively stable party democracy, the outlines of petroleum policy
closely paralleled the orientation of the successive governments in
other policy areas, especially in the state commitment to income
redistribution and citizen political participation. Two characteristics of this evolution are especially noteworthy. First, although
policy orientations changed markedly at times, especially between
dictatorial and reformist regimes, the growth of the country's participation in corporate earnings was surprisingly steady. Dictator-
ships, for example, showed no desire to renounce their inherited
sources of income. Second, to a surprising extent the conciliatory attitude of the more moderate (and authoritarian) governments toward the companies unintentionally made possible, or at
least viable, the more aggressive thrusts of succeeding reformist
regimes. Thus Gómez's "open arms" policy before 1935 allowed
a rapid growth in profits, which could then be taxed by the moderate oligarchy that followed him; the 1944–45 concessions "round"
set the companies up for the radical measures of the AD reformers;
and the 1956–57 round allowed an expansion of the industry upon
which the interim junta and the Betancourt administration could
draw. A similar process occurred at the international level. Venezuelan reforms, first in the 1940's and then in the late 1950's and
early 1960's, stimulated other oil-producing nations to make similar demands, but only after a time lag. The resulting improve-
ment in the country's bargaining position, therefore, accrued to
subsequent Venezuelan regimes rather than the ones initiating the
reforms. The "50–50" tax and the royalty "expensing" formula are
good examples of this.

Political Fragmentation and Policy Autonomy

It is clear that during the period of democratic politics since
1958 Venezuela's strategy of assertive experimentation has depended extensively on favorable political and institutional conditions. As we have seen, Betancourt began in 1959 with a strong

electoral mandate and succeeded in building a multiparty coalition government. His administration, with Pérez Alfonzo heading the Ministry of Mines, was well-equipped politically to implement a forceful search for alternative oil policies, despite unfavorable international trends and domestic economic difficulties that increased the significance of any threat to the steady flow of oil income. Pérez Alfonzo himself enlarged his political base by building a strong bipartisan coalition—parallel to but more comprehensive than the government coalition—in the *administration* of oil policy. He staffed his agencies and foreign delegations with people representing a wide political spectrum, and systematically consulted affected groups and individuals on policy issues. These steps, plus his strong working relationship with Betancourt, provided his ministry with considerable autonomy relative to the more politically charged areas of public policy. Given the dependence of every sector of Venezuela's economy on oil income, the degree of independence Pérez Alfonzo obtained was extraordinary.

This autonomy, however, eroded as the government weakened, the party system fragmented, and the foreign companies built a strong alliance with the domestic private sector. Oil policy became increasingly linked to other problems, especially budgetary requests. Bipartisan backing decreased, and the range of options narrowed rapidly. The decline in world oil prices and the companies' production decisions contributed measurably to this. Increasingly, the government had to "peg" its oil policy to domestic fiscal concerns; and its aggressive search for grand schemes to control the domestic and international systems gave way to cautious, incremental measures adopted with an eye to short-term consequences. This trend culminated late in the Leoni administration, when it seemed as though political fragmentation and economic insecurity had, for practical purposes, replaced the strategy of assertive experimentation with a pattern of conservative government-industry relations that reflected an across-the-board increase in company bargaining power.

Caldera's accession to the presidency and his decision to govern alone brought a further political twist to petroleum policy. The management of oil became caught between a weak government anxious about the economy and determined to ensure funding for its programs and a legislative group determined to reinstate a more forceful approach. This situation had developed from several circumstances: the initial passivity and administrative inexperience of the Caldera government in oil matters; the presence of several key legislative leaders committed to redirecting oil policy; and trends in the international market that eroded the bargaining power of the companies rapidly enough to allow the more experienced AD leaders to push ahead faster than the inexperienced and more cautious government. The result was a sudden wave of legislative attacks on the companies' prerogatives, which undermined the more cautious, industry-approved programs sponsored by Caldera and his advisers.

By almost any standards this was an anomalous and dangerous situation. With initiative and implementation divided both structurally and doctrinally, the subtle benefits of assertive experimentation could easily have been lost, to be replaced by raw confrontation—the executive versus the legislature, the government versus the companies—interlarded with nationalist posturing. To a considerable degree, this is precisely what began to happen, especially in 1968–70. Luckily, however, events did not spin completely out of control, for several reasons.

International events moved so rapidly that the companies were unable to undermine government income sufficiently to force the executive to its knees. Nor were they able to reactivate their defensive political alliance with the Venezuelan private sector. Repeatedly, it seemed as if the companies might gain the upper hand, but Arab and OPEC initiatives intervened. Also, Caldera himself, wavering between his accommodationist inclinations and the opposition's frontal attacks on the oil industry, gradually chose to join the attackers, cautiously at first, then more vigorously as he began to question the companies' explanations of their behavior and to interpret their actions as attempts at coercion. To a considerable extent, in fact, Caldera—to his credit—actually "relearned" the lessons about company behavior that were guiding

AD leaders in their attack; and he subsequently began to adopt their bargaining stance toward the industry, though never within as strict a conservationist doctrinal format. The best evidence of this turnabout was Caldera's parting advice to president-elect Carlos Andrés Pérez—indeed, Pérez Alfonzo or Hernández Grisanti might have ghostwritten the speech. Finally, Carlos Andrés's recent landslide victory almost surely signifies a return to more coherent and unified policy direction.

To summarize, Venezuelan democratic governments since 1958 have shown an elective affinity for assertive and experimental modes in the management of dependence; but domestic political conditions and world market trends have played an important part in determining the range of available options and the degree of success possible within that orientation. For a while it seemed that oil policy had spun out of control as a result of political fragmentation—a particularly dangerous state of affairs as the end of the concessions system drew near. However, international events, a relearning of old lessons by Caldera, and, finally, an unexpected electoral polarization headed this off.

The Multinationals and the Policy Process

To this point we have focused on the Venezuelan state and public policy, but it is also useful to consider the strategies of bargaining and self-defense adopted by the oil companies. To begin with, as far as Venezuela is concerned it would seem that many common generalizations about corporate power and the ability of foreign investors to manipulate the domestic affairs of dependent countries are wide of the mark, not so much because the influence is not there, but because of the problems involved in wielding it under conditions of uncertainty and rapid political and social change. Although the managerial skill of oilmen in handling complex economic decisions may be enormous, and although they show no lack of willingness or capacity to intervene directly in domestic affairs, their ability to skillfully orchestrate their influence is less than might be expected. Thus in Venezuela they were able to win important short-term benefits on several occasions, but they ended up paying dearly for them in the long run. The reasons for this differ from case to case; but the most satisfactory overall explanation lies in the status of the companies as subsidiaries of much larger decisional networks, a circumstance that limits the strategies they can pursue within an individual country.

As we have seen, company efforts to influence public policy can take many forms. In this case two of the most important were, first, the manipulation of economic variables, especially production rates and investments; and second, direct intervention in the domestic political process. From Venezuela's perspective, of course, the two were inseparable.

Oil companies repeatedly used economic levers to force the government to moderate its campaign to tax and control them. The principal goal was to "teach" policymakers and domestic elites in Venezuela (and elsewhere) about the dangers of pushing too hard, of asking too great a share of company profits or encroaching too far upon corporate autonomy. And to a degree the industry did constrain several Venezuelan administrations in this way, forcing upon them a moderation born of uncertainty and a sense of renewed vulnerability to corporate decisions and the international market.

But in the long run, what successive governments and opinion leaders actually "learned" was a more profound lesson: that the companies could not be trusted, and that their freedom from domestic control should therefore be terminated as quickly as possible in keeping with the overall health of the economy. It did seem for a time, with oil prices low and the OPEC able to do little, that the companies could keep Venezuela under control by wielding their economic sledgehammer. By 1974, however, the long-run implications of this approach were becoming only too painfully evident. The companies had won a few benefits, but the price they paid was an intensification of the distrust and uncertainty that spelled the death of the concessions system.

A similar relationship of short-term benefits and long-run debits obtained in company strategies of intervention in Venezuelan domestic politics. After 1958 the companies found themselves in an acutely uncomfortable relationship with the state. Instead of the old direct social contacts, they faced a hostile, independent government that was determined to ultimately replace them altogether. Isolated in this way, they sought and consolidated an institutional alliance with the domestic economic elites of Venezuela, themselves isolated and insecure vis-à-vis the state. Ensconced as a key chamber within Fedecámaras, and free to conduct massive propaganda campaigns in a sympathetic press, the companies seemed to have adapted very well to the new environment.

But when the time came to activate the alliance, during the 1966 tax reform crisis, the companies overplayed their hand, abused the relationship of confidence with their allies, and left the domestic private sector dangling in order to win concessions for themselves. This episode brought two important changes. First, Venezuelans of all sectors began to strongly resent the heavy-handed, almost bullying, role of the corporations, especially in their use of media campaigns. Second, and equally important, private economic elites came to the uncomfortable realization that the companies were willing to use them, and that the unity of interest between domestic and foreign economic groups was far less complete than company spokesmen had suggested. With time, this led many of them to consider the danger of a too-close identification with the petroleum corporations: perhaps the two need not "go down together" after all. In all this, the oilmen seem to have discounted the growing sophistication and independence of the domestic private sector in Venezuela—apart from the state, the sector of society that had changed most in the years since 1958. The companies were no longer dealing simply with a parochial group of rich families, but with commercial-industrial "empires" of considerable complexity.

The short-term benefits of this episode of intervention and alliance-building were real and important. Among other things, the companies had thwarted the government's effort to impose a selective, excess-profits tax on their earnings. But they had also isolated themselves, and had helped build among Venezuelans a much greater consensus about the need to control company actions. To be sure, the private sector continued to voice its concern about the deterioration of the oil industry; but increasingly the debate turned not upon the protection of the companies but upon the need for a new management system that would continue the developmental stimulus so important to the economy. When the real crunch came, in the early 1970's, the foreign multinationals found themselves very much alone.

Interestingly, the readiness of Venezuela's economic elites to disengage themselves politically from foreign corporate interests closely parallels a pattern in Chile described by Theodore Moran. In both cases, elitist anger at having to bear the brunt of government reformism while foreign corporations obtained seemingly preferential treatment was a key factor in provoking the cleavage. While the Chilean and Venezuelan cases differ in important ways, both demonstrate the danger of automatically assuming a united front among private powerholders in Latin America. Moreover, both examples presage the consolidation of much more concrete and restrictive "rules of the game" governing the behavior of foreign investors in their future relationships with domestic economic elites.[6]

A similar outcome can be seen in the case of company attempts to influence the electoral process. Here the evidence of direct intervention is sketchy, and in any case is far less important than the alliance-building that went on outside party ranks (parties, at least, were aware from the start of the dangers of associating with the companies). However, the companies did make financial contributions to parties, and they did little to hide their preference for Caldera in 1968 and for Carlos Andrés in 1973. Both men won, but once in office both began to view themselves as adversaries of the companies. To the extent that oil interests did influence the course of party politics—and their role was probably minor in the years before 1973—they almost surely contributed to the consolidation of a strong two-party system in Venezuela, since their financial support strengthened first one and then another of the major contenders. However, it is far from clear that the foreign corporations benefited as a result. Actually, they faced a dilemma in this respect: a weak, divided party system might produce a weak government and irresponsible nationalistic policies; on the other hand, a strong government might be better able to protect the country's interests against the corporations.

In the abstract, it is easy to imagine an entirely different strategy for the companies, one emphasizing corporate cooperation and good citizenship. Among other things, the companies might themselves have offered to coordinate their long-term decisions with government planners, offered to help build a large anticyclical fund, helped Venezuelan representatives win a hemisphere preference in the U.S. market, or taken the lead in turning over concessions to the government and establishing a new system with sufficient shared ownership and information to ameliorate the uncertainty and mistrust that poisoned the existing one. But simply listing these actions—and the list could go on—makes it clear that most of them would be fundamentally incompatible with the nature and goals of the larger multinational corporations. The reprisals policy of the late 1960's provides a good example: available evidence indicates that this was aimed as much or more at countries in the Middle East and elsewhere (e.g. Indonesia) as it was at Venezuela. The fact is that much of company behavior was and is based on much larger strategic considerations, involving many countries with conflicting domestic interests. Gains in Venezuela purchased by good citizenship and a less direct concern for profits would very likely have entailed large overall profit losses to the companies, as well as a rapid spread of restrictions on freedom of action elsewhere. The national/multinational incompatibility and the relentless drive for profits and control placed unavoidable restraints on the companies in their dealings with the government of Venezuela.

Oil and Political Development

It is one of the painful ironies of Latin American politics that despite a strong commitment to democratic ideals, civilian regimes have rarely been able to consolidate enough power and resources to firmly legitimize democratic institutions. Instead, countries of the region have shown an increasing affinity for corporatist-authoritarian rulership of some kind to relieve the tensions, conflicts, and seeming incompetence of competitive politics.[7] In this pattern of strain and tension between democratic and corporatist-authoritarian models, Venezuela had some important advantages traceable to oil. One of these was an acceleration in the breakup of the traditional agrarian economy and social structure, which released Venezuela from what might otherwise have been a much more rigid and constraining inheritance. Also, petroleum revenues allowed an unusually rapid enlargement of the state and at the same time increased the state's independence from both traditional and modern private elites.

But Venezuela has had another, more subtle, advantage. Democratic governments in Venezuela have operated for much of the time under conditions of reduced scarcity and rapid expansion of opportunities. In particular, the government's income from oil has expanded at a rate nearly double that of the economy as a whole. This has provided an important cushion, facilitating the institutionalization of conciliatory patterns of conflict resolution.[8] In game-theoretic terms, Venezuelan democracy has been an expanding-sum game; the raw edge of conflict has been softened by a growing total resource base. Compared to most developing nations, Venezuela, with government income (in constant bolívares) growing at an average annual rate of over 7 percent (since 1958), has been able to satisfy more demands and fund more programs while asking fewer sacrifices of her citizens.

More specifically, oil income has allowed political leaders since 1958 to follow a distinctive development strategy, one unavailable to societies without a resource gift of this kind and magnitude. In brief, they have moved ahead with a state-directed expansion of the economy, increasing the income and political and administrative power of the middle class; but they have done so without directly threatening the interests of established elites, instead working around these to build a modern Venezuela. Generous import-substitution protection, favorable fiscal and monetary policies (especially the absence of significant income taxation), and the government's extreme caution in foreign economic policy, especially toward ventures in economic integration—all these have made life relatively comfortable for the domestic private sector. Meanwhile, the government has concentrated on infrastructure development, educational reform, land reform, bureaucratic expansion, and the creation of export-oriented state industries. Although a dual-track development strategy of this kind can cause important problems in the long run, it is highly effective as a method of reducing social conflict and institutionalizing democratic rules of the game.

It is worth noting that the government might have gone even further with this dual approach had it not, in pursuit of other objectives, chosen to bargain so intensively with the companies. Independence and control, conservation, international cooperation, and rapid domestication of the industry all involved a potential (as it turned out, actual) sacrifice of short-term income. Such trade-offs are inherent in the choice of any array of policy objectives. From the actions of the Leoni and Caldera governments, however, it is clear that neither was willing to sacrifice its oil-revenue cushion entirely, or even to reduce it for very long. In the end, of course, neither had to.

No one who knows Venezuela well would argue that democratic procedures have become firmly established in the political culture, or that they are safe from the country's rich authoritarian legacy. But democracy is unquestionably growing stronger there, in stark contrast to trends elsewhere in the hemisphere, and there can be little doubt that oil income has contributed to this process.

The Politics of Fiscal Saturation

Although relative abundance and a growing government income may nurture democratic politics, they may also be habit-forming and leave the society vulnerable should it have to cope with scarcity. Unfortunately, it seems that exactly this has occurred in Venezuela—that is, the society and its component groups have grown accustomed to a continuing expansion of opportunities and resources. This is hardly surprising, in view of the growth that has taken place in the last four decades, but it has meant that the brief periods of relatively slow expansion or of contraction have been very difficult ones. The first part of the administration of Rómulo Betancourt (notably fiscal 1961–63, when government spending actually declined) is a case in point. Subsequent governments, with weaker legislative backing, have shown little inclination to repeat this experience, instead relying on deficit spending and external borrowing to smooth out the curve of fiscal expansion. This dependence, of course, affected petroleum policy. In the tax reform conflicts of 1966–67 and 1970, for example, we observed a growing inclination on the part of the government to turn to oil taxation after encountering problems in extracting further income from other sectors, although these were very lightly taxed. This tendency increased as a function of political fragmentation, for undertandable reasons. A weak government found it easier to attack the foreign companies than to face an alliance of opposition parties and economic elites. Obviously, this is a rather risky policy; and Caldera, in particular, was fortunate that his desire for funds paralleled so closely the desire of opposition oil strategists to increase the government's share of industry profits.

A closely related but in the long run more serious problem is that this politics of fiscal saturation, combined with a development strategy premised upon the avoidance of both income redistribution and the direct restructuring of economic activities, has led to, and may continue to produce, a failure in the long-run strategy of "sowing the oil." This of course strikes at the heart of what has for decades been the acknowledged objective of Venezuelan public policy. The problem here is that efficiency, self-reliance, and an export capacity based on a real comparative advantage in nonpetroleum products must all result from "hard" decisions about the economy and the structure of production; and the government has been unwilling to make these as long as it could buy time for itself with oil.

Continuing dependence on petroleum revenues and the concomitant lack of independence in other sectors of the economy have been a growing concern to many Venezuelans; and their fears have been magnified by the enormous new revenue windfall from oil. Although satisfactory indicators are hard to obtain, the sum of available evidence indicates that these fears are completely justified. The role of oil in the budget and the economy as a whole has remained very large, and non-oil economic activity has remained both inefficient and predisposed toward activity sustained by large doses of government capital. Per capita fiscal receipts originating from the petroleum industry, as a percentage of per capita government income, have remained remarkably constant in the last decade (Table 14). This is also true of the more significant measure of income tax from oil as a percentage of total income tax (Table 15).

The same conclusion applies to the economy as a whole, in which the percentage contribution of the petroleum sector to Venezuela's GNP has remained both large and constant for many years

TABLE 14
Oil and Government Income, 1900–1972
(Bolívares)

Year	Total income (× 1 million)		Per capita income (× 1)		Oil income per capita as % of total income
	All income[a]	Oil income	All income	Oil income	
1900	45	–	19	–	–
1910	70	–	27	–	–
1920	82	1	29	–	–
1930	210	47	67	15	22%
1940	330	98	87	26	30
1950	1,917	901	381	179	47
1960	4,968	3,001	675	408	60
1961	5,792	3,160	761	415	55
1962	5,910	3,142	751	399	53
1963	6,596	3,511	810	431	53
1964	7,133	4,693	846	557	66
1965	7,265	4,752	833	545	65
1966	7,751	4,941	858	547	64
1967	8,539	5,699	913	609	67
1968	8,775	5,824	906	601	66
1969	8,661	5,483	863	546	63
1970	9,498	5,751	913	553	61
1971	11,637	7,684	1,096	717	65
1972	12,192	7,927	1,111	723	65

SOURCE: Ministry of Finance, Ministry of Development, and Ministry of Mines, as reported in Venezuela, [9], 1966, p. 1; 1972, p. 5.
[a] Including back-tax payments but not income from foreign loans.

TABLE 15
Government Oil and Iron Income Taxes as a Percentage of
Total Income Tax, 1964–73

Year	Total income tax (Bs × 1 million)	Percent oil income[a]	Percent iron income[a]	Percent other income
1964	2,959	72.9%	3.5%	23.6%
1965	3,217	68.0	5.1	26.9
1966	3,649	64.6	8.7	26.7
1967	4,166	70.3	4.6	25.0
1968	4,338	70.2	3.6	26.1
1969	4,111	65.5	3.0	31.4
1970	4,561	62.4	5.4	32.3
1971	6,563	72.7	4.0	23.2
1972	7,062	72.1	2.4	25.5
1973[b]	11,104	80.4	1.6	18.0

SOURCE: Venezuela, [6], Appendix, p. 5.
    [a] Royalties not included.   [b] My own estimate.

(Table 16). To be sure, both economic activity unrelated to oil
and the portion of the budget coming from non-oil sources have
grown; but there is little evidence that they have made the country
any more self-sufficient than it was ten or even twenty years ago.
Indeed, in 1972—before the "crisis" price hikes—oil formed about
the same percentage of the real value of total exports as it did in
1935, 1945, 1955, and 1965 (see Appendix Table B).

The impression conveyed by these figures is confirmed by recent
studies of the overall economic development process in Venezuela,
which point to the same harsh conclusions: despite her beneficial
foreign exchange position and relative abundance of capital, Venezuela has *not* been able to use retained earnings from oil to build
a solid agricultural and industrial base for economic progress independent of petroleum.[9] What growth there has been in non-oil
sectors has taken place behind the protective barriers of stiff import-substitution legislation, and Venezuelan entrepreneurs have
remained economically inefficient, demonstrating little propensity
to generate an export capacity for the country, even though such
a capacity is essential in view of the limited potential for expansion in the domestic market. As the more profitable niches in the

TABLE 16
Oil and Gross National Product, 1956–72
(Millions of bolívares)

Year	GNP[a]	Contri-bution of oil sector	Percent contri-bution of oil sector	Year	GNP[a]	Contri-bution of oil sector	Percent contri-bution of oil sector
1956	17,930	3,693	20.6%	1965	34,434	6,957	20.2%
1957	20,596	4,605	22.4	1966	36,123	6,899	19.1
1958	22,488	4,878	21.7	1967	38,353	7,524	19.6
1959	23,668	4,802	20.3	1968	39,948	7,465	18.7
1960	23,574	4,840	20.5	1969	42,053	7,494	17.8
1961	24,675	4,927	20.0	1970	46,388	8,354	18.0
1962	26,800	5,526	20.6	1971	51,674	9,857	19.1
1963	29,333	5,250	17.9	1972	57,659	10,704	18.6
1964	32,414	6,877	21.2				

SOURCE: Venezuela, [9], 1972, p. 3. Contribution = taxes + salaries and wages + depreciation.

[a] At market prices.

domestic economy have filled, manufacturing has concentrated increasingly in services and luxuries. Planned increases in export-oriented activity are found primarily in the large-scale state enterprises involved in resource extraction and processing.[10] In sum, this economic pattern does not promise to sustain expansion or transformation by itself in the absence of continued fiscal stimulus. This is clearly illustrated by the poor performance of the economy during the episodes of fiscal decline in the 1960's.

Equally disturbing, and also attributable to the overall development strategy pursued by the government, is the persistence of an unequal distribution of the benefits stemming from petroleum. Available evidence indicates that the broad pattern of income distribution in Venezuela has remained almost unchanged since 1957.[11] During this time, of course, Venezuelans have grown richer relative to other Latin Americans. In 1970, 40 percent of Venezuelan families received an average monthly income of Bs 1,035 ($230) or more, and 30 percent received Bs 1,675 ($375) or more.[12] But this affluence has come from overall expansion, growth of the pie, not from a more equal spreading of available income. This said, however, it should be added that Venezuela is a society with a smaller concentration of wealth at the very top, and a wealthier middle class, than the other Latin American countries for which figures are available (i.e., Argentina, Brazil, Colombia, Mexico, Panama, El Salvador, and Costa Rica). The top 10 percent account for less of the income (some 41 percent) and the next 60 percent account for more (some 53 percent) than is the case in the other countries. The tragedy here is that this triumph of the middle class has been at the expense of the poorest 30 percent of Venezuelan society, who receive less of the available income than the poorer groups in the other countries mentioned.[13]

Fitting the pieces together, then, we see the convergence of oil policy, politics, and development strategy. Together they reveal a distinctive profile: assertive experimentation; fiscal saturation; fledgling democracy; and low-risk, low-threat distributive economic policy. All these intersect, and all relate to each other and to the overall pattern of national development.

Prospects

In 1974 Venezuela stands at the threshold of what seems, thanks to oil, an unbelievably bright and prosperous future. All signs point to a continuation of favorable market conditions, and forecasts of government income stagger the imagination. Tables 17 and 18 present three alternative futures based on a range of optimistic

TABLE 17
Alternative Futures: Venezuelan Fiscal Income
(Millions of 1973 dollars)

Year	High		Medium		Low	
	Total income	Oil income	Total income	Oil income	Total income	Oil income
1974	11,634	10,478	9,202	8,046	8,458	7,302
1975	10,308	9,108	8,026	6,826	6,893	5,693
1976	9,055	7,805	7,380	6,130	5,717	4,467
1977	8,854	7,554	6,139	4,839	5,717	4,467
1978	7,480	6,130	5,422	4,072	4,743	3,393
TOTAL	47,331	41,075	36,169	29,913	31,528	25,322

NOTE: Assuming: a non-oil income growth rate of 4 percent per year; fiscal income from first $3.39 of price is $1.85 per barrel; 90 percent of all price increases goes to the state. See Table 18.

TABLE 18

Alternative Futures: Venezuelan Production and Prices

(Millions of barrels daily and U.S. dollars per barrel)

Year	High Production	High Price	Medium Production	Medium Price	Low Production	Low Price
1974	3.3	$11.00	3.0	$9.50	2.9	$9.00
1975	3.2	10.00	2.9	8.50	2.6	8.00
1976	3.1	9.00	2.8	8.00	2.4	7.00
1977	3.0	9.00	2.6	7.00	2.4	7.00
1978	2.8	8.00	2.4	6.50	2.0	6.50

NOTE: These figures were used to generate those in Table 17. Forecasts my own, based on analysis of price and supply trends and my own estimate of alternative OPEC and government policies. Price estimates in TRV's.

and pessimistic assumptions about prices and production levels for the years until 1977. As these indicate, Venezuela can anticipate a veritable deluge of income, equal in 1974 alone to three times the entire budget for 1972. Assuming favorable conditions and no breakdown in production, the government may receive over the next five years some 30 or 40 billion dollars, a sum larger than the total income from oil since the beginning of its exploitation in Venezuela. To leaders of both major parties, accustomed to annual bouts of anxiety about financing the growth of next year's budget, this is a breathtaking prospect. But it means much more than freedom from year-end fiscal crunches; it also means a new freedom in designing programs and managing the economy. At the time of writing (1974), the new AD government is speaking of uniting budgetary and planning processes in the executive agency Cordiplan, thus creating a central coordinating and supervisory body to oversee new programs and long-range plans. Also under serious consideration—three decades after Pérez Alfonzo first suggested it—is a special reserve fund of oil revenues to insulate the economy from unexpected changes in the international market.

Most important, for present purposes, the new bonanza means that Venezuela can quickly terminate the concessions system and avoid many of the problems associated with its ongoing degeneration. And she can do so with a minimum of strain and conflict, paying the companies generous sums to induce their cooperation with the government after nationalization. Carlos Andrés surprised no one when he committed Venezuela to a rapid takeover of the industry in his inaugural address. The relevant questions are: how soon, with what compensation, and under what institutional arrangements? Barring surprises at the international level, the completion of nationalization with prompt, just, and adequate compensation—perhaps even more than adequate—seems assured by 1975 or 1976. And, along with the new income, the consolidation of the country's party system almost surely points to a moderation of government policy, to a much more cautious, cooperative orientation.

Along with this bright future, however, Venezuela faces a number of actual and potential problems that make complacency dangerous. To begin with, the international petroleum market is still uncontrolled and unpredictable. To be sure, the present high price levels are sustained by an income tax floor that will probably last for several years. And it seems unlikely that world demand for oil will diminish during this time enough to affect Venezuela. But with prices as high as those of 1974 ($9 to $10 realized per barrel and $11.65 TRV), many experts fear the possibility of a serious oil glut in three or four years. Such a circumstance might overstrain the tenuous unity of OPEC and lead to ruinous sales of oil at lower prices. The OPEC countries' ongoing takeover of companies within their borders may heighten rather than lessen this possibility. The potential for conflict over prices is very real, as can be seen by the history of attempts to agree on a prorationing formula. Saudi Arabia is already pushing for a lowering of prices to the point at which they will neither draw into production large amounts of more expensive oil around the world nor make profitable the use of expensive and environmentally damaging alternative sources such as atomic energy or oil shale. In contrast, Iran and many other OPEC countries with smaller reserves and larger populations are urging even higher prices.

Venezuela falls between these extremes. It is an "old" producing country as far as reserves of regular oil are concerned, and the end of its production lifetime in regular oil is not far off—probably about 20–25 years, depending on how quickly production rates decline. The company estimates indicate 11.4 years at current rates (see Table 10, p. 132); however, "proven" reserves change with oil prices, and secondary and tertiary recovery techniques can be expected to increase recoverable oil substantially. Published estimates of the geological presence of new oil in Venezuela vary between 16 and 50 billion barrels,* but it is certainly possible that major new discoveries could turn up. The most promising areas are offshore, in the Gulf of Venezuela and on the continental shelf.[14] However, to maintain her production capacity Venezuela will have to move ahead quickly in exploration and drilling, since the private companies have done little of this in recent years. Indeed, many experts estimate that Venezuelan output will inevitably drop in the early 1980's, owing to the five- to eight-year time lag in bringing regular oil into production. If prices remain anywhere near their present level, however, this is not an alarming possibility. In fact, the Venezuelan government is very likely to follow Pérez Alfonzo's advice and slow production rates down substantially. Forecasts of price trends will have an important bearing on this decision, since declining prices will reduce the value of oil left in the ground.

In the longer run, beginning in the mid-1980's, Venezuela will want to rely increasingly on her own alternative energy resource, the estimated 700 billion barrels of heavy "irregular" oil lying in the Orinoco region. Here, price is of central importance. A high price is needed to make production possible; and an even higher price is necessary to bring a sizable income to the state above costs, which may approach the $5 to $7 per barrel anticipated for shale oil. Although Venezuela, in the short run, can hardly fail to reap

* Given the uncertainty of the data available, there has been a marked tendency for estimates and projections to vary according to the needs of the analysts making them. Thus company estimates tend to be on the conservative side, whereas government estimates are more liberal. The companies, of course, are interested in figures that will provide a safe basis for future profit calculations —and will also point up the need for increasing proven reserves through added private investment. The government, by contrast, would like to dispel opposition criticism of its handling of petroleum affairs, and is therefore inclined to paint a rosier picture.

enormous profits, the issue of OPEC unity and the organization's ability to agree on a prorationing formula remains of the utmost importance.

Venezuela's position in the North American market is also an area of possible problems. Observers familiar with the history of United States oil policy cannot help but be uneasy. It is difficult to predict the degree to which the North American public will accept privations in the name of national security, and Venezuela may again find herself excluded rather than included as a partner in regional market control. And should the United States decide once again to limit imports, the resulting controls might again become as irrational and immutable as those of the old mandatory quota system.

At home, Venezuela faces a challenge of a different kind in the management of the petroleum industry. The transition from bargaining and conflict to regulation and control will require new skills and place new pressures on policymakers. The strategy of assertive experimentation involves an orientation entirely different from the one that will be necessary as the state assumes direct administrative responsibility for oil. Fortunately, the recent consolidation of the party system will permit the executive to reassert itself and reestablish a unified control of petroleum policy. The changeover itself will be especially critical, since it will necessarily occur after only superficial study and preparation. And the government will have to rely heavily upon the assistance of Venezuelans now working for foreign oil companies, many of whom have a highly critical attitude toward the state.

The lack of trained managerial manpower, in particular, will almost surely force the government to turn to the companies themselves for assistance in exploring, producing, marketing, and distributing. In this sense, Venezuela's decision to take over immediately may have provided a new source of bargaining power to the companies. Defining their role, as well as the actual administrative functions of the state, will be technically difficult and politically controversial. Many alternatives are open, ranging from mixed companies to new service contracts to much narrower "piecework" contracts with the CVP. Pérez Alfonzo, it may be noted, opposes *any* involvement of private capital, foreign or domestic, in the industry; and his judgment, as always, is likely to weigh heavily in future decisions.

Ultimately, of course, the arrangement will have to be one that places controlling participation in marketing decisions, as well as direct and comprehensive access to information about the industry, in the hands of the Venezuelan state and its agencies. Managerial problems will necessarily be immense. For Americans, it would be equivalent to having the U.S. government take control of the top 200 corporations in the country. And the regulation of domestic petroleum bureaucrats may prove as formidable, though in different ways, as handling multinational corporations.

To sum up, then, although her future does look bright, especially in comparison with that of so many other developing nations, Venezuela nevertheless faces the most difficult and challenging period in the history of her oil policy. The international petroleum system remains unstable, new reserves must be discovered and brought into production, and the administrative transition to regulation and management of the industry is sure to be troublesome. Moreover, the temptation to settle back, to postpone actually "sowing" the oil and redistributing its benefits among the less fortunate, will continue to be strong. Clearly, a lot remains to be done.

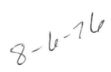

Appendix

Statistical Data

TABLE A

Financial Summary of the Venezuelan Petroleum Industry, 1947–73

(Millions of bolívares and percentages)

Item	1947	1948	1949	1950	1951	1952
Gross accum. invest.	5,320	6,697	7,641	8,027	8,526	9,312
Net accum. invest.	3,305	4,422	5,033	5,021	5,142	5,457
New invest.	1,127	1,630	1,127	561	727	967
Deprec. & amort.	190	246	325	420	495	530
Total assets	4,587	6,072	6,859	7,169	7,413	7,894
Capital	3,894	4,915	5,789	5,954	6,077	6,470
Total income	2,394	3,534	3,124	3,748	4,405	4,677
Profit after tax	745	1,060	704	970	1,201	1,262
Income tax	297	479	272	394	525	594
Other taxes	124	171	156	108	196	199
Royalties	397	640	627	519	727	751
Total to govt.	818	1,290	1,055	1,021	1,448	1,544
Govt./ind. split	52/48	55/45	60/40	51/49	55/45	55/45
Profit:						
As % income	31.11	30.00	22.54	25.88	27.26	27.00
As % av. capital[a]	21.22	24.06	13.16	16.52	19.96	20.12
As % av. net fixed assets[a]	22.54	27.44	14.89	19.30	23.63	23.81

TABLE A (cont.)

Item	1953	1954	1955	1956	1957	1958
Gross accum. invest.	9,873	10,212	10,937	13,038	15,828	17,218
Net accum. invest.	5,460	5,534	5,649	7,023	9,002	9,652
New invest.	901	933	928	1,232[b]	1,822[b]	1,788
Deprec. & amort.	558	613	680	732	812	836
Total assets	8,444	8,625	8,680	9,963	12,199	12,593
Capital	6,825	6,967	6,806	7,793	9,587	9,626
Total income	4,892	5,337	5,875	6,829	8,463	7,662
Profit after tax	1,261	1,412	1,710	2,115	2,774	1,616
Income tax	507	585	712	931	1,199	1,465
Other taxes	209	117	126	162	241	187
Royalties	786	874	1,003	1,188	1,550	1,415
Total to govt.	1,502	1,576	1,841	2,281	2,990	3,067
Govt./ind. split	54/46	53/47	52/48	52/48	52/48	65/35
Profit:						
As % income	25.78	26.46	29.11	30.97	32.77	21.09
As % av. capital[a]	18.98	20.48	24.83	28.97	31.92	16.82
As % av. net fixed assets[a]	23.10	25.69	30.58	33.38	34.62	17.33

TABLE A (cont.)

Item	1959	1960	1961	1962	1963
Gross. accum. invest.	18,803	18,987	19,155	19,417	19,353
Net accum. invest.	10,375	9,771	9,140	8,664	8,086
New invest.	1,262	730	516	474	511
Deprec. & amort.	939	948	929	1,082	986
Total assets	13,450	12,666	11,928	11,208	10,368
Capital	10,762	10,406	9,988	9,248	8,549
Total income	7,289	7,287	7,477	7,703	7,701
Profit after tax	1,335	1,282	1,477	1,694	1,679
Income tax	1,260	1,070	1,216	1,462	1,544
Other taxes	156	138	131	60	56
Royalties	1,444	1,503	1,552	1,703	1,731
Total to govt.	2,860	2,711	2,899	3,225	3,331
Govt./ind. split	68/32	68/32	66/34	66/34	66/34
Profit:					
As % income	18.32	17.59	19.75	21.99	21.80
As % av. capital[a]	13.10	12.11	14.48	17.49	18.87
As % av. net fixed assets[a]	13.33	12.73	15.62	19.03	20.05

TABLE A (cont.)

Item	1964	1965	1966	1967	1968
Gross accum. invest.	19,872	20,342	20,518	20,673	21,635
Net accum. invest.	7,778	7,553	7,043	6,576	6,853
New invest.	753	825	638	647	1,182
Deprec. & amort.	993	965	991	974	938
Total assets	11,100	11,319	10,462	9,627	10,208
Capital	8,431	8,481	7,617	7,160	7,627
Total income	10,693	10,725	10,419	10,964	11,119
Profit after tax	2,457	2,638	2,504	2,514	2,653
Income tax	2,251	2,323	2,260	2,752	2,754
Other taxes	54	50	45	45	44
Royalties	2,557	2,564	2,531	2,663	2,715
Total to govt.	4,862	4,937	4,836	5,460	5,513
Govt./ind. split	66/34	65/35	66/34	68/32	68/32
Profit:					
As % income	22.98	24.60	24.03	22.93	23.86
As % av. capital[a]	28.94	31.20	31.11	34.03	35.89
As % av. net fixed assets[a]	30.98	34.41	34.31	36.92	39.51

TABLE A (cont.)

Item	1969	1970	1971	1972	1973[e]
Gross accum. invest.	22,655	23,647	23,732	24,735	–
Net accum. invest.	7,361	7,461	7,434	7,334	7,122
Net invest.	1,574	1,294	1,287	1,000	864
Deprec. & amort.	1,009	1,070	1,211	1,140	–
Total assets	11,270	11,352	11,970	12,161	13,936
Capital	7,664	7,280	7,678	7,047	7,718
Total income	10,906	11,384	13,720	13,566	19,178
Profit after tax	2,264	1,739	2,247	1,266	2,812
Income tax	2,751	3,270	4,653	5,558	8,858
Other taxes	53	55	57	56	56
Royalties	2,722	2,875	2,836	2,797	3,496
Total to govt.	5,526	6,200	7,546	8,411	12,410
Govt./ind. split	71/29	78/22	77/23	87/13	82/18
Profit:					
As % income	20.76	16.28	16.38	9.33	14.66
As % av. capital[a]	29.61	23.27	30.04	17.19	38.10
As % av. net fixed assets[a]	31.86	23.47[d]	30.17	17.15[d]	38.90

SOURCE: Venezuela, [9], *Petróleo y Otros Datos*, 1964, p. 127; 1973, p. 152. The petroleum industry stresses the fact that the apparent increase in profits after 1964 was not entirely "real" from the companies' perspective. When the petroleum exchange rate was changed in that year (from Bs 3.09 per dollar to Bs 4.40 per dollar), the capital already invested in fixed assets was not revalued, whereas such items as gross income and costs—excepting depreciation and amortization—were calculated at the new rate. For their purpose, expressing earnings in U.S. dollars, the companies prefer to use a calculation that gives the following figures for profit as a percentage of average net fixed assets: 1964, 21.74%; 1965, 24.14%; 1966, 24.09%; 1967, 25.91%; 1968, 27.75%; 1969, 22.40%; 1970, 16.47%.

[a] Average of figures for beginning and end of each year.

[b] New investment for 1956–57 does not include the large fees paid by companies to obtain new concessions.

[e] Figures for 1973 are preliminary estimates.

[d] This figure was recalculated, and differs from the one originally given in the source.

Appendix

Government Income and Export Values, 1920–73
(Millions of bolívares and percentages)

Year	Govt. income	Govt. income[a] (1938 bolívares)	Percent change	Value of total exports (1938 bolívares)	Value of oil exports (1938 bolívares)	Oil as percent of total export value
1920	104.4	104.4	–	170.6	3.3	1.9
1921	64.8	64.8	−40.0	133.6	11.8	8.8
1922	81.6	81.6	26.0	137.2	15.7	11.4
1923	88.8	88.8	9.0	156.7	28.7	18.3
1924	111.6	111.6	26.0	213.5	65.5	30.6
1925	147.6	147.6	32.0	330.0	137.5	41.6
1926	178.8	178.8	21.0	395.4	246.6	62.4
1927	174.0	174.0	−3.0	444.1	280.8	63.2
1928	204.3	204.3	17.0	609.6	466.9	76.6
1929	256.4	256.4	25.5	778.6	593.6	76.2
1930	243.7	243.7	−6.0	762.5	643.1	83.2
1931	188.9	188.9	−22.0	651.6	547.8	84.0
1932	175.4	175.4	−7.0	628.3	531.6	84.6
1933	169.6	169.6	−3.0	617.5	553.2	89.6
1934	178.7	178.7	5.0	671.9	608.5	90.6
1935	206.4	206.4	15.5	711.7	649.3	91.2
1936	220.8	220.8	7.0	768.5	684.2	89.0
1937	312.1	312.1	41.0	871.9	770.0	88.3
1938	340.3	340.3	9.0	887.3	828.3	93.3
1939	350.9	330.4	−3.0	897.6	843.0	93.9
1940	330.1	313.8	−5.0	818.3	769.0	94.0
1941	359.2	356.0	13.5	1,052.0	991.6	94.3
1942	291.8	277.4	−22.0	675.3	604.2	89.4
1943	340.2	300.5	8.0	761.5	694.5	91.2
1944	541.9	450.8	50.0	933.0	879.2	94.4
1945	659.6	529.8	18.0	889.8	823.0	92.5
1946	855.5	630.0	19.0	853.5	762.0	91.8
1947	1,281.0	1,276.0	102.5	2,159.6	2,045.4	94.7
1948	1,776.4	1,030.0	−19.0	2,019.9	1,936.4	95.9
1949	1,979.6	1,148.9	11.5	1,950.4	1,891.0	97.0
1950	1,917.0	1,110.6	−3.0	2,020.7	1,944.4	96.2
1951	2,266.5	1,259.8	13.0	2,204.7	2,111.3	95.8
1952	2,407.8	1,363.4	8.0	2,509.2	2,369.2	94.4
1953	2,533.6	1,473.0	8.0	2,725.8	2,557.1	93.8
1954	2,631.8	1,503.0	2.0	2,923.8	2,739.3	93.7
1955	2,992.1	1,689.5	12.0	3,314.9	3,100.7	93.5
1956	4,374.7	2,484,2	47.0	3,863.5	3,605.3	93.3
1957	5,396.6	3,137.6	26.0	4,948.7	4,572.7	92.4
1958	4,706.0	2,687.6	−14.0	4,410.1	4,054.4	91.9
1959	5,743.5	3,259.6	21.0	4,152.0	3,776.4	91.0
1960	6,147.4	3,535.0	8.0	4,438.9	3,818.6	86.0

TABLE B (cont.)

Year	Govt. income	Govt. income[a] (1938 bolívares)	Percent change	Value of total exports (1938 bolívares)	Value of oil exports (1938 bolívares)	Oil as percent of total export value
1961	7,074.1	3,998.9	13.0	4,213.3	3,864.7	91.7
1962	6,589.3	3,765.3	−6.0	4,482.3	4,136.8	92.3
1963	6,618.7	3,733.0	−0.8	4,425.4	4,070.0	92.0
1964	7,217.3	3,924.6	5.0	5,899.3	5,510.8	93.4
1965	7,367.1	3,897.9	−0.7	5,780.4	5,367.2	92.9
1966	7,951.8	4,126.5	6.0	5,479.0	5,057.6	92.3
1967	8,678.8	4,585.0	11.0	5,887.0	5,423.7	92.1
1968	9,159.0	4,713.8	3.0	5,705.6	5,334.0	93.5
1969	9,676.8	4,889.7	3.7	5,578.0	5,124.3	91.9
1970	10,252.1	5,185.7	6.0	5,883.2	5,335.9	90.7
1971	12,122.6	6,001.3	15.7	6,874.3	6,343.6	92.3
1972	12,546.8	6,052.5	0.9	6,627.6	6,065.6	91.5
1973	16,054.0	7,523.0	24.3	–	–	–

SOURCES: *Government income*: 1920–64 from Central Bank, as given in Creole Corp. Rept., 1966, p. 41; 1965–72 from Venezuela, [6], App. p. 11. *Export values*: 1920–50 from Central Bank, as given in Creole Corp. Rept., 1966, p. 39; 1951–72 from Venezuela, [9], 1964, p. 9, 1971 & 1972, p. 11. Data for 1973 estimated.
[a] Figures adjusted from composite price index, Table E.

TABLE C
Venezuelan Oil Production, 1920–73
(Thousands of 42-gallon barrels per day)

Year	Production	Year	Production	Year	Production
1920	1.3	1938	515.2	1956	2,456.8
1921	4.0	1939	560.4	1957	2,779.2
1922	6.1	1940	502.3	1958	2,604.8
1923	11.9	1941	621.3	1959	2,771.0
1924	24.9	1942	405.9	1960	2,846.1
1925	54.6	1943	491.5	1961	2,919.9
1926	97.7	1944	702.3	1962	3,199.8
1927	165.5	1945	886.0	1963	3,248.0
1928	289.5	1946	1,064.3	1964	3,392.8
1929	372.8	1947	1,191.5	1965	3,472.9
1930	370.5	1948	1,338.8	1966	3,371.1
1931	320.2	1949	1,321.4	1967	3,542.1
1932	319.0	1950	1,498.0	1968	3,604.8
1933	232.8	1951	1,704.6	1969	3,594.1
1934	373.4	1952	1,803.9	1970	3,708.0
1935	406.9	1953	1,765.0	1971	3,549.1
1936	422.5	1954	1,895.3	1972	3,219.9
1937	508.9	1955	2,157.2	1973	3,366.0

SOURCE: Venezuela, [9], 1972, p. 60; Creole Corp. Rept., 1973, p. 11.

TABLE D

Average Realized Oil Prices, Exports, and Imports, 1950–73

Year	Average price for crude and products (U.S. dollars per barrel)	Price indexes (1958 = 100)		Year	Average price for crude and products (U.S. dollars per barrel)	Price indexes (1958 = 100)	
		Petroleum exports	All imports			Petroleum exports	All imports
1950	$2.11	84	91	1962	$2.08	83	119
1951	2.05	82	103	1963	2.04	82	126
1952	2.14	86	101	1964	1.95	78	130
1953	2.30	92	97	1965	1.89	75	140
1954	2.31	92	95	1966	1.87	75	145
1955	2.34	94	96	1967	1.85	74	150
1956	2.36	94	98	1968	1.87	75	153
1957	2.65	106	100	1969	1.81	72	156
1958	2.50	100	100	1970	1.85	74	160
1959	2.23	89	102	1971	2.35	94	168
1960	2.12	85	104	1972	2.52	101	176
1961	2.13	85	105				

SOURCE: Venezuela, [9], 1966, p. 173; 1972, p. 169. International Monetary Fund, *International Financial Statistics*, various issues.

TABLE E

Composite Price Index, 1938–73

(Bolívares and percentages)

Year	1938 = 100	1958 = 100	Year	1938 = 100	1958 = 100
1938	100.0	57.1	1956	176.1	100.5
1939	106.2	60.6	1957	172.0	98.2
1940	105.2	60.0	1958	175.1	100.0
1941	100.9	57.6	1959	176.2	100.6
1942	105.2	60.0	1960	173.9	99.3
1943	113.2	64.6	1961	176.9	101.0
1944	120.2	68.6	1962	175.0	99.9
1945	124.5	71.1	1963	177.3	101.2
1946	135.8	77.5	1964	183.9	105.0
1947	100.4	57.3	1965	189.0	107.9
1948	172.5	98.5	1966	192.7	110.0
1949	172.3	98.4	1967	189.3	108.1
1950	172.6	98.6	1968	194.3	111.0
1951	179.9	102.7	1969	197.9	113.0
1952	177.6	101.4	1970	197.7	113.0
1953	172.0	98.2	1971	202.0	115.5
1954	175.1	100.0	1972	207.3	118.5
1955	177.1	101.1	1973	213.4	122.0

SOURCES: For 1938–70, Venezuela, [4], 1970, p. 213. This is the government's own composite price index. It is the best available and forms the basis for all conversions of data to constant bolívares in this book. For 1971–74 the index is from International Monetary Fund, *International Financial Statistics*, adjusted.

TABLE F

Exchange Rates, 1937–73

(Bolívares per U.S. dollar)

Year	Petroleum export rate	Other export rate	Selling rate	Year	Petroleum export rate	Other export rate	Selling rate
1937	3.09	3.09	3.19	1956	3.09	3.32	3.35
1938	3.09	3.09	3.19	1957	3.09	3.33	3.35
1939	3.09	3.09	3.19	1958	3.09	3.33	3.35
1940	3.09	3.09	3.19	1959	3.09	3.33	3.35
1941	3.09	3.09	3.19	1960	3.09	3.33	3.35
1942	3.09	3.09	3.35	1961	3.09	3.33	3.35
1943	3.09	3.32	3.35	1962	3.09	3.33	3.35
1944	3.09	3.32	3.35	1963	3.09	3.33	3.35
1945	3.09	3.32	3.35	1964	4.40	4.48	4.50
1946	3.09	3.32	3.35	1965	4.40	4.48	4.50
1947	3.09	3.32	3.35	1966	4.40	4.48	4.50
1948	3.09	3.32	3.35	1967	4.40	4.48	4.50
1949	3.09	3.32	3.35	1968	4.40	4.48	4.50
1950	3.09	3.32	3.35	1969	4.40	4.48	4.50
1951	3.09	3.32	3.35	1970	4.40	4.48	4.50
1952	3.09	3.32	3.35	1971	4.30	4.38	4.40
1953	3.09	3.32	3.35	1972	4.30	4.38	4.40
1954	3.09	3.32	3.35	1973	4.20	4.28	4.30
1955	3.09	3.32	3.35				

SOURCE: International Monetary Fund, *International Financial Statistics*, monthly since 1948.

Notes

Complete authors' names, titles, and publishing data for sources cited in the Notes are given in the Bibliography, pp. 197–204. The citation "Venezuela" followed by a bracketed number indicates a Venezuelan government publication, listed under Venezuela in the Bibliography.

Introduction

1. Short but clear statements of the dependency theme may be found in Sunkel, "National Development Policy and External Dependence"; Dos Santos, "The Structure of Dependence." For greater detail and controversy, see: the essays in *Latin American Perspectives* 1 (spring 1974); Cohen, *The Question of Imperialism*; Cardoso, "Associated-Dependent Development." On multinational corporations, see: Vernon, *Sovereignty at Bay*; Kindleberger, *The International Corporation*. For case material on Latin America, see Pinelo, *The Multinational Corporation as a Force in Latin American Politics*. Moran also has provided two useful essays: "The Alliance for Progress and 'The Foreign Copper Companies and Their Conservative Allies' in Chile, 1955–70" and "Transnational Strategies of Protection and Defense by Multinational Corporations."

2. See Levin, *The Export Economies*.

3. For recent estimates, see Ruddle and Hamour, p. 299; and *Statistical Data*, p. 3. The figure given here is my own estimate, taking into account recent income increases from oil.

4. See Hirschman, *Journeys Toward Progress* and *Development Projects Observed*; Anderson, *Politics and Economic Policy in Latin America*.

Chapter 1

1. For discussion of these problems, see: Mikesell, *Foreign Investment in the Petroleum and Mineral Industries*, especially Parts I and III; Keohane and Nye, *Transnational Relations and World Politics*, especially the essays by Peter B. Evans and Raymond Vernon; Vernon, "Foreign Enterprises and Developing Nations in the Raw Materials Industries"; Tanzer, *The Political Economy of International Oil and the Underdeveloped Countries*; Penrose, *The Large International Firm in Developing Countries*; Lituak and Maule, *Foreign Investment*; Moran, "New Deal or Raw Deal in Raw Materials?"

2. Evans, in Keohane and Nye, p. 692.

3. Mikesell, *Foreign Investment*; Vernon, "Foreign Enterprises." For a different perspective, see Hirschman, *A Bias for Hope*, Ch. 11.

4. Schelling, *The Strategy of Conflict*; Iklé, *How Nations Negotiate*.

5. A more elaborate statement of this quid pro quo may be found in Huntington, "Transnational Organizations in World Politics."

6. On the world petroleum industry, see: Adelman, *The World Petroleum Market*; Hartshorn, *Politics and World Oil Economics*; Tanzer, *The Political Economy*; Penrose, *The Large International Firm*.

7. Tanzer, p. 42; Lee and Johnson, p. 32; Brown, p. 14. GNP from Venezuela, [9], 1971, p. 8.

8. Tanzer, p. 31.

9. Vernon, *Sovereignty at Bay*, is an example.

10. Creole Corp. Rept., 1972, pp. 11, 29. This publication contains basic data on the industry, compiled largely from the annual account of activities presented by the Ministry of Mines and Hydrocarbons to the Venezuelan Congress. Comparative data from Ruddle and Hamour, p. 298, and from Taylor, Hudson, et al., pp. 314–15.

11. Mikesell, *Foreign Investment*, and Vernon, "Foreign Enterprises," both analyze this shift of terms over time.

12. On profits, see: Adelman, *World Petroleum Market*; Tanzer, pp. 21–33. Profits of Venezuelan subsidiaries can be found in Appendix Table A.

13. My descriptions of political events in Venezuela draw on a large number of interpretive studies. Among the most useful are: Morón, *History of Venezuela*; Martz, *Acción Democrática: Evolution of a Modern Political Party in Venezuela*; Betancourt, *Venezuela: Política y Petróleo*; Brito Figueroa, *Ensayos de Historia Social Venezolana*; Rangel, *Capital y Desarrollo*; Blank, *Politics in Venezuela*; Bonilla and Silva Michelena, *A Strategy for Research on Social Policy*; Levine, *Conflict and Political Change in Venezuela*.

14. de Lourdes Acedo and Nones Mendoza, *La Generación Venezolana de 1928*; Martz, "Venezuela's 'Generation of '28.' "

15. For a review of this and subsequent episodes of military involvement in Venezuelan politics, see Rangel, *Los Andinos en el Poder* and *La Revolución de las Fantásias*. See also Burggraaff, *The Venezuelan Armed Forces in Politics*.

16. Powell, "Agrarian Reform or Agrarian Revolution in Venezuela?"; Martz, "Growth and Democratization of the Venezuelan Labor Movement."

17. Anderson, p. 282.

18. See Taylor, *The Venezuelan Golpe de Estado of 1958*.

19. Figures from Martz, *Venezuelan Elections*, III, 17; Blank, *Venezuela Election Factbook*, p. 35.

20. Blank, *Venezuela Election Factbook*, p. 38.

21. Ruddle and Hamour, p. 65.

22. For a comprehensive analysis of the 1968 election, see Myers, *Democratic Campaigning in Venezuela*.

23. In contrast to the rather extensive literature on political parties and elections, to date there is a paucity of studies of the private sector in Venezuela. Existing studies include: Rangel, *Capital y Desarrollo*, Vol.

III; Clark, "Fedecámaras." Much of the following, however, is based on the results of my own study (as yet unpublished) on the role of the private sector in development policymaking, conducted during 1973 while I was a visiting research professor at the Instituto de Estudios Superiores de Administración in Caracas.

24. See Mayobre, *Las Inversiones Extranjeras.*

25. See Fedecámaras, *Actuaciones del Directorio, 1972–73,* and *Aspectos Fundamentales de la Doctrina Económica de Fedecámaras.*

26. Scott, "Political Parties and Policymaking."

27. Jorge Ahumada, "Hypothesis for Diagnosing Social Change: The Venezuelan Case," in Bonilla and Silva Michelena, pp. 3–24.

28. Rangel, *Capital y Desarrollo,* III, 387.

29. For more on this, see Blank, "Planning and Political Development in Venezuela."

30. For a more detailed statement of this doctrinal orientation, see Pérez Alfonzo's own publications: *Venezuela y Su Petróleo: Lineamientos de Una Política; Petróleo: Jugo de la Tierra; Política Petrolera; El Pentágono Petrolero; Petróleo y Dependencia.* My comments are based on several hours of personal interviews with Pérez Alfonzo in 1966–67 and in 1973.

31. Pérez Alfonzo, *La Dinámica del Petróleo,* p. 75. For other analyses along these lines by Venezuelan economists, see Malave Mata, *Petróleo y Desarrollo Económico en Venezuela;* Maza Zavala, *Venezuela: Una Economía Dependiente.* See also Appendix Table C, p. 183.

32. Colin Clark, *National Income and Outlay.*

Chapter 2

1. A number of books have been written about the competition for oil and the conditions surrounding it. See: Denny, *We Fight for Oil;* Fisher, *Oil Imperialism;* Davenport and Cooke, *The Oil Trusts and Anglo-American Relations.* There are also many historical surveys of the growth of the oil industry in Venezuela and public policy responses to it. Among the most useful are: Lieuwen, *Petroleum in Venezuela: A History;* Betancourt, *Venezuela: Política y Petróleo;* Rangel, *Capital y Desarrollo,* Vol. II; Martínez, *Cronología del Petróleo Venezolano;* Vallenilla, *Auge, Declinación y Porvenir del Petróleo Venezolano;* and the various books of Pérez Alfonzo, especially *Petróleo y Dependencia.* Production and export figures appear in a number of sources: Martínez, *Cronología,* pp. 53, 64; Lieuwen, pp. 38–44. See also Appendix Table B.

2. For further financial details on this early period, see: A. Parra, "The Petroleum Industry and Its Fiscal Obligations in Venezuela"; Gertrud G. Edwards, "Foreign Petroleum Companies and the State in Venezuela," in Mikesell, pp. 101–29.

3. Lieuwen, *passim.*

4. *Ibid.,* p. 46. Income figures from Appendix Table B.

5. Martínez, *Cronología,* p. 72.

6. *Ibid.,* pp. 70–85.

7. Mikesell, p. 105.

8. For more detail on this period, see Lieuwen, pp. 70–100.

9. Wood, pp. 264–65.

10. Betancourt, *Venezuela*, pp. 130–50.

11. Martínez, *Cronología*, pp. 90–96.

12. For further details, see: Lieuwen, pp. 95–97; Hartshorn, *Oil Companies*, pp. 272–73; Mikesell, p. 107; Martínez, *Cronología*, pp. 93–94.

13. Betancourt, *Venezuela*, pp. 139–41.

14. See Medina Angarita, *Cuatro Años*, especially pp. 88–100.

15. Betancourt, *Venezuela*, pp. 935–36.

16. Pérez Alfonzo claimed that the Medina government did little to certify compliance with the income tax laws, and stated that the supervision of company accounts had progressed little since the regime of Gumersindo Torres, who was the first to begin actually *counting* the income received from the companies each year. Pérez Alfonzo, *Pentágono Petrolero*, pp. 102–6.

17. Pérez Alfonzo, *Venezuela y Su Petróleo*, p. 26.

18. Pérez Alfonzo, *Petróleo y Dependencia*, p. 22.

19. For a detailed but admittedly biased description of the conduct of policy under Pérez Jiménez, see Betancourt, *Venezuela*, Part VI.

20. For further details, see A. Parra, "The Petroleum Industry," and Mikesell, p. 106.

21. Martínez, *Cronología*, p. 144.

22. Betancourt, *Venezuela*, p. 777.

Chapter 3

1. *El Nacional*, 26.iv.58, p. 1; 23.vi.58, p. 1.

2. Betancourt, *Venezuela*, p. 741. *El Nacional*, 31.vii.58, p. 1; 12.xii.58, p. 1.

3. For details, see *El Nacional*, 23.xii.58, p. 1; 24.xii.58, p. 54.

4. *Ibid.*, 24.xii.58, p. 54.

5. *Ibid.*, 26.xii.58, p. 1.

6. Interview with Pérez Alfonzo, Jan. 1967.

7. For the CVP's chartering statute, see *El Universal*, 22.iv.60, p. 4. For Pérez Alfonzo's plans, see his comments in a university forum held on the subject and reported in *El Nacional*, 27.vii.62.

8. Creole Corp. Rept., 1973, p. 8.

9. *El Nacional*, 8.iv.59, p. 1. See Appendix Table D for prices. For further information on Venezuela's response, see Pérez Alfonzo, *Venezuela y Su Petróleo*, pp. 56–70; and Venezuela, [11], pp. 107–10.

10. See Resolution No. 557 of the Ministry of Mines, reprinted in Venezuela, [11], pp. 95–96.

11. This description of the Commission and its activities is based in part on interviews with Pérez Alfonzo, Rómulo Betancourt, members of the Commission staff and the other sections of the Ministry of Mines, and executives of the major oil companies operating in Venezuela.

12. A. Parra, "Oil and Stability," p. 14.

13. Venezuela, [11], pp. 109–10.

14. Information on this and later meetings was obtained in interviews with Pérez Alfonzo and Eduardo Acosta Hermoso, among others. For press commentary on the conference, see *El Nacional*, 25.iv.59, p. 1. See also Acosta Hermoso, *Análisis Histórico de la OPEC*.

15. As Hartshorn has pointed out (*Oil Companies*, p. 300), there have been many similar proposals to control the world oil market. During World War II, for example, the U.S. and Britain proposed a government-managed international cartel; but the project fell through because of opposition from the companies and the U.S. Senate. A number of other proposals in the 1950's suffered similar fates. For further information on the origins of the OPEC, see Acosta Hermoso, *Análisis Histórico*; Rouhani, *A History of OPEC*; Mikdashi, *The Community of Oil-Exporting Countries*.

16. Venezuela, [11], p. 13. See also *El Nacional*, 12.ix.60, 16.ix.60.

17. *N.Y. Times*, 17.i.61, p. 61.

18. For discussions of the internal conflicts and problems in OPEC, see Hirst, *Oil and Public Opinion*; Mikdashi, *The Community of Oil Exporting Countries*. Lack of will aside, OPEC countries were also technically unprepared to handle the problems involved in designing and monitoring an effective prorationing system. For an excellent analysis of these problems, see Mikdashi's Chapter 5.

19. *Newsweek*, 11.i.65, p. 65.

20. Hirst, pp. 112–13.

21. *Economist*, 23.i.65, p. 352.

22. *Ibid.*, p. 351.

23. *N.Y. Times*, 28.xii.64, p. 38.

24. For more detailed discussions of U.S. oil import policy, especially as it relates to Venezuela, see: Adelman, pp. 148–55; Balestrini, "Las Restricciones Petroleras"; Venezuela, [14], *Mesa Redonda*; U.S. Cabinet, *The Oil Import Question*; Wilkins, "Effects on the Economy of Venezuela of Actions by the International Petroleum Industry and the United States Regulating Agencies."

25. *United States Statutes at Large* 69 (Washington, D.C.: G.P.O., 1955), p. 1966.

26. *N.Y. Times*, 26.i.58, sect. III, p. 1; 6.iv.58, sect. III, p. 1 (columns by J. H. Carmichael).

27. The act had been amended in 1958; *United States Statutes at Large* 72 (Washington, D.C.: G.P.O., 1959), I, 678–79. For details of the regulations, see U.S. Presidential Proclamation 3279, "Adjusting Imports of Petroleum and Petroleum Products into the United States," *Federal Register* 24, No. 42, pp. 178–84.

28. *N.Y. Times*, 11.iii.59, p. 57.

29. *El Nacional*, 12.iii.59, p. 48.

30. Pérez Alfonzo, *Venezuela y Su Petróleo*, pp. 63–64. *El Nacional*, 3.v.59, p. 1; 6.v.59, p. 1.

31. Pérez Alfonzo, *Venezuela y Su Petróleo*, pp. 62–64.

32. See *N.Y. Times*, 8.vi.61, sect. III, p. 1.

33. Interview with Rómulo Betancourt, 6.ii.67.

34. *El Nacional*, 2.vi.61, p. 1; 9.vi.61, p. 1; 14.vi.61, p. 1.

35. *El Universal*, 3.iv.60, p. 1; Peter R. Odell, "Oil and State in Latin America," *International Affairs* 40 (Oct. 1964), p. 667.

36. *N.Y. Times*, 10.xii.60, p. 39.

37. Fedecámaras's criticism has been repeated over and over again since 1961, and can be found in most of the organization's publications. My discussion draws chiefly on *Las Principales Actuaciones, 1961–62* (presented before the 18th Annual Assembly, held in Merida in 1962). See especially "Documento Preliminar de Fedecáras [sic] Sobre el Plan de Medidas Fiscales," pp. 29–38; "La Federación Venezolana de Cámaras y Asociaciones de Comercio y Producción ante las Recientes Modificaciones Cambiarias," pp. 51–60. For press comment, see *El Nacional*, 29.v.62, p. 1. The most elaborate analysis of all was produced in the spring of 1966 under the direction of Pedro R. Tinoco as a result of a decision by the 22d Annual Assembly to publish under the same cover the various papers that were presented at the meeting. See Tinoco, *Análisis de la Política Petrolera Venezolana.*

38. In 1966 Uslar Pietri published *Petróleo de Vida o Muerte*, a collection of his writings and public statements on the topic of petroleum. It is the best source, outside the newspapers, for statements of his position on the subject. The documents collected range from 1955 to 1966. Especially interesting is the transcript of a television debate between Uslar and Pérez Alfonzo that took place in May 1963, very near the peak of the antigovernment criticism in this first phase. The following discussions draws heavily on the information that came out in this direct confrontation.

39. The best information on production cost is found in Adelman, Chapter 2 and its appendixes. Adelman uses sophisticated measures of long-run supply costs, and these can be found in his Table II-8 (p. 76). The production cost of U.S. oil, it might be noted, is nearly three times the Venezuelan figure.

40. Adelman, pp. 69, 146. My emphasis.

Chapter 4

1. *El Nacional*, 18.xi.66, p. 1.

2. Pérez Alfonzo, *Petróleo y Dependencia*, p. 120.

3. See Tinoco, *Análisis.*

4. Calculations based on information provided in Pérez Alfonzo, *Pentágono Petrolero*, pp. 128–29.

5. Shoup, et al., p. 5.

6. For some of Uslar's best, see: *Petróleo de Vida o Muerte*; *El Nacional*, 7.viii.66, p. 1, 9.viii.66, p. 1; *El Universal*, 25.viii.66, p. 1. For Caracas Chamber statements, see *El Universal*, 26.viii.66, p. 1; *El Nacional*, 7.ix.66.

7. *El Universal*, 23.ix.66, p. 1.

8. *El Nacional*, 15.viii.66, p. 1.
9. *El Universal*, 8.ix.66, p. 1.
10. *El Nacional*, 12.xi.66, p. 1.
11. *El Universal*, 29.viii.66, p. 1.
12. My description, unless otherwise indicated, is based on Leoni's speech as given in *El Nacional*, 29.ix.66, pp. D1–D2, and the elaboration by Minister Pérez Guerrero, *ibid.*, 8.x.66, p. C8, as well as on interviews with persons involved.
13. *El Nacional*, 27.x.67, p. D1.
14. *Ibid.*, 29.x.66, p. D1.
15. *El Universal*, 4.x.66.
16. *El Nacional*, 29.ix.66, p. 1.
17. *Ibid.*, 15.xi.66, p. D1.
18. *Ibid.*, 31.xii.66, p. D1.
19. For Pérez Alfonzo's arguments in favor of the reform, see *Pentágono Petrolero*, pp. 117–39; for his comments on the outcome of the crisis and company profits, see *Petróleo y Dependencia*, pp. 55–64, 119–27.
20. Pérez Alfonzo, *Petróleo y Dependencia*, p. 127.
21. Interview with Ministry of Mines official Alirio A. Parra, 7.vi.73.
22. Pérez Alfonzo's assessment of the agreement, which is a bit short on detailed calculations to back up his estimates of loss to the government, can be found in *Petróleo y Dependencia*, pp. 115–210. The charges are summarized on pp. 165–68. The text of the agreement is in *Memoria, 1968* (Caracas: Ministerio de Minas e Hidrocarburos, 1969).

Chapter 5

1. My information on the controversy over service contracts, as well as on subsequent struggles in the legislature, is based in part on interviews with key participants: Pérez Alfonzo; Arturo Hernández Grisanti, Enrique Tejera París, and other legislators; company and government representatives; and journalists who covered the events.
2. For further details, see *Petroleum Intelligence Weekly*, 20.vii.70. The terms were published in Venezuela, Congreso Nacional, *Gaceta Oficial*, 10.ix.70. Administration of exploration and production was to be supervised by joint CVP-company committees.
3. *Petroleum Intelligence Weekly*, 20.iv.70.
4. *Ibid.*, 2.viii.71.
5. *Latin America*, 3.x.69, p. 319.
6. My description of the political events leading up to the tax reform is based on journalistic accounts and on interviews with persons involved. Also helpful was a chronological account of the events prepared by Mariluz Bascones R. and Hilda Herrera, two master's candidates at the Instituto de Estudios Superiores de Administración, and presented in their paper "Análisis de un Proceso de toma de decisiones: Aumento de la tributación y distribución del ingreso" (1973).
7. *Latin America*, 27.x.70, p. 378.

8. W. J. Levy, p. 654; Adelman, p. 251.

9. Interview with Pérez Alfonzo, 20.vi.73.

10. Interviews with company executives and with Kim Fuad, oil specialist and *Petroleum Intelligence Weekly* stringer in Venezuela.

11. My conclusions here are based on interviews with private-sector representatives and oil company officials, as well as on a careful review of Fedecámaras and Petroleum Chamber activities. Further commentary on this issue, including a textual analysis of private-sector position papers on oil policy, may be found in Vallenilla, pp. 390–405. Since he served for many years as president of the Venezuelan Association of Executives, Vallenilla's own critical comments on the past passivity of Fedecámaras in allowing the foreign companies to determine its positions on oil is one of the clearest statements of the reorientation alluded to: "The petroleum industry being an *activity of public interest and fundamental economic importance for the country, controlled by foreign interests,* it was not, nor is it, proper that Fedecámaras—a Venezuelan entrepreneurial guild organization of great national import—echo positions representing the petroleum companies, positions that were, at the very least, in need of some discussion" (pp. 391–92, my emphasis).

12. Interview with Kim Fuad, 16.iv.73.

13. For company statements and public reaction to the bill, see *El Nacional,* various issues between 7.xii.70 and 18.xii.70.

Chapter 6

1. For the best information on this debate, see *Proceedings of the Second Venezuelan Oil Congress,* 4.xii.70 (mimeo.), especially the papers presented by Alvaro Silva Calderon and Juan José Navarrete Senior, by Aristides Rangel and Luis Guillermo Arcay, and by former Minister of Development Manuel Egaña. The proceedings were covered in *El Nacional* and *El Universal* during the first week in December. Information on the debates was also provided to me by Kim Fuad.

2. For further details, see *Venezuela,* [9], 1971, pp. ix–xiii; *Petroleum Intelligence Weekly,* 28.vi.71.

3. *Petroleum Intelligence Weekly,* 14.vi.71.

4. *Latin America,* 16.vii.71, p. 231; *Petroleum Intelligence Weekly,* 28.vi.71.

5. *Petroleum Intelligence Weekly,* 28.vi.71.

6. *Latin America,* 23.vii.71, pp. 236–37.

7. *Ibid.,* 31.iii.72, p. 103.

8. Fuad, "Oil Penalties," p. 10.

9. Decree 832, 17.xii.71. Venezuela, [9], 1971, pp. xvii–xviii.

10. *Petroleum Intelligence Weekly,* 23.iv.73.

11. *Ibid.,* 3.i.72.

12. *Ibid.,* 28.ii.72.

13. *Latin America,* 4.ii.72, p. 33.

14. *Petroleum Intelligence Weekly,* 16.x.72.

15. See Fuad, "The Haunting Prospect."

16. For further details, see *Petroleum Intelligence Weekly*, 22.iii.71 and 4.x.71.

17. For the text of the law, see Venezuela, [9], 1971, pp. xiv–xv. For further comments, see *Petroleum Intelligence Weekly*, 30.viii.71 and 4.x.71.

18. The best analysis I have seen of the problems involved is that in Mikdashi, Ch. 5.

19. For the Government's position on this, see Venezuela, Presidencia, *Cuarto Mensaje del Presidente de la República Dr. Rafael Caldera al Congreso Nacional, 12 Marzo, 1973* (Caracas: Oficina Central de Información, 1973), pp. 201–3. See also *Petroleum Intelligence Weekly*, 29.iii. 71, 15.xi.71, 28.ii.72, and 25.ix.72, among others.

20. *Latin America*, 26.vi.70, p. 204.

21. *Petroleum Intelligence Weekly*, 11.i.71.

22. *Latin America*, 18.ii.72, pp. 54–55.

23. U.S. Cabinet, *The Oil Import Question*, p. 10.

24. See Table 5, p. 68.

25. See Akins, "The Oil Crisis."

26. Martínez, *Recursos Hidrocarburos*, p. 119. The study is J. A. Galarvis and H. Velarde, "Geological Study and Preliminary Evaluation of Potential Reserves of Heavy Oil of the Orinoco Tar Belt, Eastern Venezuelan Basin," a paper presented at the Seventh World Petroleum Congress (Mexico, 1967) and published in its *Proceedings*, I, 229–34.

27. *El Nacional*, 16.v.73, p. 1.

28. Akins, "The Oil Crisis."

29. *El Universal*, 1.iv.73, p. 1; 23.iv.73.

30. *Daily Journal* (Caracas), 28.iii.73, p. 1.

31. Richard M. Nixon, "The President's Message to the Congress Announcing Executive Actions and Proposing Enactment of Bills to Provide for Energy Needs, April 18, 1973," *Weekly Compilation of Presidential Documents* 9, No. 16 (23.iv.73), pp. 389–406.

32. *El Nacional*, 8.v.73, p. D1.

33. *Latin America*, Christmas 1973, p. 409.

34. Quoted in Norman Gall, "Changing the Guard in Venezuela," *Wall Street Journal*, 3.i.74, p. 10.

Chapter 7

1. One example of this attitude is Vallenilla, *Auge, Declinación, y Porvenir*, especially, pp. 294–314.

2. Lindblom, "The Science of Muddling Through," *Public Administration Review* 19 (1959), pp. 79–88, and *The Intelligence of Democracy: Decision-Making Through Mutual Adjustment* (New York: Free Press, 1965); Hirschman, *Journeys Toward Progress.*

3. Hirschman, *Development Projects*, Ch. 1.

4. Leff, *Economic Policymaking in Brazil* (New York: Wiley, 1968).

5. See Wolfgang Stolper and Wilfred Malenbaum, "Political Ideology and Economic Progress," *World Politics* 12 (Apr. 1960), pp. 413–21.

6. Moran, "The Alliance for Progress." Similar tendencies existed in

the relationship of domestic and foreign elites with regard to the International Petroleum Company in Peru. See Pinelo, *The Multinational Corporation*, Conclusion.

7. See Schmitter's provocative essay "Paths to Political Development in Latin America."

8. For an assessment of the degree of institutionalization of such patterns in Venezuela, see Levine, *Conflict and Political Change in Venezuela*.

9. The most important of these is the study completed by an independent UN Mission to Venezuela in the late fall of 1971. It was prepared for the national planning agency Cordiplan under the direction of Dr. Meir Merhav. Once completed, however, its circulation was restricted by the government. See Merhav, *Posibilidades de Exportación*. Also useful here is an article by William G. Harris, "The Impact of the Petroleum Export Industry on the Pattern of Venezuelan Economic Development," in Mikesell, pp. 129–57.

10. See Merhav, *Posibilidades de Exportación*.

11. This conclusion is based on a review of four studies of income distribution in Venezuela for the years 1957, 1962, 1968, and 1970. They are: Shoup, et al., p. 37; William R. Cline, *Potential Effects of Income Distribution on Economic Growth: Latin American Cases* (New York: Praeger, 1972), pp. 107–8, 208; United Nations Economic Commission for Latin America, *Economic Survey of Latin America, 1968* (New York, 1970), p. 13; Mariluz Bascones R. and Hilda Herrera, "Análisis de un Proceso de Toma de Decisiones: Aumento de la Tributación y Distribución del Ingreso" (unpubl. paper, Instituto de Estudios Superiores de Administración, 1973), graphs 2 and 3, between pp. 7 and 8. The last study takes the categories suggested in the UN study and uses 1970 income data provided by the *Informe* of the Central Bank of Venezuela. One further source, Taylor, Hudson, et al., p. 263, comes to a conclusion compatible with those suggested in the above sources.

12. See Bascones and Herrera, *Análisis*.

13. United Nations, p. 13.

14. For some representative estimates, see: Martínez, *Recursos de Hidrocarburos en Venezuela*, pp. 75–88; Alirio A. Parra, "La Demanda Mundial," p. 12; Venezuela, [9], various years; Venezuela, [13], *Plan de la Nación: 1965–68*, p. 188.

Bibliography

Acción y Reacción: Compilación Hemerográfica. Tema: El Petróleo Vene-zolano. Caracas: Asociación Pro-Venezuela, 1973.

Acosta Hermoso, Eduardo. *Análisis Histórico de la OPEC.* 2 vols. Cara-cas: Editorial Arte, 1969–70.

———— *La Comisión Ecónomica de la OPEC.* Caracas: Editorial Arte, 1971.

———— *Este Petróleo es Venezolano.* Caracas: Editorial Arte, 1964.

———— *Fundamentos de Una Política Petrolera Racional para Vene-zuela.* Mérida: Universidad de los Andes, 1967.

———— "La Organización de Países Exportadores de Petróleo," *La Esfera* (Caracas), 14.iii.62.

———— "The Venezuelan Coordinating Commission for the Conserva-tion and Commerce of Hydrocarbons." Paper presented to the Third Arab Petroleum Congress, Alexandria, 16–22.x.61 (mimeo).

Adelman, M. A. *The World Petroleum Market.* Baltimore: Johns Hop-kins Press, 1972.

Akins, James. "The Oil Crisis: This Time the Wolf is Here," *Foreign Affairs* 51, No. 3 (spring 1973): 462–90.

Alexander, Robert J. *The Venezuelan Democratic Revolution.* New Brunswick, N.J.: Rutgers University Press, 1964.

Anderson, Charles W. *Politics and Economic Policy in Latin America: Governing Restless Nations.* Princeton, N.J.: Van Nostrand, 1967.

Balestrini C., César. *La Industria Petrolera en América Latina.* Caracas: Universidad Central de Venezuela, 1971.

———— "Las Restricciones Petroleras en los Estados Unidos," *Economía y Ciencias Sociales* 7 (Jan.–Mar. 1965): 10–25.

Baloyra, Enrique A. "Oil Policies and Budgets in Venezuela, 1938–1968," *Latin American Research Review* 9, No. 2 (summer 1974): 28–72.

Betancourt, Rómulo. *Diálogo con el País.* Caracas: Imprenta Nacional, 1963.

———— *Posición y Doctrina: Conferencias y Discursos.* Caracas: Editorial Cordillera, 1959.

———— *Problemas Venezolanos.* Santiago: n.p., 1940.

——— *Rómulo Betancourt: Pensamiento y Acción.* Mexico City: V. de
Silva, 1951.
——— *Venezuela: Política y Petróleo,* 2d ed. Caracas: Editorial Sende-
ros, 1969.
Blank, David E. *Planning and Political Development in Venezuela.*
Unpubl. dissertation, Columbia University, 1969.
——— *Politics in Venezuela.* Boston: Little, Brown, 1973.
——— ed. *Venezuela Election Factbook.* Washington, D.C.: Institute
for Comparative Study of Political Systems, 1968.
Boletín Informativo. Caracas: Cámara de la Industria del Petróleo,
yearly.
Bonilla, Frank, and José A. Silva Michelena, eds. *A Strategy for Research
on Social Policy, I: Studying the Venezuelan Polity.* Cambridge, Mass.:
M.I.T. Press, 1967.
Brito Figueroa, Federico. *Ensayos de Historia Social Venezolana.* Cara-
cas: Universidad Central de Venezuela, 1962.
Brown, Lester R. *The Interdependence of Nations.* New York: Foreign
Policy Assoc., 1972.
Burggraaff, Winfield J. *The Venezuelan Armed Forces in Politics, 1915–
1959.* Columbia, Mo.: University of Missouri Press, 1972.
Cardoso, Fernando Enrique. "Associated-Dependent Development: The-
oretical and Practical Implications," in Alfred Stepan, ed., *Authori-
tarian Brazil: Origins, Policies, and Future.* New Haven, Conn.: Yale
Univ. Press, 1973.
Carrillo Batalla, Tomás Enrique. *Política Fiscal.* Caracas: Ediciones Dis-
trito Federal, 1968.
Chilcote, Ronald H. "A Critical Synthesis of the Dependency Litera-
ture," *Latin American Perspectives* 1, No. 1 (spring 1974): 4–29.
Clark, Colin. *National Income and Outlay.* London: Macmillan, 1937.
Clark, Robert P., Jr. *Fedecámaras en el Proceso de la Formulación de
Política en Venezuela.* Caracas: Centro de Investigaciones Adminis-
trativos y Sociales de la Comisión de Administración Pública, 1966.
——— "The LAFTA Debate in Venezuela: A Test-Case in Consensus-
Building." Unpubl. dissertation, Johns Hopkins School of Advanced
International Studies, 1966.
Cockcroft, James D., A. G. Frank, and Dale L. Johnson. *Dependence and
Underdevelopment: Latin America's Political Economy.* Garden City,
N.Y.: Anchor, 1972.
Cohen, Benjamin J. *The Question of Imperialism: The Political Econ-
omy of Dominance and Dependence.* New York: Basic Books, 1973.
Creole Petroleum Corporation Report. *Data on Petroleum and Economy
of Venezuela.* Caracas: Creole Petroleum Corp., yearly.
Davenport, E. H., and H. Russell Cooke. *The Oil Trusts and Anglo-
American Relations.* New York: Macmillan, 1924.
de Lourdes Acedo de Sucre, María, and Carmen Margarita Nonès Mendoza. *La Generación Venezolana de 1928: Estudio de Una Élite Política.* Caracas: Ariel, 1967.

Denny, Ludwell. *We Fight for Oil.* New York: Knopf, 1928.

Dos Santos, Theotonio. "The Structure of Dependence," *American Economic Review, Papers and Proceedings* 60 (May 1970): 231–36.

Engler, Robert. *The Politics of Oil: A Study of Private Power and Democratic Directions.* New York: Macmillan, 1961.

Fedecámaras (Federación Venezolana de Cámaras y Asociaciones de Comercio y Producción). *Actuaciones del Directoria.* Caracas. Published annually.

———— *Aspectos Fundamentales de la Doctrina Económica de Fedecámaras.* Caracas, 1973.

———— *La Industria Petrolera Venezolana en la Década del '60: Situación Actual y Perspectivas.* Maracay, 1970.

———— *Las Principales Actuaciones, 1961–62.* Presented before the 18th Annual Assembly in Merida, 1962.

Feinstein, Otto. "Foreign Investment and the Development of Venezuela." Unpubl. dissertation, University of Chicago, 1965.

Fisher, Luis. *Oil Imperialism.* New York: International, 1926.

Foro Presupuesto Nacional y Finanzas Públicas. Caracas: Asociación Venezolana de Ejecutivos, 1971.

Frank, Helmut J. *Crude Oil Prices in the Middle East: A Study in Oligopolistic Price Behavior.* New York: Praeger, 1966.

Fuad, Kim. "The Haunting Prospect of Permanent Penalties," *Business Venezuela,* Jan.–Feb. 1973: 15–18.

———— "Oil Penalties: Damned if You Do, Damned if You Don't," *Business Venezuela* 18 (1972): 9–14.

Gilmore, Robert L. *Caudillism and Militarism in Venezuela, 1810–1910.* Athens, O.: Ohio University Press, 1964.

Gómez, Henry, and Ignacio Olcoz. "The Venezuelan Petroleum Industry: A Case Study in Economic Innovation and Adaptation." Paper presented at the 1966 National Fall Conference of the American Marketing Association, Bloomington, Ind., Sept. 1966 (mimeo).

Harris, William G. "The Impact of the Petroleum Export Industry on the Pattern of Venezuelan Economic Development." Unpubl. dissertation, University of Oregon, 1967.

Hartshorn, J. E. *Politics and World Oil Economics.* New York: Praeger, 1962.

———— *Oil Companies and Governments.* New York: Praeger, 1968.

Hirschman, Albert O. *A Bias for Hope: Essays on Development and Latin America.* New Haven, Conn.: Yale University Press, 1971.

———— *Development Projects Observed.* Washington, D.C.: Brookings Institution, 1968.

———— *Journeys Toward Progress: Studies of Economic Policy Making in Latin America.* New York: Twentieth Century Fund, 1963.

———— *National Power and the Structure of Foreign Trade.* Los Angeles: University of California Press, 1945.

Hirst, David. *Oil and Public Opinion in the Middle East.* New York: Praeger, 1966.

Huntington, Samuel P. "Transnational Organizations in World Politics," *World Politics* 25, No. 3 (Apr. 1973): 333–69.

Iklé, Fred. *How Nations Negotiate.* New York: Harper & Row, 1964.

Issawi, Charles, and Muhammed Yaganeh. *The Economics of Middle Eastern Oil.* New York: Praeger, 1962.

Keohane, Robert O., and Joseph S. Nye, Jr., eds. *Transnational Relations and World Politics.* Special issue of *International Organization* 25, No. 3 (summer 1971).

Kindleberger, Charles, ed. *The International Corporation.* Cambridge, Mass.: M.I.T. Press, 1970.

Labouisse, Henry R., et al. *The Economic Development of Venezuela.* Baltimore: Johns Hopkins Press, 1961.

Lee, Robert D., Jr., and Ronald W. Johnson. *Public Budgeting Systems.* Baltimore: University Park, 1973.

Lenczowski, George. *Oil and State in the Middle East.* Ithaca, N.Y.: Cornell University Press, 1960.

Levin, Jonathan. *The Export Economies: Their Pattern of Development in Historical Perspective.* Cambridge, Mass.: Harvard University Press, 1960.

Levine, Daniel H. *Conflict and Political Change in Venezuela.* Princeton, N.J.: Princeton University Press, 1973.

Levy, Fred D. *Economic Planning in Venezuela.* New York: Praeger, 1968.

Levy, Walter J. "Oil Power," *Foreign Affairs* 49, No. 4 (July 1971): 652–69.

Lieuwen, Edwin. *Petroleum in Venezuela: A History.* Berkeley: University of California Press, 1954.

Lituak, Isaiah A., and Christopher J. Maule. *Foreign Investment: The Experience of Host Countries.* New York: Praeger, 1970.

López Contreras, Eleazar. *Proceso Político-Social, 1928–1936,* 2d ed. Caracas: Editorial Ancora, 1955.

Luzardo, Rudolfo. *Notas Histórico-Económicas, 1928–63.* Caracas: Editorial Sucre, 1963.

Magallanes, Manuel Vicente. *Partidos Políticos Venezolanos.* Caracas: Tipografía Vargas, 1960.

Malave Mata, Héctor. *Petróleo y Desarrollo Económico de Venezuela.* Caracas: Universidad Central de Venezuela, 1962.

Martínez, Aníbal R. *Cronología del Petróleo Venezolano.* Caracas: Ediciones Librería Historia, 1970.

———— *Nuestro Petróleo, Defensa de un Recurso Agotable.* Madrid: Gráficas Minerva, 1963.

———— *Petróleo: Seis Ensayos.* Caracas: Edreca, 1971.

———— *Recursos Hidrocarburos de Venezuela.* Caracas: Edreca, 1972.

Martz, John D. *Acción Democrática: Evolution of a Modern Political Party in Venezuela.* Princeton, N.J.: Princeton University Press, 1966.

———— "The Growth and Democratization of the Venezuelan Labor Movement," *Inter-American Economic Affairs* 17 (autumn 1963).

────── *The Venezuelan Elections of 1963*. Washington, D.C.: Institute for Comparative Study of Political Systems, 1964.

────── "Venezuela's 'Generation of '28': The Genesis of Political Democracy," *Journal of Inter-American Studies* 6 (Jan. 1964).

Mayobre, José Antonio. *Las Inversiones Extranjeras en Venezuela*. Caracas: Monte Avila, 1970.

Maza Zavala, D. F. *Venezuela: Una Economía Dependiente*. Caracas: Universidad Central de Venezuela, 1964.

Medina Angarita, Isaías. *Cuatro Años de Democracia*. Caracas: Pensamiento Vivo, 1963.

────── *La Nueva Lucha y la Acción Nueva*. Caracas: Oficina Nacional de Presa, 1943.

Mejía Alarcon, Pedro Esteban. *La Industria del Petróleo en Venezuela*. Caracas: Universidad Central de Venezuela, 1972.

Merhav, Meir. *Posibilidades de Exportación de la Industria Venezolana: Informe Preliminar*. Caracas: Cordiplan, 1971.

Mikdashi, Zuhayr. *The Community of Oil-Exporting Countries: A Study in Governmental Cooperation*. Ithaca, N.Y.: Cornell University Press, 1972.

Mikesell, Raymond F., ed. *Foreign Investment in the Petroleum and Mineral Industries: Case Studies of Investor-Host Country Relations*. Baltimore: Johns Hopkins Press, 1970.

Montiel Ortega, Leonardo. *Nacionalismo e Industrialización: Programa para el Rescate del Petróleo y para el Desarrollo de las Industrias Básicas en Venezuela*. Caracas: Pensamiento Vivo, 1962.

────── *Petróleo y Soberanía*. Caracas: Ediciones Congreso, 1971.

Moran, Theodore J. "The Alliance for Progress and 'The Foreign Copper Companies and Their Local Conservative Allies' in Chile, 1955–70," *Inter-American Economic Affairs* 25 (spring 1972): 3–25.

────── "New Deal or Raw Deal in Raw Materials," *Foreign Policy* 5 (winter 1971–72): 119–36.

────── "Transnational Strategies of Protection and Defense by Multinational Corporations: Spreading the Risk and Raising the Cost for Nationalization in Natural Resources," *International Organization* 27, No. 2 (spring 1973): 273–87.

Morón, Guillermo. *A History of Venezuela*. New York: Roy, 1963.

Myers, David J. *Democratic Campaigning in Venezuela: Caldera's Victory*. Caracas: Fundación La Salle, 1973.

Nash, Gerald D. *United States Oil Policy, 1890–1964: Business and Government in Twentieth-Century America*. Pittsburgh: University of Pittsburgh Press, 1965.

OAS (Organization of American States). *América en Cifras, 1972*. Washington, D.C.: OAS, 1972.

Parra, Alirio A. "Oil and Stability." Paper presented to the Third Arab Petroleum Congress in Alexandria, Oct. 16–22, 1961 (mimeo).

────── "The Petroleum Industry and Its Fiscal Obligations in Venezuela." Paper presented to the First Congress of the Society of Petroleum Engineers of Venezuela, Mar. 24, 1962 (mimeo).

———— "Some Aspects of the International Price Structure of Crude Petroleum." Unpubl. thesis, George Washington University, 1957.

Parra, Francisco R. "A Role for OPEC," *World Petroleum* 32 (Aug. 1961): 28–31.

———— "Venezuela's Changing Oil Policy," *World Petroleum* 31 (Dec. 1960): 41–42.

Penrose, Edith T. *The Large International Firm in Developing Countries: The International Petroleum Industry.* London: Allen & Unwin, 1968.

Pérez Alfonzo, Juan Pablo. *Exposición del Ministro de Minas e Hidrocarburos al Congreso Nacional.* Caracas: n.p., 1959.

———— *La Dinámica del Petróleo en el Progreso de Venezuela.* Caracas: Universidad Central de Venezuela, 1965.

———— *El Pentágono Petrolero.* Caracas: Ediciones Revista Política, 1967.

———— *Petróleo y Dependencia.* Caracas: Síntesis Dos Mil, 1971.

———— *Petróleo, Jugo de la Tierra.* Caracas: Ediciones del Arte, 1961.

———— "El Petróleo Ruso No Es una Amenaza para Venezuela," *Mundo Económico* 8 (Sept. 1961): 7–10.

———— *Política Petrolera.* Caracas: Imprenta Nacional, 1962.

———— *Venezuela y Su Petróleo.* Caracas: Imprenta Nacional, 1962.

Pérez Guerrero, Manuel. "Política Petrolera Venezolana," *Cuadernos de la Corporación Venezolano de Fomento* 1 (Apr.–June 1964): 149–65.

El Petróleo y la Economía Venezolana. Caracas: Asociación Venezolana de Ejecutivos, 1968.

Pinelo, Adalberto J. *The Multinational Corporation as a Force in Latin American Politics: A Case Study of the International Petroleum Company in Peru.* New York: Praeger, 1973.

Powell, John D. "Agrarian Reform or Agrarian Revolution in Venezuela?," in Arpad von Lazar and R. R. Kaufman, eds., *Reform and Revolution.* Boston: Allyn & Bacon, 1969.

Rangel, Domingo Alberto. *Los Andinos en el Poder.* Merida: Talleres Gráficos Universitarios, 1966.

———— *Capital y Desarrollo. I: La Venezuela Agraria. II: El Rey de Petróleo. III: La Oligarquía del Dinero.* Caracas: Vols. I & II, Caracas: Universidad Central de Venezuela, 1969, 1970; Vol. III, Editorial Fuentes, 1972.

———— *La Revolución de la Fantásias.* Caracas: Ediciones Ofido, 1966.

Rouhani, Faud. *A History of OPEC.* New York: Praeger, 1971.

Ruddle, Kenneth, and M. Hamour, eds. *Statistical Abstract of Latin America.* Los Angeles: UCLA Latin American Center, 1971.

Salera, V. "Venezuelan Oil: Facts, Fancies, and Misinterpretations," *Inter-American Economic Affairs* 11 (spring 1958): 37–48.

Schelling, Thomas. *The Strategy of Conflict.* New York: Oxford, 1963.

Schmitter, Philippe. "Paths to Political Development in Latin America," in Douglas A. Chalmers, ed., *Changing Latin America: New Interpretations of Its Politics and Society.* New York: Proceedings of the Academy of Political Science 30, No. 4, Columbia University, 1972.

Scott, Robert. "Political Parties and Policymaking in Latin America," in Joseph LaPalombara and Myron Wiener, eds., *Political Parties and Political Development.* Princeton, N.J.: Princeton University Press, 1966.

Shaffer, Edward H. *The Oil Import Program of the United States: An Evaluation.* New York: Praeger, 1968.

Shelden, Ruth. "New Venezuelan Administration Reassures Oil Interests," *World Petroleum* 16 (Dec. 1945): 36–37.

Shoup, Carl S., et al. *The Fiscal System of Venezuela.* Baltimore: Johns Hopkins Press, 1959.

Sommerfeld, Raynard M. *Tax Reform and the Alliance for Progress.* Austin: University of Texas Press, 1966.

Statistical Data on the Latin American and Caribbean Countries. Washington, D.C.: Inter-American Development Bank, 1973.

Sunkel, Osvaldo. "National Development Policy and External Dependence in Latin America," *Journal of Development Studies* 6 (Oct. 1969): 23–48.

———— "Big Business and 'Dependencia,' " *Foreign Affairs* 50, No. 3 (Apr. 1972): 517–31.

Tanzer, Michael. *The Political Economy of International Oil and the Underdeveloped Countries.* Boston: Beacon, 1969.

Taylor, Charles L., Michael C. Hudson, et al. *World Handbook of Political and Social Indicators,* 2d ed. New Haven, Conn.: Yale University Press, 1972.

Taylor, Philip, Jr. *The Venezuelan Golpe de Estado of 1958; The Fall of Marcos Pérez Jiménez.* Washington, D.C.: Institute for Comparative Study of Political Systems, 1968.

Taylor, Wayne C., and John Lindeman. *United States Business Performance Abroad: The Case of Creole Petroleum Corporation in Venezuela.* Washington, D.C.: National Planning Association, 1955.

Tejera París, Enrique. "Los Precios Internacionales Justos y el Ejemplo de la OPEC," *Política* 16 (June–July 1961).

Tinoco, Pedro, R., ed. *Análisis de la Política Petrolera Venezolana.* Caracas: Fedecámaras, 1966.

United States Cabinet Task Force on Oil Import Control. *The Oil Import Question: A Report on the Relationship of Oil Imports to the National Security.* Washington, D.C.: Govt. Printing Office, 1970.

United States Oil Imports: A Case Study in International Trade. New York: Petroleum Industry Research Foundation, 1958.

Uslar Pietri, Arturo. *Petróleo de Vida o Muerte.* Caracas: n.p., 1966.

Vallenilla, Luis. *Auge, Declinación y Porvenir del Petróleo Venezolano.* Caracas: Editorial Tiempo Nuevo, 1973.

Venezuela, Government Agencies:
[1] Banco Central de Venezuela. *Informe Económico.* Caracas, yearly.
[2] Comisión de Administración Pública. *Informe sobre la Reforma de la Administración Pública Nacional,* Vols. I–II. Caracas: Imprenta Nacional, 1972.
[3] Congreso, Contraloria General. *Informe Anual.* Caracas: Imprenta Nacional, 1971.
[4] Ministerio de Fomento. Dirección General de Estadística y Censos Nacionales. *Anuario Estadístico de Venezuela.* Caracas. Yearly.
[5] Ministerio de Hacienda. *Compilación de Leyes, Decretos y Demas Disposiciones dictadas en Materia de Impuesto sobre la Renta, 1942–1966.* Caracas, 1968.
[6] ——— *Memoria Correspondiente al Ejercicio Anual.* Caracas, yearly.
[7] Ministerio de Minas e Hidrocarburos, División de Economía Petrolera. *Actividades Petroleras.* Caracas: Oficina Técnica de Hidrocarburos, 1965–66.
[8] ——— División de Economía Petrolera and División de Economía Minera (in collaboration). *Carta Semanal.* Caracas, 1958–73.
[9] ——— Dirección General. *Petróleo y Otros Datos Estadísticos.* Caracas: Oficina de Economía Petrolera, yearly.
[10] ——— *Petróleos Crudos de Venezuela y Otros Paises,* 2d ed. Caracas, 1959.
[11] ——— *Venezuela and the OPEC.* Caracas: Imprenta Nacional, 1961.
[12] Ministerio de Relaciones Exteriores, Dirección de Comercio Exterior y Consulados. *Inversiones de Capitales Extranjeros en Venezuela.* Caracas, 1963.
[13] Oficina Central de Coordinación y Planificación. *Plan de la Nación: 1963–1966.* Caracas, 1962 and subsequent plans.
[14] Universidad Central de Venezuela. *Mesa Redonda Sobre Restricciones Petroleras.* Caracas, 1958.

Vernon, Raymond. "Foreign Enterprises and Developing Nations in the Raw Materials Industries," *American Economic Review, Papers and Proceedings* 60 (May 1970): 122–31.
——— *Sovereignty at Bay: The Multinational Spread of U.S. Enterprises.* New York: Basic Books, 1971.
Wilkins, Billy Hughel. "Effects on the Economy of Venezuela of Actions by the International Petroleum Industry and the United States Regulating Agencies." Unpubl. dissertation, University of Texas, 1962.
——— "Foreign Investment and Internally Generated Funds: A Venezuelan Case," *Inter-American Economic Affairs* 16 (spring 1963): 3–10.
Wood, Bryce. *The Making of the Good Neighbor Policy.* New York: Columbia University Press, 1960.

Index

AD (Acción Democrática), 19–31
passim, 44, 86, 99–106 *passim*, 142f,
156f; political strength, 76–77; and
tax reform proposal, 111–16; and
Hydrocarbons Reversion Bill, 119;
attacks natural gas bill, 129
Additional Tax, 45
Agricultural sector, 2, 49, 164f, 169;
reform, 17ff; political influence,
21–24 *passim*
Akins, James, 139f
Andean Pact, 136
Andrés Pérez, Carlos: as Minister of
the Interior, 27; as President, 28,
119, 142ff, 159, 162, 171–72
Anticyclical fund, 46, 85, 163, 171
Arab countries: war with Israel, 100,
127; embargo on oil shipments, 127,
138
Arab Petroleum Congress (First), 60–
61. *See also* OPEC
ARPEL (Asociación de Asistencia
Recíproca Petrolera Estatal
Latinoamericana), 131n
Assertive experimentation, 50–54, 86,
96, 146–51, 153, 157f, 174. *See also*
Coordinating Commission

Bargaining: impact on policy, 4, 14,
165, 174; Medina's posture, 42;
under dictatorship, 47; by OPEC,
64–66, 104, 127; positions altered,
141; oil as weapon, 144; in learning,
146–51; flexibility, 153f; capital investment control, 154; risks, 155–59
passim. *See also* Concessions;
Interdependent bargaining
Barrios, Gonzalo, AD candidate, 102
Betancourt, Rómulo, 27, 156f; President, 21f; assassination attempt,
24; at 2d OPEC conference, 62; and
President Kennedy, 75

Betancourt Administration, 96, 156;
and CVP, 53–54; and Coordinating
Commission, 54–60; and OPEC, 62,
66; proposes oil agreement to U.S.,
73–74; bipartisan coalition, 76, 157,
166; attacked by companies, 77–85;
austerity program, 77; assertive
experimentation, 86
Budget: cuts, 23; anticyclical fund
(reserves), 46, 171; deficits, 50, 52n,
108f, 122–27 *passim*, 151; proposal,
105, 109ff, 113n; linkage with oil,
157, 164, 168; predicted, 170–71

Caldera, Rafael, 100ff, 111–15 *passim*,
119–34 *passim*, 139, 143, 157ff, 162,
167; elected President, 25ff
Caldera Administration: petroleum
policy, 101f; service contracts, 105–
8; tax reform, 111–16; Hydrocarbons
Reversion Bill, 119–20; export
volume penalties, 124–25; TRV's
and penalties increases, 126; state
gas monopoly, 127–29; OPEC influence, 129–31; relations with Latin
American state-owned companies,
131; relations with U.S., 133–38; and
faja bituminosa, 139f; U.S. quota
system abandoned, 141; changes in
oil policy, 142, 147, 154
Canadian oil, 68, 73, 135f
Chamber of the Petroleum Industry,
80, 100, 114, 120
Civil-military junta, 19. *See also*
Revolutionary junta
Committee of the Middle Class, 91
Companies, petroleum, *see* Multinational corporations
Competition of Venezuela with
Middle East, 64, 78, 83, 97–98, 131n,
134, 136; comparative costs, 82
Concessions, 9f; terms changed, 14–17